SAGE was founded in 1965 by Sara Miller McCune to support the dissemination of usable knowledge by publishing innovative and high-quality research and teaching content. Today, we publish more than 850 journals, including those of more than 300 learned societies, more than 800 new books per year, and a growing range of library products including archives, data, case studies, reports, conference highlights, and video. SAGE remains majority-owned by our founder, and after Sara's lifetime will become owned by a charitable trust that secures our continued independence.

Los Angeles | London | New Delhi | Singapore | Washington DC

SPORT, CULTURE

and

NATION

SPORT, CULTURE
and
NATION

Perspectives from Indian Football
and South Asian Cricket

Kausik Bandyopadhyay

Maulana Abul Kalam Azad
Institute of Asian Studies

www.sagepublications.com
Los Angeles • London • New Delhi • Singapore • Washington DC

First published in 2015 by

 SAGE Publications India Pvt Ltd
B1/I-1 Mohan Cooperative Industrial Area
Mathura Road, New Delhi 110044, India
www.sagepub.in

SAGE Publications Inc
2455 Teller Road
Thousand Oaks, California 91320, USA

SAGE Publications Ltd
1 Oliver's Yard, 55 City Road
London EC1Y 1SP, United Kingdom

SAGE Publications Asia-Pacific Pte Ltd
3 Church Street
#10-04 Samsung Hub
Singapore 049483

Published by Vivek Mehra for SAGE Publications India Pvt Ltd, typeset in 10/12pt Times New Roman by Zaza Eunice, Hosur, India and printed at Saurabh Printers Pvt Ltd, New Delhi.

Library of Congress Cataloging-in-Publication Data Available

ISBN: 978-93-515-0302-6 (HB)

The SAGE Team: Shambhu Sahu, Sanghamitra Patowary, Rajib Chatterjee and Rajinder Kaur

For

Arun Bandopadhyay
and
Bhaskar Chakraborty

Bulk Sales

SAGE India offers special discounts
for purchase of books in bulk.
We also make available special imprints
and excerpts from our books on demand.

For orders and enquiries, write to us at

Marketing Department
SAGE Publications India Pvt Ltd
B1/I-1, Mohan Cooperative Industrial Area
Mathura Road, Post Bag 7
New Delhi 110044, India

E-mail us at **marketing@sagepub.in**

Get to know more about SAGE

Be invited to SAGE events, get on our mailing list.
Write today to **marketing@sagepub.in**

This book is also available as an e-book.

Contents

List of Illustrations

Tables

Figures

List of Abbreviations

ACC	Asian Cricket Council
ACF	Afghanistan Cricket Federation
AFC	Asian Football Confederation
AFSPA	Armed Forces Special Power Act
AGM	annual general meeting
AIFF	All India Football Federation
AMFA	All Manipur Football Association
AMSA	All Manipur Sports Association
ANDS	Afghanistan National Development Strategy
AOC	Afghanistan Olympic Committee
AREU	Afghanistan Research and Evaluation Unit
BCCI	Board of Control for Cricket in India
BJP	Bharatiya Janata Party
CAB	Cricket Association of Bengal
CIA	Central Intelligence Agency
CPI-M	Communist Party of India-Marxist
CSBM	confidence- and security-building measure
FIFA	Federation Internationale de Football Association
ICC	International Cricket Council
ICL	Indian Cricket League
IFA	Indian Football Association
IPCS	Institute of Peace and Conflict Studies
IPFA	Indian Premier Football Association
IPL	Indian Premier League
LTTE	Liberation Tigers of Tamil Eelam
MAKAIAS	Maulana Abul Kalam Azad Institute of Asian Studies
MRF	Madras Rubber Factory
MSC	Mohammedan Sporting Club
NCP	Nationalist Congress Party
NFL	National Football League
NSCN	National Socialist Council of Nagaland

NWFP	North-West Frontier Province
ONGC	Oil and Natural Gas Corporation
PCB	Pakistan Cricket Board
PLA	People's Liberation Army
PPP	Pakistan Peoples Party
RAW	Research and Analysis Wing
SAARC	South Asian Association for Regional Corporation
SAF	South Asian Federation
SAFF	South Asian Football Federation
SAI	Sports Authority of India
TFA	Tata Football Academy
UNLF	United National Liberation Front
UNMACA	United Nations Mine Action Centre for Afghanistan
UPA	United Progressive Alliance

Acknowledgements

This book comprises of a set of essays, mostly written or conceived, while I was a Fellow at the Maulana Abul Kalam Azad Institute of Asian Studies (MAKAIAS), Kolkata, between 2006 and 2009. I am grateful to a number of persons for making it possible to collate the essays into a publishable manuscript—Jayanta Kumar Ray, Arun Bandopadhyay, Bhaskar Chakraborty, Hari S. Vasudevan, Muntassir Mamoon, Boria Majumdar, Ahmed Kabir, Amit Kumar Biswas, Kajal Debnath, Sarwar Hossain, Michael Roberts, Md Mowsil, Mahinda Wijesinghe, Ranjit Fernando, Neil Wijeratne, Trevor Chesterfield, Javed Ahmed Hamim, Sayed Mahmood Zia Dashti, Attaullah Asim, Dan Rath, Ehsan Mani, Ajay Chakraborty, Amiya Chaudhury, Rakhee Bhattacharya, Arpita Basu Roy, Binoda K. Mishra, Priya Singh, Anirban Mukherjee, Ashoke Ranjan Thakur, Kamales Bhaumik and Paritosh Kanjilal. I would like to extend sincere thanks to my colleagues at North Bengal University, Siliguri, and West Bengal State University, Barasat, and my special thanks to the colleagues at MAKAIAS for making my stint there truly enjoyable. I also recall with gratitude the phenomenal support I have received from some of my friends at times of personal crisis in the last few years: Sreemoyee Tarafder, Satyajit Ash, Urvi Mukhopadhyay, Sipra Mukherjee, Arunabha Adhikari, Arun Hota, Soma Sur, Subhamita Chaudhury, Shamee Bhattacharya, Debaprasad Mandal, Aatrayee Mukherjee, Jayati Gupta and Sayantan Bose.

I am thankful to the authorities and staff of all the libraries and institutions wherever I have worked to collect research materials: British Library and School of Oriental and African Studies Library (London); Central Library, Dhaka University and Central Public Library (Dhaka); Sri Lanka Cricket Library (Cricket Board of Sri Lanka, Colombo); Afghanistan Research and Evaluation Unit (AREU) and Afghanistan National Development Strategy (ANDS) (both in Kabul); Olympic Study Centre, International Olympic

Committee, Lausanne (Switzerland); Nehru Memorial Museum and Library (New Delhi); National Library, Ramakrishna Mission Institute of Culture Library, Department of History Seminar Library of the Calcutta University, MAKAIAS Library, the Indian Football Association (IFA) Archives and the Cricket Association of Bengal Library (all in Kolkata); and North Bengal University Central and Departmental Libraries and Udayan Memorial Sports Library (Siliguri, West Bengal). Thanks are also due to the IFA, Indian Olympic Association, International Olympic Committee, Bangladesh Football Federation, Bangladesh Cricket Board, Sri Lankan Cricket Board, Pakistan Cricket Board, Afghanistan Football Federation and Afghanistan Olympic Committee (AOC) for providing valuable sources. The feedback I received at various seminars in India and abroad have enriched the manuscript immensely. I am also thankful to the reviewers of the manuscript for their comments and suggestions.

Some of the essays in this book were earlier published in different journals or edited works and have been either kept intact or revised to suit the purpose of the present book, while others are written solely for this book. Chapters 1 and 2 were first published in *Soccer and Society*, Vol. 9, No. 3 (Routledge, July 2008), pp. 377–393 and *Sport in Society*, Vol. 12, No. 6 (Routledge, August 2009), pp. 792–810, respectively. Chapter 3 is a revised version of an article with the same title published in Jayanta Kumar Ray and Rakhee Bhattacharya (eds), *Development Dynamics in Northeast India* (Delhi: Anshah Publications, 2008), pp. 163–185. Chapter 4 is a much revised work of my article 'Feel Good, Goodwill and India's Friendship Tour of Pakistan, 2004: Cricket, Politics, Diplomacy in Twenty-First-Century India', first published in *The International Journal of the History of Sport*, Vol. 25, No. 12 (Routledge, October 2008), pp. 1654–1670. Similarly, Chapter 7 is a reworked version of my essay 'Cricket under Siege: Terrorism, Security and Diplomacy in Contemporary South Asia with Particular Reference to Pakistan', published in *Asia Annual 2009* (New Delhi: Manohar, 2011), pp. 155–180.

I express my sincere debt to MAKAIAS for funding my trips to Bangladesh, Sri Lanka, Afghanistan and New Delhi in 2007 and 2008. Thanks are also due to the staff of MAKAIAS, who pampered many of my unreasonable requests during my tenure at the institute.

Finally, I would thank Dr Sreeradha Dutta, Director, MAKAIAS, for taking keen interest in my research and giving me the opportunity to publish this work with MAKAIAS; and of course, it has been a pleasure to work with the SAGE team.

My parents have been a constant source of sustenance all through. The support I have enjoyed from Mono, Mingki, Kumaresh, Papui, Jhuma, Darshan, *Mama, Kaku* and *Kakima* has been most precious. However, without love and care from Tania, this book could never have been written.

Kausik Bandyopadhyay
Kolkata

Introduction

When James Walvin wrote his influential essay 'Sport, Social History and the Historian'[1] for the first volume of the *British Journal of Sports History* in 1984, he was fully convinced that 'the history of a particular game had an importance which far transcended the game itself' and that 'ultimately, sport could (and perhaps ought to) provide a reflection of wider issues and relationships in society at large.'[2] In the past three decades, Walvin's inspiration led to the emergence of diverse historical perspectives on sport across the world. While South Asia is not an exception in this regard, most studies on the history of sport in this region have an Indian enclave in their scope and perspective. And again, it is Indian cricket in its myriad forms which has drawn greatest attention from scholars. Hence, there is much scope left for the historian to explore various aspects of the history of sport in South Asia, viewing sport as what Ramachandra Guha calls 'a *relational idiom*, a sphere of activity which expresses, in concentrated form, the values, prejudices, divisions and unifying symbols of a society.'[3]

It is probably important at the outset to clarify what this book intends to offer and address. This book is a collection of essays that try to redress some hitherto unexplored dimensions of the history of sport in South Asia (football and cricket in this case) in the context of issues such as culture, politics, identity and regional cooperation, which actually provide the thematic preoccupation of the text. First and foremost, Indian football has been treated quite separately in this book, and the chapters on Indian football do not make any claim to focus on South Asia in general. Rather, the Indian experience is intended to generate future forays into similar/different experiences/contexts in other nations/parts of South Asia. While using the term 'South Asia' in the context of cricket, the usage has been confined to cricket's spread in the subcontinent, and intends to provide a comparative perspective on the patterns of cricket culture in the subcontinent with Bangladesh and Pakistan as specific case studies. In fact, the phrase 'South Asian cricket' commonly denotes cricket in the subcontinent, including India, Pakistan, Sri Lanka, Bangladesh and, now, Afghanistan. As the volume does not in any way intend to make a holistic appraisal of cricket in South Asia, I find it irrelevant to engage readers with the origins and nature of disparate evolution of cricket in other parts of South Asia, for example, in Nepal, Maldives or Bhutan. More importantly, when it comes to sports in general and football and cricket in particular, I look at 'South Asia' both as a space and as a community in terms of regionalism and regional cooperation as in usage in discourses of international relations.[4]

Sport in colonial and postcolonial South Asia has been closely linked to wider historical processes that have shaped the society and culture of the region since the twentieth century. It has been a powerful vector of forces, such as imperialism, nationalism, communalism, regionalism, decolonization, partition, immigration, violence, diplomacy, interstate relations and commercialization. Quite simply, patterns of history and society have transformed sport in the region while simultaneously sport has shaped the history and society of South Asia. It is, therefore, relevant to explore and analyze the intricate relationships between sport, culture, politics, identity and regional cooperation in the context of South Asia. In other words, the major objective of this book is to establish the legitimacy of sport as a viable theme in historical research on identity, culture, nationalism and regional cooperation in South Asia. How sport can shape the history and culture of colonial and postcolonial South Asia becomes clear from recent publications on the social history of cricket and soccer, the Olympic movement and the Commonwealth Games in India.[5] In colonial India, sports, such as cricket or football, reflected the ethos of nationalism, communalism, colonial culture and so on.[6] In time, sport became a contested terrain where sentiments pertaining to imperialism, nationalism, communalism, regionalism, culture and so on came to be produced and reproduced. Chapter 1 of the book charts this contestation in football in colonial and postcolonial India. The transition from the colonial to the postcolonial era affected certain shifts in sport's status and significance in the spheres of polity, society and culture in South Asia. In the postcolonial scenario, the new nation states had to cope with the changed priorities of governance and economy in which initially sport could not find a legitimate place of serious worth. Football's status in postcolonial India bears testimony to this point and Chapter 2 of the book elaborates it. However, with time, particularly as the century came to its end, the states in South Asia began to realize sport's importance as an integral part of popular culture and social life. Sports such as football, in such context, have sometimes proved to be a viable career option to people of politically sensitive and socially turbulent north-eastern states of India, as shown in Chapter 3. The question of identity is addressed in the chapter from an entirely different angle with emphasis on profession and economic dimension, making out a case for a merger/convergence of national and regional identities.

From the 1980s, cricket in India, alias South Asia, went through a spell of commercialization, which raised its status as a tool of economic transformation. Against this backdrop, in the midst of traditional enmity in Indo-Pakistan (Indo-Pak) relations, as Chapter 4 argues, cricket began to be looked upon as a key confidence-building measure at the turn of the century. Cricket's rising importance as a socio-economic force also makes way for its political appropriation evident in cricket board elections at both central and regional levels in India, which is discussed in Chapter 5.

The importance of sport as a political instrument, cultural tool or emotional bond in other South Asian nations, such as Bangladesh, Pakistan, Afghanistan and Sri Lanka, has not been given adequate attention in studies on society and culture of the region. The book will try to redress this imbalance by focusing on specific aspects of sports culture with particular reference to cricket in these countries and relating those aspects to the notions of nationalism, politics, identity and regional cooperation in the region as a whole. The question of forming/achieving national identity through a particular sport or sports in general is a complex and problematic aspect. In a few sports, such as cricket, India seems to assert its national identity at the international stage. In most other South Asian countries, too, as the last three chapters of the work intend to show, cricket as an integral part of national popular culture provides a legitimate space for examining the issues of national identity, popular culture and regional cooperation in relation to peoples' pursuit of the game and the country's participation in international contests.[7]

Football has been one of the central components and an insepa-rable part of popular culture in colonial and postcolonial India with wider and reciprocal ramifications for polity, society and economy. It has been integrally connected with wider historical processes that have influenced the society and culture of the region since the nine-teenth century. At the same time, the history of Indian football shows that formation of community connections and identities was strongly articulated through the game at different points of time. In India, foot-ball started as a marker of nationalist identity against British imperi-alism. This unitary social identity, however, gave way to a series of fragmentations in terms of new forms of community formations or connections or identities. These relate to social differences expressed through communal and sub-regional overtones represented through club loyalties, premised upon which football thrived as a mass spec-tator sport in colonial and postcolonial India. Chapter 1 examines the ways in which the notion of 'community' can be theoretically re-conceptualized in the context of Indian football, thereby also trying to establish football's credibility as a viable theme in the study of national/regional/local dichotomies in Indian social history and cul-tural studies.

Football has been a mass spectator, sport in India since the turn of the nineteenth century. During colonial rule, India's true potential as a soccer power remained mostly undetermined. After independence, however, India emerged as an important Asian representative in inter-national football scenario. India's performance in Olympic soccer between 1948 and 1960 was promising, barring a huge defeat against Yugoslavia in the Helsinki Olympics of 1952. When India won the gold medal in Jakarta Asian Games in 1962, the nation seemed ready to perform impressively at the international level. But it could not keep the momentum, and a long trend of decline set in. Since 1960, the Indian football team has not qualified for the Olympics. Therefore, Indian football came to be regarded as a sleeping giant. Chapter 2, looking deep into this much-publicized metaphor of 'sleeping giant', seeks to understand the long-term underlying processes and the cul-tural politics of soccer that explains both the legacies and the pros-pects of Indian football in the Olympic Games, linking thereby its past, present and future. In the process, it also argues that Indian soc-cer's failure to make a mark in the Olympics reflects the nation's failure to develop an enduring Olympic culture over time.

India's Northeast has internalized over the years a state of political insurgency, economic dependence and cultural isolation not conducive to integrated development strategies at all. In the age of globalization, commercialism and professionalism are the two most crucial weapons by which the underdeveloped states of the region could cope with political instability (insurgency and counter-insurgency), economic backwardness (infrastructural debilities and unemployment) and social maladies (drug abuse and spread of AIDS). It is in this context that sports, such as soccer, can be looked upon as a lucrative career option generating new avenues of employment as well as sources of livelihood to the youth of the region. Chapter 3 takes up the case of Manipur, where soccer has done wonders to provide the young generation with a viable professional alternative amidst political instability and social maladies. Men's soccer in the state has attained such a standard in the last one and half decade, thanks mostly to the efforts of All Manipur Football Association (AMFA) and the Sports Authority of India (SAI), that young football players from Manipur have opted either for playing outside Manipur in different club teams throughout India, or for the local clubs of Manipur, thereby creating for themselves alternative career options and earning a decent living. Instead of destroying their ethnic identity by any means, as the chapter would argue, this has given wider recognition to their professional expertise and has enhanced the prestige and status of their community at the national stage.

The pre-eminence of cricket in Indian life has led to its construction and interpretation in terms of political transition, social tension, economic transformation, diplomatic relations or cultural development. When it comes to India's cricketing relations with Pakistan, it begins to signify different meanings and convey different messages to different people in India: nationalism, communalism, war, infiltration, insurgency, terrorism, diplomacy, peace, election, cultural exchange, commercial boom, cricketing conflict and so on. The Indian team's tour to Pakistan in 2004 evoked a plethora of responses in the public life of India and Pakistan. From the learned to the laity, people on both sides of the border began to consider cricket as a means to various ends: a diplomatic ploy to accelerate peace process, a political instrument to generate electoral confidence, an economic means to ameliorate the nation's pecuniary distress, a cultural arena to assert cricketing muscle, an emotional tool to soothe traditional rivalry and so on. Chapter 4 analyzes the representations of the tour both in popular media and in popular perception as part of a broader diplomatic initiative to stabilize India–Pakistan relations and in the wider context of domestic political debates and cricketing rivalry. It also argues, even with a note of caution on the possible exaggeration of such a role of sport, that sport can go some way forward to create an ambience of fraternity to address and resolve outstanding issues that continue to complicate India–Pakistan relations.

In twenty-first-century India, cricket is not a mere sport; its implications have moved far beyond the rubric of leisure or entertainment. Rather, cricket is more about politics, about economy. While cricket signified various connotations in twentieth-century India, its importance as a political tool has rarely attracted that much attention. In the new century, cricket is intricately linked to politics, intrigue and business. Chapter 5 shows that the recent trends of operation and development in the organization and control of the game in India both at central and regional levels are clear proof of this comment. The elections of Board of Control for Cricket in India (BCCI) in 2004 and 2005 marked the steady intrusion of mainstream politics into the fold of cricket, thereby making it 'political cricket', while the Cricket Association of Bengal (CAB) election of 2006 provided an occasion for not only the clash of this new trend with traditional 'cricketing politics' but also a serious rift within mainstream politics on the desirability of political intervention in sport. The chapter intends to explore the intricate relationship between cricket, power and politics in the context of the BCCI elections of 2004–2005 and the CAB elections of 2006 in West Bengal.

Bangladesh could boast of a rich heritage of cricket in terms of tradition, culture and mass following. During British as well as Pakistan rule, there were attempts to appropriate the game to serve subversive, nationalist purposes, and thereby to decolonize the game. Post-Independence, in the absence of their national team at the international level, common Bangladeshis began to support either Pakistan or India and worship cricketing icons of these nations. However, with the country's rising status as a cricket-playing nation at the turn of the twentieth century, the masses of Bangladesh began to support 'their' national team and worship their 'own' players as icons in the new century. This trend of cricket culture, well established with the experience of the 2007 World Cup, marked the rise of Bangladesh as a cricketing nation and the decolonization of Bangladesh cricket. The hosting of the International Cricket Council (ICC) World Cup in 2011 and its impact on the everyday life of Bangladesh may be said to have completed this process of decolonization, thereby transforming cricket into a nationalist obsession and establishing the game as a marker of its national identity. Chapter 6 intends to throw light on this complex and shifting process of decolonization of Bangladeshi cricket in a historical perspective.

Cricket has become one of the most abiding national passions in South Asia in the last few decades. Pakistani cricket is an integral part of the subcontinental cricket culture and economy now being led by India at the international level. However, as Chapter 7 argues, there is one non-cricketing factor which is going to decide the fate of Pakistan as a cricketing nation in the twenty-first century: the question of terrorism and human security. Pakistan's image as a stable political entity began to face unpleasant questions relating to its alleged links with acts of global terrorism since the destruction of the World Tower on 11 September 2001. Post 9/11 incident, most cricket-playing countries sans the South Asian nations refused to play in Pakistan for security reasons. As a result, cricket began to suffer not only as a game but also as commerce. As cricket exchanges between Pakistan and other South Asian nations depend mainly on bilateral relations based on the reciprocity of political goodwill on both sides, the latter continued to play in Pakistan to allay security fears embedded in the Western mind. However, in the aftermath of the terrorist attacks in Mumbai (November 2008), the process of confidence building between India and Pakistan received a major blow as evidences clearly pointed to Pakistan's strong hands in the plot of the terror. Finally, the terrorist attack on the Sri Lankan cricketers and officials at the Gaddafi Stadium, Lahore, on 3 March 2009, may be regarded as the last nail in the coffin of Pakistan as a host cricketing nation as Pakistan was deprived of its status as one of the co-hosts of the 2011 World Cup. This has proved to be, as the chapter will suggest, a major blow to the cricketing solidarity of South Asia. More importantly, as this chapter would argue, from the point of view of Pakistan, given Pakistan's lack of credibility in the avowed objective of containing terrorism, and the strong presence and growing influence of the Taliban in the country, security threats emanating from continuous acts of terror in the country, coupled with ever-rising social instability, religious fundamentalism and political tension, pose serious concerns for the nation in any efforts to recreate its image as a peaceful democratic society where cricket could be pursued without fear.

The last chapter offers an ethnographic commentary on the nature of sports culture in contemporary Sri Lanka and Afghanistan drawn from my personal experiences during field trips to these two South Asian countries. This chapter has been intended as an exercise in ethnographic observation and commentary in the domain of sports culture with a focus on cricket in Sri Lanka and Afghanistan. While it does not offer any serious/rigorous research based on empirical sources, it hints at a number of important inferences and posits a range of potential arguments for future research. I do not claim the commentary to be rich in terms of ethnographic thickness; yet, selective oral sources I have used to engage the readers in a discussion on the culture of sports/cricket in two South Asian nations are from some of the best representatives of that domain. It shows how cricket has truly become an emblem of national pride as well as a unifying force in an ethnic-strife-ridden Sri Lanka, particularly since Sri Lanka's historic World Cup victory in 1996. While the story of Sri Lankan cricket shares similarity with other South Asian counterparts like India and Pakistan on more counts than one, this chapter would argue the culture of cricket that has evolved in Sri Lanka over the last two decades has proved to be an aberration in South Asia. Compared to its more illustrious subcontinental counterparts, which are known for their over-the-top behaviour and excesses of passion over cricket and its attendant nationalism, cricket worship and fan culture in Sri Lanka have always shown a sense of proportion and mature appreciation of the game. Afghanistan, on the other hand, has been a hotbed of political turmoil over the past three decades, accompanied by tribal clashes, religious dissensions, social cleavages and cultural purges from time to time. The Taliban rule in the late 1990s marked a distinct phase in Afghan history as it, apart from its self-defined political massacres and religious prosecution, imposed a series of restrictions and bans on sociocultural life of the Afghan people, including sporting activities. The end of Taliban rule in late 2001 after the 9/11 incident raised hope for a restoration of peace and security, as it was followed by a constitutional process to establish democracy in the country. In the process of transition from a fundamentalist authoritarian rule to a progressive democratic state in Afghanistan, as this chapter would argue, sport plays a critical role. While for Afghan men, sport has become an arena for the assertion of national identity, women have taken it as a means of emancipation and empowerment. Sport's instrumentality in contemporary Afghan society is also linked with the nation's urge for peace, development and progress, as Afghan youths have increasingly preferred to replace guns with bats, and bullets with balls. The chapter will further argue that sport can play a positive role in the state's changing international image as a stable developing progressive nation.

Finally, a note on the methodology of the work. Barring a few chapters (say, Chapters 1 and 6), most of the essays in the volume are works on contemporary history, which requires methodological novelty and empirical nuance. That is why I have used three major types of primary sources/tools for analysis—print media, including newspapers and periodicals/magazines; oral sources, including interviews, discussions, conversations and interactions; and internet resources, including the social media. Since not much work has been done in most of these areas of research, the citation of relevant academic texts is sometimes scanty. Similarly, I have not preferred any superimposition of theoretical structures only for the sake of serious contextualization as I do not consider this to be advisable at this early stage of research on themes discussed in some of the chapters.

In South Asia, sport has long been a site, albeit ignored by social scientists, which articulates the complexities and diversities of the everyday life of the nation. In view of the complexities of sport in the region, it is easy to comprehend that a single research work can only scratch the surface. The present study has attempted to reveal at least part, if not the whole, of the process of how significant sports, particularly football in India and cricket in South Asia, have become—politically, socially, culturally and emotionally. The book is compiled with the premise that social history of sport can be meaningfully understood only by looking beyond the sports field, and the work attempts to appeal not only to those interested in the history of sport in the region but also to those who might be uninterested in sport per se, but are interested in the broader themes of the history of South Asia. Some of the essays in the present book are being published without any revision or modification, in conformity with the copyright agreement with the publishers of the journals or books, where they first appeared,[8] while a few others are revised to suit the purpose of the present volume. Hence, the dates of their first publication should be considered in any critical appreciation of these writings. Yet, there are some others I have written solely for the book. I would be most delighted if scholars and sports enthusiasts across the world find this work interesting and worth reading.

Notes

1. James Walvin, 'Sport, Social History and the Historian', *British Journal of Sports History*, Vol. 1, No. 1 (1984), pp. 5–13.
2. Ibid., p. 6.
3. Ramachandra Guha, 'Cricket and Politics in Colonial India', *Past and Present*, No. 161 (November 1998), p. 157.
4. For interesting reflections on the idea of South Asia as a viable entity, see Sridhar K. Khatri, 'The Politics of Becoming a Community: Stages and Prerequisites', *South Asian Survey*, Vol. 6, No. 2 (1999), pp. 197–229; I.P. Khosla, 'Constructing the South Asian Community', *South Asian Survey*, Vol. 6, No. 2 (1999), pp. 181–196; Rajiv Kumar Bhatia, 'South Asia's Destiny: Conflict or Cooperation?', *Indian Foreign Affairs Journal*, Vol. 6, No. 2 (April–June 2011), pp. 152–164.
5. See, for example, Ramachandra Guha, *A Corner of a Foreign Field: The Indian History of a British Sport* (Delhi: Picador, 2002) and Boria Majumdar, *Twenty-Two Yards to Freedom: A Social History of Indian Cricket* (New Delhi: Penguin/Viking, 2004) for cricket; Boria Majumdar and Kausik Bandyopadhyay, *Goalless: The Story of a Unique Footballing Nation* (New Delhi: Penguin/Viking, 2006) and Kausik Bandyopadhyay, *Scoring Off the Field: Football Culture in Bengal, 1911–80* (New Delhi: Routledge, 2011) for football; and Boria Majumdar and Nalin Mehta, *Olympics: The India Story* (New Delhi: HarperCollins, 2008) for the Olympic movement in India.
6. Guha, *A Corner of a Foreign Field*; Majumdar, *Twenty-Two Yards to Freedom*; Majumdar and Bandyopadhyay, *Goalless*; Bandyopadhyay, *Scoring Off the Field*.
7. In some of the important recent works on the subject, namely, Boria Majumdar and J.A. Mangan, eds. *Sport in South Asian Society: Past and Present* (London: Routledge, 2005) and James Mills, ed. *Subaltern Sports: Politics and Sport in South Asia* (London: Anthem Press, 2005); and Subhas Ranjan Chakraborty, Shantanu Chakrabarti and Kingshuk Chatterjee, eds. *The Politics of Sport in South Asia* (London: Routledge, 2009), sports in Pakistan, Bangladesh or Afghanistan do not find any worthy place. Only a few works have recently tried to fill this gap. See, for example, Shamya Dasgupta, 'Bangladesh Cricket: Scoring on Passion, but Little Else...', *Sport*

in Society, Vol. 10, No. 1 (2007), pp.162–181; Kausik Bandyopadhyay, *Bangladesh Playing: Sport, Culture, Nation* (Dhaka: ICBS/Subarna, 2012); Chris Valiotis, *Cricket and Identity in Pakistan and Anglo-Pakistan: Sporting Nations of the Imagination* (London: Routledge, 2012); Chris Valiotis, 'Cricket in "a nation imperfectly imagined": Identity and tradition in postcolonial Pakistan', in Stephen Wagg, ed. *Cricket and National Identity in the Postcolonial Age—Following On* (London: Routledge, 2005); Kausik Bandyopadhyay, 'Pakistani Cricket at Crossroads: An Outsider's Perspective', *Sport in Society*, Vol. 10, No. 1 (January 2007), pp. 101–119. So far as sports in Sri Lanka, especially Sri Lankan cricket, are concerned, scholars seem to have paid a little greater attention. See, for example, Jayadeva Uyangoda, ed. *Cricket, Lovely Cricket! Sports in Culture, Class and Nation in Sri Lanka* (Colombo: Social Scientists Association, 2007); Michael Roberts, 'Ethnicity in Riposte at a Cricket Match: The Past for the Present', in Michael Roberts, *Exploring Confrontation: Sri Lanka—Politics, Culture and History* (Switzerland: Harwood Academic Publishers, 1994); J.A. Mangan, 'Imperial Origins: Christian Manliness, Moral Imperatives and Pre-Sri Lankan Playing Fields—Beginnings and Consolidation', in J.A. Mangan and Fan Hong, eds. *Sport in Asian Society: Past and Present* (London: Frank Cass, 2003); Suvendrini Perera, '"Cricket with a Plot": Nationalism, Cricket and Diasporic Identities', *Journal of Australian Studies*, June 2000; Trevor Chesterfield, 'Cricket in Sri Lanka: In Need of a Messiah', in Boria Majumdar and J.A. Mangan, eds. *Cricketing Cultures in Conflict: World Cup 2003* (London: Routledge, 2004); Michael Roberts, 'Sri Lanka: The power of Cricket and the Power in Cricket', in Wagg, ed. *Cricket and National Identity in the Postcolonial Age*; Michael Roberts, 'Landmarks and Threads in the Cricketing World of Sri Lanka', in John Gemmell and Boria Majumdar, eds. *Cricket, Race and the 2007 World Cup* (London: Routledge, 2007); Michael Roberts, 'Wunderkidz in a Blunderland: Tensions and Tales from Sri Lankan Cricket', *Sport in Society*, Vol. 12, Nos. 4–5 (2009), pp. 566–578.

8. See 'Acknowledgements' for first publication dates of relevant essays.

1

'The Nation and Its Fragments'*:
Football and Community in India

Introduction: Football and Community in the Indian Context

Football has been one of the central components and an inseparable part of popular culture in colonial and postcolonial India. Throughout the game's history, it has been closely linked to wider historical processes that have shaped the society and culture of the region since the late nineteenth century. These include imperialism, nationalism, communalism, regionalism, decolonization, partition, immigration, hooliganism, violence, diplomacy, interstate relations, commercialization and professionalism.[1] The history of Indian football has also been inextricably linked with the formation of community connections and identities, which have been strongly articulated through the game in different ways during different points of time. While the notion of 'community' is itself ambiguous and debatable, it can be meaningfully analyzed—in the context of this chapter—through concepts such as nationalism, communalism and sub-regionalism.[2] In India, football started as a marker of nationalist identity and

---

* This title is taken from Partha Chatterjee's celebrated work *The Nation and Its Fragments: Colonial and Postcolonial Histories* (Calcutta: Oxford University Press, 1995). Chatterjee used the title to denote a larger historical context of nationalism in colonial and postcolonial India. Sport, however, has no place in his scheme of understanding and representation of nation and its fragments.

community against British imperialism. This, however, gave way to a series of fragmentations in terms of new forms of community connections or identities. These related to social 'differences' expressed through communal and sub-regional identities represented through club loyalties. Indeed, it is in relation to the expression of these differences that football thrived as a mass spectator sport in colonial and postcolonial India.

This chapter examines the ways in which the notion of 'community' can be theoretically reconceptualized in the context of Indian football. By doing so, it will establish football's credibility as a viable theme in the study of national/regional/local dichotomies in Indian social history and cultural studies. It will also bring forth the pertinent question of 'the autonomy of sport as a manifestation of indigenous popular culture, and local, regional and national negotiation and resistance in the face of global movements.'[3]

Football in India: The Beginnings

It is reasonably clear that football came to India with the East India Company. Football's early pioneers were the officers and men of trading firms and regimental battalions, European professors of educational institutions and naval men who used to play the game at ports, such as Calcutta, Bombay, Madras and Karachi.[4] Tony Mason and Paul Dimeo, following the most overarching and widely popular theory of 'games ethic' popularized by J.A. Mangan, explain football's introduction and organization in Calcutta primarily in terms of public school games-playing ethos[5] learnt by the educated Bengali upper-middle and middle classes at the British-run Anglo-Indian colleges.[6] The concept of 'games ethic'—in common with the notion of 'muscular Christianity'[7] propagated by moral missionaries—had a firm belief in sport as an instrument of imperial moral persuasion. This belief was clearly discernible in the efforts of evangelicals, such as Theodore Leighton Pennell and Cecil Earle Tyndale-Biscoe, who used football in the North-West Frontier Provinces and in Kashmir, respectively, as a 'key weapon in the battle to win over local populations and to begin transforming them from their "uncivilized" and "heathen" state to one where they might be considered "civilized" and "Christian".[8] In Bengal, especially in Calcutta, Anglo-Indian schools certainly utilized sports, including football, as integral elements of their educational curriculum. To these early missionaries, as well as public school teachers, the game was a moral tool to inculcate 'a series of moral lessons, regarding hard work and perseverance, about team loyalty and obedience to authority and, indeed, involving concepts of correct physical development and "manliness".'[9]

Despite the initial importance of middle-class schools and colleges in the development of football in India, their ultimate role in the widespread promotion of the game should not be overstated. Indeed, football's appropriation by the Indian public in the late nineteenth century was a distinctly complex process, especially in Bengal where the game came to be embroiled in identity politics and cultural resistance.

During the mid-to-late nineteenth century, the Bengali 'community' was stereotyped by its British colonizers as an effeminate non-military race.[10] The response to this was uniquely 'cultural'. The Bengali people reacted to this stereotype through the promotion of a 'neo-traditional physical culture' to efface the 'self-image of effeteness'.[11] This promotion was led by a number of noted Bengali intellectuals and middle-class cultural nationalists who urgently led resurgence in traditional Bengali physical culture and traditional indigenous games. This movement—led and popularized in Bengal by Nabagopal Mitra's Hindu Mela in the 1860s and 1870s—began to promote the rejuvenation of ancient Hindu principle of physical culture.[12] However, the physical culture movement was marked by a conspicuous lack of any competitive element which exemplified modern Western sports, such as football, cricket or hockey. Moreover, even if rigorous physical exercise was looked upon as a plausible weapon to counter British stereotype of local physical weakness, it did not afford Bengalis the opportunity to compete with their colonizers on even terms. Middle-class Bengalis quickly realized the futility of the traditional physical culture movement as a form of cultural resistance, and sought new ways to reassert their physical prowess and redeem their masculinity. Western sports, and especially football, provided the ideal tools. Dimeo has argued that by adopting modern sports in this fashion, Bengalis followed a 'route of mimicry'.[13] But he fails to identify that these sports were adopted explicitly as a form of resistance which would enable Bengalis to show their physical worth by competing with Europeans on an equal plane. Football's adaptation was, therefore, more a cultural ploy than a simplistic form of mimicry.

In the 1880s and 1890s, football in India was solidly regarded as a cultural weapon to reassert Bengali/Indian physical prowess and masculinity. By the end of the nineteenth century, the game had developed from being an occasional recreation for military men and a school sport/leisure activity among other Europeans to being an arena for competition and conflict between the British and the Indians.[14] To suggest that Indian football clubs of the 1880s and 1890s from their very inception began to reflect or represent nationalist instincts on the sports field is almost certainly overbold. However, at the turn of the century, football in India can be described as a new and unique cultural nationalist force, although the approach of different clubs to the game was not always uniform.

It was the Mohun Bagan Club which rose among its contemporaries to symbolize the clearest nationalist response of the injured 'cultural self' of Indians during this period. Originally founded in 1889 by a few idealistic North Calcutta gentlemen at Mohun Bagan Villa, it proved, from its very inception, to be more than a simple sports club. It was an institution with the avowed objective to not only produce excellent sportsmen, but also to impart in them impeccable moral and social values. The ideals that the founders set before themselves were novel for Indians at that time.[15] The executives of the club saw to it that each member combined the development of the body with the development of their 'mind'. Little did the pioneers envisage, however, that the club would, through its epic victory over the East York Regiment in the 1911 IFA Shield final, bring about a national reawakening!

One Club, One Nationalism: Football and Nationalist Community in Colonial India

Within a span of three decades, football had become an important part of Bengali popular culture in colonial India. It transcended simple recreational practices and became a cultural weapon to fight British imperialism. At the turn of the century, Bengali youth came to look upon football 'as an avenue through which they would be able to retrieve their sinking political prestige and establish their superiority over the semblance of power the Raj represented.'[16] Indeed, the sight of 'puny', barefooted, Bengali players matching heavily built and better-equipped Europeans soon took on the form of a cultural battle against foreign rulers. In the shifting socio-political context of the early twentieth century, when Bengal was engulfed by a spate of nationalist fervour in the wake of the anti-Partition movement during 1905–1908,[17] football came increasingly to be looked upon as a novel instrument of cultural nationalism in Bengal. The game became a weapon to use on the cultural battlefield of *maidan*[18] and an emblem around which nationalist consciousness could be fostered. In the wake of vehement anti-partition agitation, Bengalis looked towards the game with a new purpose. Any success against British teams on the football field began to be viewed as a victory of the spirit of nationalism over the evil of colonialism.

The trend of barefoot on-field battle against European civil and military teams was set in the context of political agitation and social unrest that grew in response to the Partition of Bengal in 1905. From that year onwards, the Mohun Bagan Club came to prominence with successive wins in the Cooch Behar Cup in 1904–1905 and a Gladstone Cup success in the same season. From 1906 to 1908, the club won the Trades Cup three times in a row. This was in addition to winning the Gladstone Cup in 1908, the Cooch Behar Cup in 1907 and 1908, and the Lakshibilas Cup in 1909 and 1910. More importantly, Mohun Bagan achieved a series of victories against strong European sides during this period, stirring up a passionate blend of nationalist fervour amongst the Bengali community.

The rise of Mohun Bagan to fame had a clear impact on the emotional involvement of Indian people with the game. The Indian crowd became enmeshed with the on-field tensions of soccer encounters between 'their' teams and various European outfits. People all over Bengal appreciated these victories in the context of a surge of anti-British sentiments in the political realm and in July 1911, Mohun Bagan—comprising 10 barefooted Indian players[19]—created sporting history when it defeated European civil and military teams one by one to lift the coveted IFA Shield.[20] The enthusiasm that Mohun Bagan's march into the final created was unique. It was the 'the moment of departure'[21] in Indian football history, when an Indian nationalism started appropriating a Western sport to assert its

distinctive identity. The crowd which attended the game was esti-
mated between 80,000 and 100,000 string. As one newspaper noted,
'The spectators who packed every inch of the Maidan simply defied
calculation. They might have been eighty thousand or they might
have been more.'[22] Thus, when Mohun Bagan actually entered the
final of the IFA Shield, signs of a great mass awakening in Bengal
were quite visible. People became obsessed with the dream of beating the ruling British at its own national game. The dream became
reality when Mohun Bagan defeated the East Yorks team 2–1 in the
historic final of 29 July 1911.

Mohun Bagan's victory was hailed as a blow struck not only for
Indian football, but also for Indian nationalism. However, it is difficult to ascertain whether the 'nation' appealed to was Bengal or
India. Most of the press reports, in celebrating the victory, used the
terms 'Bengali' and 'Indian' interchangeably,[23] thereby indicating
the ambiguous nature of footballing nationalism in colonial India.
However, it is clear from the reports that Indian people—irrespective
of class, caste or community—were supposed to connect with a victory over the British ruling class.

Recent observations on the 1911 Mohun Bagan victory largely
confirm the view that it had a strong impact on Indian society. Indeed,
attempts have even been made to relate the Shield triumph to the
moving of capital of India from Calcutta to Delhi later in the same
year. Ramachandra Guha, noted Indian sports historian, states:

> Oddly enough, it was in the same year, 1911, that the British shifted the
> capital of the *raj* from Calcutta to Delhi. Recent memorialists of Mohun
> Bagan's victory have, alas, failed to notice this coincidence. *If* it is a coin-
> cidence, for it is highly likely that one was the cause of the other and
> that to pre-empt further humiliation the British adroitly and deliberately
> moved the seat of power from Bengal, away from its skillful footballers
> and its bomb-wielding nationalists. The link between sporting prowess
> and militant anti-imperialism was thus undermined, to be finally rent
> asunder by Gandhi and the Bombay capitalists.[24] (emphases in original)

A similar interpretation is offered by Rudrangshu Mukherjee, a
scholar-turned-journalist:

> The victory seems, in retrospect, to have been a triumph of the moral
> force which Gandhi extolled and advocated in *Hind Swaraj*. For Bengalis

who had seen only a few years age their land partitioned and their young men and women imprisoned and punished during the Swadeshi movement, the win over a white team in football seemed a moment of national pride. It appeared as some sort of recovery of dignity and self-respect in the year that Calcutta was to lose its status as the capital. It was the inherent inequality of the encounter in which the apparently weak trounced the obviously strong that made Mohun Bagan's victory the stuff of legends.[25]

In contrast to this assessment, Mason is more circumspect in his analysis of the events of 1911:

Mohan Bagan's victory did not produce a bombardment of Fort William by Bengali athletes, nor did it provoke a military revolt against peace and order. It clearly injected some confidence into some of the native peoples of Calcutta and convinced them that they were as good as their masters. But it also seems to have reinforced admiration for those masters. Perhaps that is the essence of the mystery of hegemony.[26]

This view aside, however, it is largely accepted that in the aftermath of the Mohun Bagan victory, football not only came to represent a novel cultural sporting nationalism for Indian people, but also contributed to the formation of a unique footballing identity. In the wake of the triumph, the game became a rallying point around which nationalist consciousness gained momentum. Indeed, in the first three decades of the twentieth century, the maidan became an arena where spontaneous effusion of nationalist sentiment found ready expression as and when a native team—especially Mohun Bagan—played against British civilian or regimental sides. Playing and watching the game cut across the affiliations of indigenous caste, class and community in Indian society and provided a social bond for nationalist-minded Indians. Football as a cultural weapon to fight and defeat the British added a new dimension to the anti-British national consciousness of Indians, particularly in Bengal. Thus, parallel to the political struggle against an oppressive colonial power, there began a social struggle of national liberation organized around a specific cultural component. In that context, the football maidan, as a national cultural territory, began to reflect an Indian nationalist impulse that found heroic expression in the effort of the footballers.

In the aftermath of Mohun Bagan successes, football gradually came to present an outlet for the 'pent-up nationalism' of Bengali professionals and students. A large section of the Bengali community were affluent, educated, practical and decent, but were hesitant to actively take part in the freedom struggle. As such, they came to view the football field as an ideal place to confront British imperialism. Similarly, the Bengali youth, many of whom were reluctant to participate in politics of direct confrontation, came to view football as a potent nationalist gesture and beating the British produced an immense emotional satisfaction for them. Urban and suburban middle-class Bengalis, who served the British as officials, clerks or professionals, could not show their anti-British resentment in public, and working-class people, who were not drawn into the fold of nationalist politics until the late 1920s, could only really express their nationalism in covert ways. This 'pent-up' nationalism of the Bengali middle class and sections of working-class people thus found prolific expression through emotional outbursts experienced during Mohun Bagan's matches.

On the football field, it was considered to be an act of great courage to shove an elbow or a fist into the face of a sahib or a soldier, or kick him under the guise of tackling. Those who could get away with it were respected as great players. Footballers, such as Gostho Paul, Abhilash Ghosh and Balai Chatterjee, earned glamour and fame in Bengali society for their reputation of successfully executing 'reverse hits' or *palta mar*. Off the field, it was also claimed that some Indian spectators would deliberately pick quarrels with the 'superior' British. Sometimes these encounters would turn violent and afford the Bengalis the opportunity of giving the *gora* (white) sahibs a 'sound beating'. Indeed, the nationalist element within Bengali football culture during this period was often most obvious among spectators. Spontaneous effusion of nationalist feeling found prolific expression in specific forms of fan behaviour, including pitch-side language; jokes and doggerels; erratic vocal outbursts; peculiar physical gestures; tearing shirts, throwing sandals and stones into the ground; torching papers and clothes; and, occasionally, spectator violence.

For European scholars, such as Mason and Dimeo, Indian victories over colonial masters were little, but a sign of the success of British cultural imperialism.[27] They read in such football victories Indians' unwitting admiration for, acceptance of and submission to such cultural imperialism. Richard Cashman has raised a pertinent question as to whether we can analyze the spread of colonial sports solely in terms of the ideology of colonialism and games ethic.[28] For him, the indigenous appropriation (domestication) of modern sports (cricket in his case) calls for more logical explanation.[29] Cashman's conclusion is that, 'while games are an effective vehicle for proselytization in some circumstances, they can be subverted in others.'[30] The appropriation of football in colonial India for nationalist purposes, as this section has shown, certainly suggests a colonial reformulation of the imperial model of the games ethic. It points towards football's transformed role as an instrument of reaction, resistance and subversion configured in one club and represented by one national community.

Communalism on the Maidan: Football and Communal Identity in Colonial India

By the early-twentieth century, football came to provide a potential source of coalescence for Indian people, irrespective of caste, class, religion or community affiliation. Players' or spectators' identities had the capacity to cut across traditional social categories and express a form of nationalism. However, the game could not hold on to this apparent unifying influence for long. Differences and conflicts based on social, religious, regional and sub-regional affiliations split the coherent footballing identity of the country into fragments. From mid-1930s onwards, India's anti-British footballing nationalism came to be fractured and with the rise of the Mohammedan Sporting Club (MSC) to football fame in the early 1930s, rivalry in Indian football was no longer confined to Briton versus Indian. Instead, it came to express divisions between Hindu versus Muslim communities for the first time.

Muslim representation in Indian football began in the last decade of the nineteenth century when MSC[31] rose to prominence, thanks to the efforts of a number of Muslim individuals. The club, established in 1891, was quickly understood as a Muslim institution which gradually carved out a niche in the Indian football scene.[32] It would, however, be a mistake to argue that the club reflected divisive sectarianism at its inception. According to *The Musalman*, in the aftermath of Mohun Bagan's famous Shield victory, the members of Mohammedan Sporting 'were almost mad and rolling on the ground with joyous excitement on the victory of their Hindu brethren'.[33] Another Muslim journal, *The Comrade*, of which Maulana Mohammed Ali was the founder and editor at that time said: 'We hereby join the chorus of praise and jubilation over the splendid victory of Mohun Bagan. The team did remarkably well throughout the tournament and won the Shield by sheer merit.'[34] Recounting Mohun Bagan's status as a team beloved by both communities, Achintya Kumar Sengupta wrote:

> Till then communalism had not entered the sports-field. Mohun Bagan then belonged to both the Hindu and the Muslim. The green galleries that burnt in the football stadium of the Calcutta that day carried the mark of both Hindu and Muslim hands. One brought the petrol and the other the matches.[35]

When MSC began to emerge as a powerful team in Indian football in the early 1930s, it was perhaps inevitable that the atmosphere around the club would change. While its achievements were undoubtedly 'Indian' success stories, Hindu football-lovers felt only a mixture of respect and fear with no real sensation of joy.[36] The Muslim League, by then a force hostile to the Congress, was the ruling party in Bengal in the 1930s and had the support of the British. Muslim nationalists could soon be seen holding the Congress flag in one hand and the black-and-white banner of Mohammedan Sporting in the other, and the Muslim League itself came to use the club as cultural example of Muslim superiority in Bengal. From the second half of the 1930s, rivalry in Indian football was no longer confined to the British versus the Indians, but had extended to include Hindus versus Muslims, adding definite sectarian overtones to the sport.

In 1932, 'a group of young, energetic, patriotic and progressive men' in Calcutta formed the New Muslim Majlis.[37] The main driver behind this development was Khwaja Nooruddin, cousin and brother-in-law of Khwaja Nazimuddin, who later played a heroic part in making the MSC a premier football club. One of the immediate aims of the Majlis was to co-opt the MSC and to develop it into the nation's premier club. The socio-political successes of the Majlis went hand in hand with the success on the football field achieved by the MSC.

When the club went on to win the first division league in its first year at that level, the repercussions were overwhelming. The club souvenir published in 1935 noted:

> In the 44th year of its existence we find the club not only makes its own history but history in Indian Football by winning the championship of the Calcutta Football League. When the Calcutta League, 1934, opened, the Mohammadan Sporting team were styled as the babes of the League owing to their promotion from the second division. From babes through the evolution of victory after victory and holding the top place on the League table they became the giants of the League and earned the coveted and unique distinction of being the first Indian team to win the League.[38]

The club souvenir also pointed to enormous enthusiasm that the victory brought in its wake:

> With their progress in the League there was unbounded enthusiasm among the Muslim public of Calcutta and the team were responsible for increasing the gates at which ever match they played fourfold. But not only in Calcutta was this enthusiasm manifested. In the mofussil thousands followed each game with the greatest of interest, so much so that many used to walk miles to the railway station to meet incoming trains with Calcutta newspapers in order to get the results as soon as possible.
>
> After their the team was lionized in the city of Calcutta and it was not for some weeks after that they could call an evening their own without having to attend some function in their honour. They were given a civic reception at the Town Hall when an address was presented to them by the Mayor of Calcutta.[39]

In 1935 when Mohammedan Sporting lifted the League for the second consecutive time, it was deemed to be a great achievement by Calcutta Muslims. The club souvenir thus recorded the immediate reaction to the victory: 'Tumultuous scenes were witnessed on the Calcutta ground after the match. The joy of the crowd was unbounded and each of the players was carried shoulder high while their bus was escorted in triumphant procession by thousands of Mohammadans wild with joy.'[40]

The success of Mohammedan Sporting in lifting the Calcutta Football League had a mixed impact on Indian society. For some— irrespective of their caste, creed or community—it was a worthy victory for Bengalis, alias Indians, on the sporting field. Indeed, the supremacy the club mastered over British sides was hailed as a unifying Indian victory in many quarters. For some Hindus, however, the victory was a cause for concern as it represented a victory of Muslim confidence and superiority.

There were tributes and messages, as gathered from the club's souvenir, which clearly hailed Mohammedan's victory as a success for the Muslim community. The Mayor of Calcutta, A.K. Fazlul Huq, commented: 'The marvelous achievements of the Mohammadan Sporting Club on the football field have earned a name and fame for Muslims in the sporting world, of which the community may justly be proud.'[41] Syed Abdul Hafeez, a member of the Council of State, wrote in his message: 'The Muslims of the sporting world take pride in the initiation taken by the Mohammadan Sporting Club of Calcutta. The club came into existence to fulfil a long felt want of the sporting spirit of the community.'[42] Another Muslim gentleman, M. Rafique, spoke of the importance of the club's success in terms of a great community service:

> Games and sports play a vital part in moulding and shaping the character and ultimately the destinies of individuals, no less than that of communities. The success of the Mohammadan Sporting Club will be a harbinger of greater successes in the *self-realisation of our great community in other branches of human endeavour.*[43] (emphasis added)

After a second year of league success, the MSC was clearly established as a symbol of Muslim identity and confidence across India. This is evident in the congratulatory messages it received from different corners of Bengal and the whole of the country.[44] As K. Nooruddin, one of the revivers of the club in the 1930s, remarked, 'Their spectacular performance, in recent years, is the turning point for the Mussalmans of Bengal in the field of sports.'[45] More importantly, in terms of how Muslim fans reacted to the victories, the club souvenir recorded the following:

> Ever since their (the club's) chances were rosy (in clinching the League) in the League last year and throughout this year, they have had the solid backing of thousands of supporters who rain, cloud or sunshine, have mustered to a man to see them play and encourage them.
> Club football fans would be amazed to see who some of these supporters are. Businessmen who leave their firms and shops to witness the

games, old men who have lost interest in football for years, but who have had it resuscitated with the enthusiasm for Mohammadans.[46]

Commenting upon the MSC's huge following during this period, Mohammad Nasiruddin, editor of *Saugat*, wrote:

Calcutta maidan used to witness large gathering on the days of Mohammadan Sporting's match. The crowd comprised educated and uneducated youth and old men along with maulavis and maulanas. When space on the sidelines of the ground proved insufficient, diehard fans climbed upon trees and sat on the branches to witness the matches of their favourite club. Kaji Najrul Islam, the famous Muslim bard, called these over-enthusiastic fans 'branch-monkeys'.[47]

In the changing political equation in Bengal during the 1930s, Mohammedan Sporting was discriminated against by the IFA. Despite the club's gallant performances against leading European teams, it was not given anywhere near the recognition accorded to Mohun Bagan after its victory in the IFA Shield in 1911. Key to the IFA's discriminatory attitude against Mohammedan Sporting was the Muslim political ascendancy in Bengal in the 1930s.[48] The Bengali *bhadralok*s (gentlemen) began to feel threatened by the Muslim political ascendancy in Bengal in the mid-1930s.[49] With the accession of the Krishak Praja Party–Muslim League ministry led by Fazlul Huq in 1937,[50] in almost every domain of the public sphere from higher education to administrative and political appointments, the Hindu bhadralok preserves were under threat. It was this situation that led the IFA to oppose the dominance of Mohammedan Sporting and ultimately to look favourably upon British rule.[51]

This atmosphere of hostility failed to deter the club from registering its fifth straight league triumph in July 1938. These performances escalated tensions between the IFA and the club, and in 1938, Mohammedan Sporting again suffered from seemingly unfair treatment from the authorities. The central grievances of the club were 'maximum punishment for minimum offences, repeated bad referring, arbitrary decision with regard to the venue of matches and generally the tyranny of the majority of the council of the IFA against our club.'[52] While Mohammedan Sporting did compete in the 1938 IFA Shield under extreme duress, the governing body's derisive attitude finally took its toll and forced the Mohammedans to withdraw from the Calcutta Football League in 1939. Interestingly, this withdrawal was not confined to the MSC alone. East Bengal Club and Kalighat Club also joined together against the discriminatory attitude adopted by the IFA, which continued to favour the Mohun Bagan Club. Though a temporary truce was once again arrived at in 1940, resulting in the re-entry of these clubs into the Calcutta Football League, the temporary parting of ways did have a lasting effect.

Thus, a potential situation of extreme social tension developed in Indian football in course of the 1930s when peaceful coexistence of two communities in challenging British supremacy on the soccer field gave way to serious rift between Hindus and Muslims. It was the oppositional perception of identity of two communities in a tense socio-political context which led to the fracture of footballing nationalism from the 1930s. This transition from 'community' to 'communal' in Indian football had several delicate moments, subtle shifts and points of convergences.

Regardless of the administrative confrontations, victories by Mohammedan Sporting and other Muslim clubs over strong European and Hindu teams certainly instilled a spirit of self-confidence and pride in the Muslims of Bengal; the vast majority of whom, through years of persecution and humiliation, had lost faith in the future.[53] It can be argued, therefore, that MSC contributed significantly to an atmosphere which enabled the Muslim League to gather increasing popular support in Bengal.[54] The series of victories achieved by the club, even in the all-India competitions, considerably increased the prestige of the party. The club's effect on Muslim fans was said to be consistently 'electrifying',[55] and a number of new Muslim sporting clubs in the districts and subdivisional towns were established as a result.

Along with this new Muslim interest in football came a more aggressive form of support teams such as Mohammedan Sporting. Indeed, the Muslims who were said to be 'rolling on the ground with joy' in 1911 at the victory of their Hindu brothers all appeared to disappear, and were replaced by a new breed of supporters who came to watch games carrying knives and bottles of soda water. Indians had never displayed such aggressive spirits on the Calcutta sports field before. Suranjan Das notes, 'reverses suffered by the Mohammadan Sporting Club in football matches enraged Muslim feelings which were expressed in sporadic violence against the Hindus',[56] and Moti Nandy comments, 'with each victory, a communal wedge was driven deeper into Calcutta football if not into Calcutta society.'[57] This transition of Indian football from nationalist force to promoter of separatist, communal identities can be situated in the wider context of nationalist movement and the rise of communal politics leading ultimately to the Partition of 1947, although this is not the place to discuss the historical debate concerning questions of partition and the role of different communities, groups or parties in it.

The Quit India Movement of 1942, the economic insecurity generated by the Second World War, the panic evacuation of Calcutta caused by the fear of Japanese bombs, the famine, restlessness among the youth and the communal riots that broke out on the day of call for 'direct action' by the Muslim League—the stress of all these events gradually reduced enthusiasm for football in India. Because of the riots, there was no competition for the Shield in 1946 and the Calcutta League was not played in 1947. Immediately after the partition in August 1947, having finally achieved their desire of creating a separate homeland for themselves in the form of Pakistan, many of the patrons of Mohammedan Sporting left for either East or West Pakistan. As a result, the club lost much of the financial support it enjoyed till that time. The club's fame of success was extinguished, never to be revived in quite the same way again. Since independence, Mohammedan Sporting has not enjoyed another period of success like that experienced during the 1930s and 1940s, and has only won the League championship on three occasions.

Confrontation and Assimilation: Host and Migrant Communities in Indian Club Football

In colonial India, Indians employed football to express first nationalist and later separatist, communal identities. The move from colonialism to independence, however, added a further fragmentary dimension to Indian football. In the aftermath of the Partition of Bengal that accompanied independence, large-scale Hindu immigration from East Pakistan (now Bangladesh) to West Bengal created a new socio-demographic tension which resulted in a distinct socio-cultural conflict in Bengali society. The sub-regional identity of the East Bengali Hindus clashed with that of the established Hindu settlers of West Bengal. To the West Bengali Hindus, who used to refer East Bengali Hindus derisively as *Bangals* (immigrants), the new immigrants disrupted the normal patterns of local life. Hence, they strongly disapproved of according them any prominent positions in local society, culture or business. The Bangals, with their common memory of a homeland, culture and a shared experience of suffering and migration, fought hard to earn their living, economic strength, social position and cultural recognition to ensure survival in a hostile environment. They ultimately came to refer to the locals as *Ghotis* (settlers). While the Ghoti–Bangal conflict certainly epitomized a cultural rivalry in Indian society, the identities, however, seemed more 'instrumentalist', that is, that were more constructed than 'primordialist'.

The Ghoti–Bangal conflict certainly came to express itself in the football arena. As immigrants sought to preserve their cultural identity and integrity in a new society, they searched for new avenues to assert themselves. In this context, East Bengali Hindus appropriated football as a cultural tool to establish their social identity and cultural excellence. Consequently, the maidan became a cultural space where the opposed identities of the Ghotis and Bangals came to be produced and reproduced through a bitter rivalry between Mohun Bagan, the club of the Ghotis, and East Bengal, the club of the Bangals.

The differences between Ghoti and Bangal was clearly discernible in terms of dialect, manner, dress, food habits, rites and rituals and even appearance, transcending wider similarities of religion, language and a common cultural past. These mostly 'cultural' differences, though not rigid, had the potential to create sharply distinctive 'social' identities in times of heightened socio-political tension. The Partition of Bengal in 1947, followed by a massive influx of East Bengali Hindu refugees into West Bengal, created the occasion for a sub-regional social conflict to flourish. In the aftermath of partition, the East Bengali refugees found in East Bengal a club of their 'own', representing their cultural 'self' to fight and win against the 'other' (West Bengali Hindus). As the latter mockingly named East Bengal 'the club of the Bangals', in turn, the East Bengali Hindus renamed Mohun Bagan 'the club of the Ghotis'. Consequently, the Ghoti–Bangal rivalry on the maidan divided Bengali Hindu society into two camps during every match between the two respective clubs. Interestingly, as Moti Nandy writes:

> these two communities even divided the aquatic population in a symbolic manner—the prawn for the *Ghotis* and the hilsa for the *Bangals*. In the evening after a football derby, the prices of prawn and hilsa used to rise or fall depending on the result of the match.[58]

While the rivalry between East Bengal and Mohun Bagan was most pronounced after the partition, it began when the East Bengal Club was formed in 1920 by East Bengalis keen to ameliorate the continuous discrimination waged against them by Calcutta's Bengali clubs.[59] By the 1930s, however, East Bengal lost some of its exclusive sub-regional character and fielded no more East Bengali players than Mohun Bagan or any other club.[60] Even during this period, though, the name and banner of East Bengal continued to inspire the East Bengali population, and they had a clear emotional attachment to the club. At the height of communal tension in Bengal on the eve of the partition, the IFA was alarmed at the increasing spectator violence at Mohun Bagan versus East Bengal matches. For example, a 1946 League match between the two which resulted in East Bengal's League triumph witnessed rampant hooliganism and violence.[61]

The degree of social sensitivity and cultural divergence evidently visible in Mohun Bagan–East Bengal rivalry before the partition, however, should not be exaggerated either. This bitter and fanatical rivalry between supporters of the two clubs shifted from a fluid to a rigid/exclusive state only after the Partition of Bengal in 1947. Hindu refugees started to arrive in droves in West Bengal from East Bengal/ Pakistan. Moti Nandy catches the tragedy of this refugee exodus brilliantly:

> Searching for a roof over their heads in the city and its surrounds and a fistful of rice twice a day, they began their struggle for survival under conditions of unbearable hardship. Lost and impoverished in an unknown territory and hostile environment, faced with severe adversities, they would sometimes lose the battle and fall back, then return once more to dream of settling down to a secure and normal existence.[62]

A more recent observation by a subaltern historian may be of more value here:

> The experiences of the refugees after being uprooted and upon their arrival in West Bengal were far from pleasant. They were forced to live in cramped government-run relief camps. There small sums were handed out to them as doles and they were given meagre family rations. In overall terms they were treated no better than beggars. No efforts were made to create employment opportunities to enable them to eke out a living.[63]

It was under the stress of such plight in everyday life that the Hindu refugees discovered a football club called East Bengal which was waging another battle on the sports field and, surprisingly enough, winning! 'For these ravaged and embittered masses,' remarks Nandy, 'the one source of hope, pride and victory lay in the triumphs of the Club named after their abandoned homeland.'[64] In fact, a spell of five years (1949–1953) in the immediate aftermath of the Partition and the refugee influx witnessed the spectacle of a dazzling display of football by the famous 'Five Pandavas' of East Bengal forward line, namely, Vengkatesh, Apparao, Dhanraj, Ahmed Khan and Saleh, leading to the club's series of successes in all national level tournaments.[65] These victories, for the uprooted Bangal migrants, leapt from the boundaries of sports field to become a cultural weapon to fight against settlers' discrimination. In other words, the Ghotis being identified as antagonists in their subconscious, the club's victory over Mohun Bagan on each occasion instilled a new confidence into their hearts. Naturally, they all began to assemble under the club's red-and-yellow banner. The city of Calcutta thus came to be divided into two clearly defined camps in football. As Berry Sarbadhikary noted in 1951:

> If a gallop-poll in the matter of football partisanship were taken today it would reveal a Calcutta split into two distinct camps, one for Mohun Bagan and the other for East Bengal; Mohun Bagan for their premiership amongst Indian football clubs, their hoary tradition and a uniformly high standard of play, and East Bengal for their solid, nearly all-conquering performances in recent years not only in Calcutta but all over the country. And so, if one half of Calcutta is glad, the other half inevitable becomes sad. Joy and sorrow constitute the pattern of life itself and are all in the game as long as these are tainted with fun-warranted boastfulness on the one side, and bitterness and malice on the other.[66]

It has been argued with some justification, if 'Mohammedan Sporting Club had brought with it hatred through its aggressive communalism born of a minority's natural instinct for self-preservation', 'East Bengal brought anger through regional, cultural and language differences in the backdrop of a hostile social, economic and political environment.'[67] Press reports on matches between the East Bengal and Mohun Bagan in the 1950s and 1960s confirm their importance through comments on the presence of exceptionally large crowds. The IFA Shield final between East Bengal and Mohun Bagan in 1947 had to be abandoned on the first day due to spectator violence.[68] In the Shield final between the two clubs in 1950, a huge police force had to be stationed at the ground to avert violence.[69] These skirmishes gradually extended to engulf the whole of the Calcutta maidan, so much so that the IFA decided to continue with the League only with regular assistance from the Calcutta Police in 1951.[70] East Bengal, however, objected to this decision and a bitter rivalry ensued between the club and the police. The matter assumed such a controversial dimension that the chief minister had to intervene to settle matters.[71] The chief minister also expressed concern over the question of the organization and control of the game in 1955. Disappointed with the IFA's role in the process, he proposed the formation of a central organization to control the game in Calcutta.[72] The very next year, East Bengal along with a few other clubs filed a petition to the IFA against biased refereeing in the League. The referee's bias, according to the petition, was intended to favour one particular club. They demanded that the IFA must end the favouritism within a week.[73] Needless to say, the favoured club was Mohun Bagan.

Throughout the 1950s and 1960s, the rivalry between Mohun Bagan and East Bengal continued to prosper along sub-regional and cultural lines. While the refugees, backed strongly by the Communists, waged a pitched battle against the Congress-led West Bengal government on the political plane,[74] East Bengal led the onslaught on the cultural plane, that is, on the football field. The situation became so alarming in the late 1950s that Dr B.C. Roy, then chief minister of West Bengal, suggested a change in club names which carried religious, regional or ethnic overtones.[75] Further, football's politicization in the context of increasing spectator violence in the 1950s was a major source of discord between the IFA on the one hand and clubs like East Bengal, Mohammedan Sporting or Aryan on the other. In such context, the Ghoti–Bangal war around football in the 1950s and 1960s probably came to reflect an invisible association between football and politics. However, this is not to deny that football hooliganism on the ground, in the galleries or on the streets had its own autonomous domain without any political undertones; that is, it was generated at many points by field experiences of the game, including most commonly referee's decisions.

The configuration of Indian football along sub-regional lines took an aggressive turn in the 1970s. The war of liberation in East Pakistan and the emergence of Bangladesh in 1971 led to a fresh wave of immigration of Hindus into West Bengal. This added substantially to East Bengal Club's support base as the club served as a rallying point for the immigrants' shared cultural identities. May be as a result, the first half of the 1970s was a glorious period for the club.[76] More importantly, during the six years from 1970 to 1975, the club conceded only one defeat at the hands of Mohun Bagan.[77] Naturally, therefore, the supporters of the club dominated the maidan in this period.

The immigration of the early 1970s coincided with a period of intensive social tension and political turmoil in West Bengal in the wake of the anti-establishment Naxalite Movement that used violence and terror as a means to achieve its end. The football field failed to isolate itself from this violence. As a result, spectator behaviour began to undergo qualitative changes. As Surojit Sengupta, the footballer-turned-sports journalist, has remarked, 'In the context of the Naxal Movement in the early 1970s, political uncertainty and social depression often turned Calcutta's football ground hot and violent.'[78] Emotional bonding with a club rapidly acquired more extreme expressions as aggression became more pronounced and victories and defeats were met with equally hysterical reactions. Spectators routinely stood in queues for days at a time to obtain tickets to watch matches. Skirmishes and feuds were common during these long waits, and people would frequently become injured or fall ill. In the 1975 Shield final, East Bengal defeated Mohun Bagan 5–0. After the fourth goal was scored, one East Bengal supporter had a heart attack out of sheer ecstasy and had to be taken to hospital immediately.[79] For a 25-year-old young Mohun Bagan supporter named Umakanto Palodhi, the ignominious defeat aroused so much dejection that he committed suicide. The suicidal note he left said: 'By becoming a better Mohun Bagan footballer, I wish to take revenge of this defeat in my next birth.'[80] Two years later, when East Bengal defeated favourites Mohun Bagan in a 1977 League encounter,[81] a young Mohun Bagan supporter poisoned himself by drinking a bottle of pesticide.[82] The post-match report pointed to extremely unruly behaviour among the crowd and mentioned that the East Bengal supporters after the match had become uncontrollable.[83] Instances of the crowd going overboard are galore in contemporary press reports. What these trends of crowd behaviour bring to light is that behind the facade of eternal enmity between the two clubs inspired by a long-term cultural conflict lay a deeper and more intense force of club loyalty. Matters between the two clubs came to a head in 1980 when, during a relatively unimportant League match between the two teams at the Eden Gardens in Calcutta, clashes between supporters led to widespread violence in the stadium, resulting in a stampede that cost 16 fans their lives.[84]

While supporters of East Bengal and Mohun Bagan viewed their assumed cultural differences extremely seriously, the players never conformed strictly to the Ghoti–Bangal divide. Ghotis, such as Arun Ghosh, earned fame playing for East Bengal, while Bangals such as Gautam Sarkar rose to prominence as players for Mohun Bagan. Both later noted that identification of the clubs with Ghotis or Bangals depended entirely on the extreme feelings of some supporters and a few club officials, and that players hardly played any role at all.[85] Since the early 1980s, the supporters' rivalry on sub-regional lines, too, began to fade away, as memories of the partition and the old homeland grew weaker. As Dimeo notes:

> By the 1980s, though, identity markers were becoming less distinct. The memory of East Bengal as 'home' was the preserve of a fading generation of migrants, their sons and daughters more at home in West Bengal. Inter group relationships became more common, dialects less pronounced, and cultural traditions passed away. There are cases of fans with East Bengali parents supporting Mohun Bagan. Thus, a liminal, in-between space developed that contravened the polarity of previous years.[86]

While relations between East Bengal and Mohun Bagan have undoubtedly improved in recent decades, there is still a continuing and unique enmity between the two clubs. The tradition of a long-term rivalry, the consolidation of oppositional identities and the conventions of supporters' cultures and intensifications with their clubs have all helped sustain the excitement of the 'battle royal' of Indian football.[87] What still differentiates this rivalry from other Indian club rivalries is the intense emotional attachment of the clubs' supporters towards 'their' club and vehement opposition to the 'others' club.[88] This oppositional perception of 'self' and 'other' continues to shape the most fascinating rivalry in Indian football.

Nation versus Club: The Dichotomy Continues!

In the transition from colonialism to postcolonialism, football in India acted as a platform for social networks, community connections and identity formations of various types. Whenever the game mobilized or unified a community for a cause, be it national, religious or sub-regional, it always created intense club loyalty that led to the game's widespread social popularization as a mass spectator sport. The three clubs—Mohun Bagan, Mohammedan Sporting and East Bengal—while representing respective identities and commonalities of nationalism, communalism and sub-regionalism also heightened the social viability and commercial prospects of football in India. The intense support bases of the three clubs sustained the mass craze around the game all over India until the 1980s when club teams from Punjab, Maharashtra, Kerala and Goa began to challenge Bengal's supremacy in domestic tournaments. This new challenge also signalled the beginning of new rivalries between club-based regional communities across India. With the launch of the new National League in 1996, these rivalries have now a perfect stage on which to be played out.

Since the fragmentation of Indian sporting nationalism in the 1930s, club loyalties in football have become dominant over national interests. Even in the peculiar amateur (semi-professional since the mid-1990s) set-up of Indian football, the clash of interests between India's leading clubs and the national team has been a constant problem for the game's administrators, resulting in India's dismal showing in international football over the last four decades. And now with the slow but steady commercialization of football in twenty-first-century India, club communities are increasingly growing strong. The introduction of theme songs and websites; the promotion of merchandising such as club jerseys, flags and symbols; and the formation of local fan clubs and satellite communities are all aimed at strengthening and widening the geographical fan base of the clubs within India and beyond. It is the responsibility of the All India Football Federation, the apex controlling body of football in India, and its affiliated state units to ensure that the interest of the national team must not be destroyed entirely by the growing strength of these club communities: a situation which is likely to plague Indian football for quite some time yet. Last but not least, the gradual penetration of global capital into Indian football scene, apparent with the onset of the Indian Super League on the model of Indian Premier League cricket, has the potential to transform the future of this club–nation relation for ever.

Notes and References

1. For a broad discussion on some of these aspects, see Boria Majumdar and Kausik Bandyopadhyay, *A Social History of Indian Football: Striving to Score* (London: Routledge, 2006).
2. The discussion on these aspects in this essay has some resonance to the author's earlier writings on the subject. For details, see Kausik Bandyopadhyay, 'Race, Nation and Sport: Footballing Nationalism in Colonial Calcutta', *Soccer and Society*, Vol. 4, No. 1 (2003), pp. 1–19; '1911 in Retrospect: A Revisionist Perspective on a Famous Indian Sporting Victory', *The International Journal of the History of Sport*, Vol. 21, Nos. 3/4 (2004): 363–383; and 'Ghoti Bangal o Bangalir Football (Ghoti-Bangal and Bengalis' Football)', Aniruddha Roy, ed. *Itihas Anusandhan-20* (Kolkata: Firma KLM, 2006), pp. 496–504.
3. J.A. Mangan, 'Series Editor's Foreword', in G. Armstrong and R. Giulianotti, eds. *Fear and Loathing in World Football* (Oxford: Berg, 2001), p. viii.
4. For a brief discussion on the beginnings of football in India, see Bandyopadhyay, 'Race, Nation and Sport', pp. 1–4.
5. The accepted definitive study of public school games as moral training is J.A. Mangan's *Athleticism in Victorian and Edwardian Public School: The Emergence and Consolidation of an Educational Ideology* (Cambridge: Cambridge University Press, 1981 and London: Frank Cass, 2000 with a new introduction).
6. Tony Mason, 'Football on the Maidan: Cultural Imperialism in Calcutta', in J.A. Mangan, ed. *The Cultural Bond: Sport, Empire, Society* (London: Frank Cass, 1992), p. 144; Paul Dimeo, 'Football and Politics in Bengal: Colonialism, Nationalism, Communalism', in Paul Dimeo and James Mills, eds. *Soccer in South Asia: Empire, Nation, Diaspora* (London: Frank Cass, 2001), p. 62.
7. For a reflective discussion on this theme in Asian context, see J.A. Mangan, 'Imperial Origins, Christian Manliness, Moral Imperatives and Pre-Sri Lankan Playing Fields— "Beginnings" and "Consolidation"', in J.A. Mangan and Fan Hong, eds. *Sport in Asian Society: Past and Present* (London: Frank Cass, 2003), pp. 1–49.

8. J.A. Mangan, 'Soccer as Moral Training: Missionary Intentions and Imperial Legacies', in Dimeo and Mills, eds. *Soccer in South Asia*, p. 41.

9. Ibid.

10. In fact, throughout the nineteenth century, British imperialists, perhaps out of their deep dislike for the climate, topography and inhabitants of Bengal, made the Bengali a butt of satiric criticisms for their supposed physical effeteness—a stereotype that ran all through the period of Imperial rule. This colonial construction of 'effeminate Bengali' could be found in everyday British attitude towards commonplace Bengalis, in their various speeches and most prolifically in their writings, namely, contemporary Anglo-Indian literature.

11. For an in-depth study of this concept, see John Rosselli, 'The Self-Image of Effeteness: Physical Education and Nationalism in Nineteenth-Century Bengal'. *Past and Present*, Vol. 86 (1980): 121–148.

12. For a detailed history of this movement, see Jogesh Chandra Bagal, *Hindu Melar Itibritta* (Calcutta: Maitrayee, 1945).

13. Paul Dimeo, 'Colonial Bodies, Colonial Sport: "Martial" Punjabis, "Effeminate" Bengalis and the Development of Indian Football', *The International Journal of the History of Sport*, Vol. 19, No. 1 (March 2002): 84.

14. This transformation of football's social dimension has been elaborately discussed by Soumen Mitra in his unpublished MPhil dissertation, 'Nationalism, Communalism and Sub-regionalism: A Study of Football in Bengal, 1880–1950', Centre for Historical Studies: Jawaharlal Nehru University, 1988, Chapter 3.

15. *Mohun Bagan Club Platinum Jubilee Souvenir* (Calcutta: Mohun Bagan A.C., 1964), pp. 1–5.

16. Soumen Mitra, 'Babu at Play: Sporting Nationalism in Bengal, 1880–1911', in Nisith Ray and Ranjit Roy, eds. *Bengal: Yesterday and Today* (Calcutta: Papyrus, 1991), p. 46.

17. The best work on the anti-Partition movement till date is Sumit Sarkar's *The Swadeshi Movement in Bengal* (New Delhi: People's Publishing House, 1973).

18. A sports field.

19. Only Sudhir Chatterjee played in boots for the club.

20. Details on the results of all these matches can be found in *Mohun Bagan Platinum Jubilee Souvenir*, pp. 15–17; also see Nandy, *Mohun Bagan 1911* (Calcutta: Karuna Prakashani, 1976).

21. I have taken this term from Partha Chatterjee's celebrated work *Nationalist Thought and the Colonial World: A Derivative Discourse?* (London: Zed Books, 1986), pp. 54–84. Chatterjee, however, used the term in an entirely different context.

22. *Amrita Bazar Patrika*, 31 July 1911, p. 8.

23. Newspapers that stressed 'Bengali' identity were *Amrita Bazar Patrika*, *Nayak*, *Times of India Illustrated Weekly* and *Basumati*. On the other hand, *London Reuter*, *The Englishman* and *The Musalman* reckoned the victory to be an 'Indian' one.

24. *The Telegraph* (Calcutta), 20 June 1998.

25. Rudrangshu Mukherjee, 'Elegy on the Maidan', *The Telegraph*, 5 March 2002.

26. Mason, 'Football on the Maidan', pp. 150–151.

27. Ibid.; Dimeo, 'Football and Politics in Bengal', p. 71. For the most authoritative discussion of British cultural imperialism on the sports field, see Allen Guttman, *Games and Empires: Modern Sports and Cultural Imperialism* (New York: Columbia University Press, 1994).

28. Richard Cashman, 'Cricket and Colonialism: Colonial Hegemony and Indigenous Subversion', in J.A. Mangan, ed. *Pleasure, Profit, Proselytism: British Culture and Sport at Home and Abroad, 1700-1914* (London: Frank Cass, 1988), pp. 259–260.
29. Ibid.
30. Ibid.
31. In 1887 was established the Jubilee Club, a sporting organization for the Muslims in Calcutta. The club changed its name twice in the next few years, first to the Crescent Club and then to the Hamidia Club. Finally, in 1891, the latter culminated into the Mohammedan Sporting Club. For details, see Mohammedan Sporting Club Records, Mohammedan Sporting Club, Calcutta.
32. The initiative of some Muslim youths, both of Calcutta and the mofussil, who felt the need of the Muslim youth having its own sporting club founded the Crescent Club in 1889. It is, however, said that the club had its predecessor in the Jubilee Club founded in 1887 in Calcutta at the initiatives of Khan Bahadur Aminul Islam, Maulavi Abdul Ghani of Malda and Maulavi Muhammad Yasin of Burdwan. In 1890, the club's name was changed again into Hamidia Club. In 1891, finally, the club came to be transformed into the Mohammedan Sporting Club. For further details on the origin of the club, see 'History of the Club', *Mohammedan Sporting Club. Calcutta League Champions 1934-35. A Souvenir* (Calcutta: Mohammedan Sporting Club, 1935), pp. 27, 35–39.
33. Quoted in *Mohun Bagan Club Platinum Jubilee Souvenir*, p. 25.
34. Ibid.
35. Achintya Kumar Sengupta, *Kallol Yug* (Calcutta: M.C. Sarkar & Sons, 1950), p. 66.
36. Comments of Muhammad Nasiruddin, the editor of *Saugat*, a periodical published from Dacca, quoted in Lutfar Rahman Ritan, *Football* (Dacca: Bangla Academy, 1985), p. 21.
37. M.A.H. Ispahani, *Qaid-E-Azam Jinnah—As I Knew Him* (Karachi: Forward Publications, 1965), p. 4; Kenneth McPherson, *The Muslim Microcosm: Calcutta, 1918–1935* (Wiesbaden: Franz Steiner Verlag, 1974), p. 121.
38. 'History of the Club', in *Mohammedan Sporting Club. Calcutta League Champions 1934–35. A Souvenir*, p. 36.
39. Ibid.
40. Ibid.
41. Ibid., p. 12.
42. Ibid., p. 25.
43. Ibid., p. 26, emphasis added.
44. Hundreds of messages came from Muslim clubs and organizations of different parts of India, including Shillong, Sylhet, Dacca, Rangpur, Tippera, Dinajpur, Jalpaiguri, Darjeeling, Purnea, Cuttack, Benares, Bombay, Bangalore and Calcutta. For details, see *Mohammedan Sporting Club. Calcutta League Champions 1934–35. A Souvenir*, p. 28.
45. Ibid.
46. 'Tribute from the Green Stands', in ibid., p. 34.
47. Comments of Mohammad Nasiruddin quoted in Ritan, *Football*, pp. 20–22.
48. Majumdar and Bandyopadhyay, *A Social History of Indian Football*, Chapter 5.
49. Ibid.
50. Led by Abul Kasem Fazlul Huq, the Krishak Praja Party drew its strength from the mass following it enjoyed among Bengal's Muslim peasantry and intermediate shareholders.

51. Majumdar and Bandyopadhyay, *A Social History of Indian Football*, Chapter 5.

52. *Mohammedan Sporting Club Souvenir* (Calcutta: Mohammedan Sporting Club, 1939), pp. 66–68, quoted in ibid., p. 101.

53. Ispahani, *Qaid-E-Azam Jinnah—As I Knew Him*, p. 12.

54. Abul Kalam Shamsuddin, *Atit Diner Smriti (Memories of Olden Days)* (Dacca: Nowroje Kitabistan, 1968), pp. 154–158.

55. Humaira Momen, *Muslim Politics in Bengal: A Study of Krishak Praja Party and the Elections of 1937* (Dacca: Sunny House, 1972), p. 72.

56. Suranjan Das, *Communal Riots in Bengal: 1905–1947*, New Delhi: Oxford University Press, 1991, p. 170. Also see *Amrita Bazar Patrika*, 8 July 1946, 4; File-5/27/46 Poll (I), the IB Daily Summary Information of 8 July 1946.

57. Moti Nandy, 'Calcutta Soccer', in Sukanta Chaudhuri, ed. *Calcutta: The Living City, 2: The Present and Future* (Calcutta: Oxford University Press, 1990), p. 318.

58. Nandy, 'Football and Nationalism', translated by Shampa Banerjee, in Geeti Sen, ed. *The Calcutta Psyche* (New Delhi: India International Centre, 1990), p. 249.

59. Historians of the East Bengal Club have all noted this aspect of discrimination waged against the East Bengali players and people and unanimously pointed to the exclusively regional character of the club at its birth and its impressive beginning in Calcutta football. For details, see Santipriya Bandyopadhyay, *Cluber Naam East Bengal* (The name of the club in East Bengal) (Calcutta: New Bengal Press, 1979); Jayanta Dutta, *Glorious East Bengal* (Calcutta: Sahitya Prakash, 1975); Paresh Nandy, *East Bengal Club, 1920–1970: Ponchas Bochhorer Sangram o Safalya* (East Bengal Club, 1920–70: Fifty years' struggle and successes) (Calcutta: Bichitra, 1973); Pandit Mashai, *East Bengal Cluber Itihas*; Rupak Saha, *Itihase East Bengal* (East Bengal in history) (Calcutta: Deep, 2000).

60. A number of worthy footballers from eastern Bengal played for Mohun Bagan throughout the first half of the twentieth century. The list includes names such as Nagen Kali, Hemango Basu, Rabi Basu, Bagha Som, Sanmatha Datta and K. Datta. For details, see Sen, *Kheladhular Bichitra Kahini* (Peculiar stories of games and sports) (Calcutta: R.M. Gupta/Geetanjali Book Centre, 1983), pp. 21–29.

61. *Amrita Bazar Patrika*, 7 July 1946.

62. Nandy, 'Football and Nationalism', pp. 249–250. The experience of suffering, deprivation and impoverishment of the East Bengali refugees in the aftermath of the Partition has been vividly delineated in a rich crop of Bengali literature. Historically, most important and memorable of these novels, dramas and short stories are: *Arjun, Atmaprakash* (Sunil Gangopadhyay); *Nonajal Mithemati* (Prafulla Roy); *Aranyadandak, Bakutala P L Camp, Balmik* (Narayan Sanyal); *Sona Fasoler Pala, Meghe Dhaka Tara* (Shaktipada Rajguru); *Notun Ihudi* (Salil Sen); *Ranipalangka, Gotrantar* (Bijan Bhattacharyya); *Epar Ganga Opar Ganga* (Jyotirmoyi Debi); *Madhab o tar Pariparshik, Jaal* (Sirshendu Mukhopadhyay); *Nilkantha Pakhir Khonje, Abad, Manusher Gharbari, Iswarer Bagan, Aloukik Jaloyan, Mrinmoyi* (Atin Bandyopadhyay); *Sthaniya Sambad* (Sankar); *Suchander Swadeshjatra, Adab* (Samaresh Basu); *Hasubanu* (Probodh Kumar Sanyal); *Lalmati, Bidisha, Maryada* (Narayan Gangopadhyay); *Shada Ghora* (Ramesh Chandra Sen); *Badwip, Swaralipi* (Sabitri Ray); *Sanko, Dalil* (Hritvik Ghatak); *Ei Swadhinata* (Sachindranath Sengupta); *Gar Srikhanda, Nirbas* (Amiyabhushan Majumdar); *Ghoorni* (Sambhu Mitra); *Gosthabiharir Jibanjapan* (Amalendu Chakraborty); *Ora Aajo Udbastu* (Dulalendu Chattopadhyay); *Manaskanya* (Jarasandha); *Nischitpurer Manush* (Jyotirindra Nandi); *Panchaparba* (Banaful); *Bipasha* (Tarasankar Bandyopadhyay);

Sarbajanin, Upay, Subala (Manik Bandyopadhyay); *Duekti Ghar Duekti Swar* (Loknath Bhattacharyya); *Doorbhashini* (Narendranath Mitra); and *Nil Agun* (Saroj Kumar Roychaudhury).

63. Gyanesh Kudaisya, 'Divided Landscapes, Fragmented Identities: East Bengal Refugees and Their Rehabilitation in India, 1947–79', in D.A. Low and Howard Brasted, eds. *Freedom, Trauma and Continuities: Northern India and Independence* (New Delhi: Sage, 1998), p. 118.

64. Moti Nandy, 'Calcutta Soccer', in Sukanta Chaudhuri, ed. *Calcutta: The Living City*, Vol. II (Oxford: Oxford University Press, 1990), p. 319.

65. Thanks to this legendary forward line, during this period, East Bengal won both the IFA League and Shield thrice (League–1949, 1950, 1952 and Shield–1949, 1950, 1951); Durand Cup and DCM Trophy twice (Durand–1951, 1952 and DCM–1950, 1952); and the Rovers Cup once (1949).

66. Berry Sarbadhikary, 'Sports Commentary', *Amrita Bazar Patrika*, 11 June 1951.

67. Nandy, 'Football and Nationalism', p. 250.

68. *The Statesman*, 5 October 1947.

69. *Amrita Bazar Patrika*, 17 September 1950.

70. Ibid., 31 May 1951.

71. Ibid., 22 and 23 June 1951.

72. Ibid., 29 June 1955.

73. Ibid., 22 June 1956.

74. For a useful study of the relationship between Communist political ascendancy in West Bengal and refugee politics, see Prafulla Chakrabarty, *The Marginal Men: The Refugees and the Left Political Syndrome in West Bengal* (Calcutta: Lumière Books, 1990).

75. See the *Amrita Bazar Patrika*, 17, 18 and 24 July 1957. The chief minister, by these terms, apparently referred to Mohammedan Sporting, East Bengal and the Rajasthan Clubs respectively.

76. East Bengal won the League title six times in a row from 1970 to 1975—still a record. It won the IFA Shield in 1970, and then with a gap of a year in 1971 won every year from 1972 to 1976. The club bagged the Durand Cup in 1970 and 1972; Rovers Cup in 1972, 1973 and 1975; DCM Trophy in 1973 and 1974; and Bordoloi Trophy in 1972 and 1973.

77. This sole occasion when Mohun Bagan got the better of their arch-rivals was in the 1974 Durand Cup semi-final. Mohun Bagan won the match by a solitary goal.

78. Interview with Surojit Sengupta, 25 August 2002. For Sengupta's fuller views on football culture that grew around the East Bengal–Mohun Bagan rivalry in India, see Sengupta, *Back Center*. Incidentally, Sengupta who was a worthy right-winger of East Bengal team in the 1970s has recently left his job to take charge as the sports editor of *Khela*, the foremost sports vernacular magazine of Bengal.

79. *Ananda Bazar Patrika*, 30 September 1975.

80. Ibid., 1 October 1975. Also see Manas Chakrabarty, 'Mohun Bagan-East Bengal Reshareshi' (Mohun Bagan-East Bengal conflict), *Anandamela*, 19 July 2000, p. 118.

81. East Bengal won the match 2–0.

82. *Ananda Bazar Patrika*, 10 July 1977. The report said that the person was taken to the PG Hospital in a very critical condition.

83. According to the same newspaper report, 'total chaos resulted in the streets and different quarters of the city as the euphoric supporters ran wild with *mashal*s (fire torch) in their hands from one place to another. There were several complaints against the

jubilant crowd, which stopped private cars and scooters on the streets. Bricks were thrown into the ground and on another club's tent resulting in the injury of at least two dozens of people, three of them being rushed to Shambhunath Pandit Hospital. According to the police, eight persons were arrested on that evening.' *Ananda Bazar Patrika*, 10 July 1977.

84. The pre-match press reports suggested possibilities of chaos and violence on the match day. In fact, the Federation Cup final between the two teams on 8 May 1980 witnessed extremely unruly behaviour of not only the fans but also the players and club officials. See *Ananda Bazar Patrika*, 15 August 1980; *Khelar Asar*, 16 May 1980.

85. Tanaji Sengupta, 'Nirapade Bhinna Clube', *Desh* (Binodon sankhya), 1988, pp. 184–189.

86. Dimeo, '"Team Loyalty Splits the City into Two": Football, Ethnicity and Rivalry in Calcutta', in Armstrong and Giulianotti, eds. *Fear and Loathing in World Football* (Oxford: Berg, 2001), p. 106.

87. Despite radical changes in Indian sporting map in the 1980s—organization of Asian Games in Delhi (1982), India's World Cup victory in cricket (1983) followed by Mini World Cup triumph two years later (1985), live telecast of World Cup football since 1982 and of European and Latin American league and cup matches (since 1987), organizational laxity of All India Football Federation and, most important of all, utter failure of the national and regional football bodies as well as the two great Calcutta clubs to adapt to the challenge of globalization, commercialism and professionalism till the mid-1990s—the intensity of rivalry between Mohun Bagan and East Bengal showed no signs of abatement. However, the rivalry faced a real challenge in 1997 when both the clubs came to be sponsored and marginally controlled by the same company, namely, the United Breweries Group. After this sponsorship deal, there arose a large apprehension among the supporters of the clubs that their age-old enmity would come to an end. Yet what still continues to dominate Indian football is a desperate rivalry between the two Bengali outfits.

88. A more recent incident is conclusively revealing on this point: In late May 2003, Mohun Bagan Club, bogged down by internal strife and court cases, could not arrange for the money to retain its star players, including the club's heart-throb Jose Ramirez Barreto, the Brazilian forward. Learning this from newspaper reports, one ardent supporter of the club decided to sell off his ancestral house and came to the club authority to know the formalities of payment. The club officials understandably refused the offer but take pride in it as a reflection of the club's continuing tradition and glory. As East Bengal, the foremost enemy of his club, won all the five tournaments they participated in the previous season, including the all-important National League title with a nearly all-win record against Mohun Bagan, the fan could not bear the thought of a repeat of the same story next year. Hence, to retain the star forward, who he believed could only ameliorate the plight of the club against their arch-rival, he committed his only asset for the sake of the club. For details, see *Ananda Bazar Patrika*, 3 July 2003.

Rupak Saha narrates a similar incident of 1991 when an East Bengal fan mortgaged his house and took his wife's gold ornaments to rope in a few good players for the club in times of the club's financial crisis. For details, see Rupak Saha, 'Bangalir Football', *Desh*, 28 August 1993, pp. 23–24.

2

Uncovering the Sleeping Giant Syndrome: India in Olympic Football

Introduction

.... There is still a temptation to classify this, the world's second most populous nation, in the familiar category popularly and vaguely known as 'sleeping giants'. The term has been applied, with varying degrees of justification, to many other countries, especially to those in Africa, where the giant has woken and has startled others into doing so. In China, to take another example, the giant appears to be awake but is seemingly incapable of getting out of bed.

The Indian colossus remains mostly in slumber, despite intermittent bouts of insomnia, reacting to the occasional attempts to rouse it. But such awakenings have seldom had sufficient effect as to transcend regional frontiers.[1]

In the valedictory session of the Conference of Indian Football held in March 2003 at New Delhi, Dato Peter Velappan, general secretary, Asian Football Confederation (AFC), exuded confidence in India's future potential: 'The time to act is now, for yesterday was past, tomorrow is the future and the present is the transition. Decide where you wish to be in the Asians Cup final or the World Cup?'[2] The immediate antecedent of this confidence is important. Velappan presented in the same conference a paper titled 'Vision India: The Way Forward', which, when implemented, was expected to revolutionize football in the country. He said 'if there is a will then blessings begin to shower. A nation of over one billion population with 33% of them in the U-14 years category presents a vast segment of potential footballers who need to be tapped, moulded and brought up on the right lines.'[3] He also highlighted the 11 elements, like 11 men of a team on a football field, which need to be looked into for a way forward: national state associations, marketing, youth development, coaches' education, referees, sports medicine, men's football, women's football, futsal, media and communications and fans.[4] Later on the project started, as he had affirmed, with the building of a permanent headquarters of the All India Football Federation (AIFF) in the capital, and would be followed by football offices in various states and expertise at every step.

Urs Zanitti, Head of the Development Division of Federation Internationale de Football Association (FIFA), who was a delegate in the conference, lamented a few months later: 'It's a scandal from an outsider's point of view. FIFA's job is to provide the money but, in countries like India, we are forced to deal directly with the people to whom the money is paid eventually.'[5] Pointing to the FIFA House project, the plan to build a permanent office and much more for the AIFF in New Delhi's Dwarka area, he exclaimed: 'We are dealing directly with the architects and contractors, because nothing seems to get done otherwise. It was supposed to have been built a year or so ago, but it's still not in functioning condition.' His experience with the AIFF top brass has been more revealing:

> They seem interested enough but where's the administration? Where are the administrators? You have some people in Delhi. Some in Kolkata. Some in Goa. There are no people. The human resource is very poor. The financial resources are poor also, but that's where we come in. But here we need to take part in creating the human resource also.[6]

In terms of the genealogy of soccer as a modern sport, India certainly ranks as a giant. So long as she was a colony, her true potential as a soccer power remained undetermined. After Independence, however, India emerged as a formidable Asian force on the international stage. The story of India's tryst with Olympic football offers an interesting repertoire of stunning performances, including modest success, appalling defeat and long absence, ranging from India's decent start in the London Olympics of 1948 through a huge defeat in the Helsinki Olympics of 1952 to a stirring performance in 1956. And when India's spirited display in the Rome Olympics of 1960 was followed by the startling victory in the Jakarta Asian Games in 1962, the nation seemed ready to have a crack at the international level. But the momentum was lost quite astonishingly within a decade. The decline set in and the giant had fallen asleep again. Yet the slumber has been mostly dreamy with intermittent magic spells of insomnia, albeit without any sustained impact on the nation's Olympic soccer fortune. Since 1960, Indian football team never qualified for the Olympics. This chapter, looking deep into this much-publicized metaphor of 'sleeping giant', deciphers the long-term underlying processes and the cultural politics of soccer that explains both the legacies and the prospects of Indian football in the Olympic Games, thereby linking its past, present and future. In the process, it also argues that Indian soccer's failure to make a mark in the Olympics reflects the nation's failure to develop an enduring Olympic culture over time.

From Asian Force to Spent Force: India in International/Olympic Football[7]

The concept of an Indian nation in international football is arguably a postcolonial development. Since the late 1920s, Indian teams began to undertake soccer tours to countries such as Australia, South Africa, Burma, Singapore, Malay, China, Japan and Ceylon, while Indian national and club teams played against invited foreign teams in the 1930s. These friendship matches could by no means judge the true worth and standard of Indian players. The results of the annual Indians–Europeans matches since 1920, however, did testify to the quality and standard of Indian football to a certain extent. Yet there was no question of India's participation in any international tournaments of worth under colonial rule.

After gaining independence, India got its first toast of participation in international competition in the London Olympics of 1948. The Indian football team raised high promises of a good show in their pre-Olympic trial/friendly matches.[8] The team also played bare feet in order to see how they fared on soft ground without boots. As one report argued:

> According to their trainer, B.D. Chatterjee, they have boots with them in case the ground proves too yielding, but they prefer to play in barefeet.
>
> The way they performed without boots tonight surprised many spectators and the match can be summed up in the words of a police supporter who said, 'They are even better without boots than our boys are with them.' The clever footwork and ball control often baffled opposition but shooting was very weak.[9]

India met France at Ilford in its first ever Olympic match on 31 July 1948. India played well to match a far superior French side, although it ultimately lost the game 1–2, but only after missing two penalties awarded to her.[10] Berry Sarbadhikari gave a first-hand account of India's performance in the match:

> On a bone-dry ground, shining in oriental splendour, the Indians with their phenomenal speed, barefooted ball-control and jugglery had literally swamped France so that the panting Frenchmen eventually were reduced to marking the man—not the ball.
>
> And I have never seen before or since the vanquished team given as big a hand as the Indians were that evening at Ilford, nor the victors booed and heckled most bitterly as they entered the pavilion with their heads hung in shame.
>
> In the Indian team, all but the right full-back Taj Mohamed, were barefooted and it must have been a strange sight indeed in England—and in Olympic football too.[11]

India continued with the good work by performing well against some amateur sides that she played in a post-Olympic tour of Europe. Barefooted display of quality football impressed many in the West. On one occasion,[12] when Stanley Rous, secretary of the British Football Association, complimented the Indian Team Manager Manindra Dutta Ray on the Indian performance, the latter asked for a suitable coach from England to come to India for further improvement. In reply, Rous stated: 'You don't need a coach from outside, you play excellent football and surely your experienced men could look after your boys and brush them up.'[13] However, as Jaydeep Basu has rightly pointed out, 'the experience in the London Olympics made it amply clear that India was still not ready to challenge the best in the world.'[14] According to him, 'the barefoot approach only raised curiosity, but not the standard of the game.' And he goes on to argue: 'The call of the time was to discard the old tactics and learn quickly from the mistakes. But no one gave much thought to it till the team courted disaster in the next Olympics at Helsinki.'[15] Meanwhile, India had qualified for the World Cup in 1950 to be held in Brazil. Despite having a rich band of footballers, however, she could not take part in the World Cup she had only qualified for. Most commonly ascribed reasons for this withdrawal are: faulty role of the AIFF, lack of foreign reserves, barefooted playing style, the long sea journey and apprehension about India's chances against world's topmost teams.

On the Asian circuit, India began with a bang. She clinched the gold medal in the first Asian Games soccer in 1951 by beating a booted Iran side in the final by a solitary goal. This success, it may be surmised, made the Indian soccer administration complacent. The AIFF failed to realize the changing priorities of the global game and did not really object to the barefoot playing style, which, increasingly becoming out-of-date would prove fatal to quality sides in the future. The illusion of barefooted brilliance was shattered in the Helsinki Olympics of 1952 when a formidable Yugoslavia drubbed India 10–1. True, Yugoslavia was one of the strongest football sides of that time. That is why Indian Team Manager M. Dutta Ray admitted just before the match that 'India did not stand the slightest chance of defeating one of the strongest teams he had ever seen.'[16] *Amrita Bazar Patrika* wrote thus:

> Indian team tried hard and in their efforts to break Yugoslav defence they were cheered by more than 10,000 spectators but their forwards were too slow in taking advantage of few chances they got.
>
> Seven of Indian players did not wear boots. But their intricate footwork, which puzzled Yugoslavs did not have the effect which it would have had in football fields like the ones they were used to in India.
>
> Olympic football rules permit a slightly smaller field and as Mr. Dutta Ray feared, had a telling effect. Though surprisingly, Indians enjoyed fullest sympathy of huge crowd. All the spectators rose when Ahmed Khan netted the only goal for India.[17]

Interestingly enough, the Indian team drew favourable comments from the Yugoslav press despite their huge defeat. Commenting on India's big reverse, the Yugoslav news agency, Tanjug, argued that the defeat 'does not represent the true picture of Indian skill'.[18] Another leading Belgrade paper pointed out that 'considering the technical perfection of the Indian players, the result should have been a difference of two goals.'[19] *Nas Sport*, the leading Belgrade sports journal, praised the Indian outside-right Venkatesh, describing him as 'the best player on the field'. The paper also added that 'Yugoslav's success was not due to the weakness of the Indian defence, but to the Yugoslav goalkeeper Bearai who more than once saved goals from Venkatesh's onslaught.'[20] Another newspaper, *Politika*, found the fault in the combination of the Indian team and expressed surprise at the selection of Anthony in goal and Sattar in forward ahead of Varadraj and Mewalal.[21]

The debacle, despite creating large dejection among players, officials and football-lovers, drove home the most important point: time had come to bid adieu to barefooted football. As Basu puts it excellently, 'The pampered and officially encouraged barefoot approach of India football was truly and thoroughly buried at Helsinki's Olympic stadium that evening.'[22] The AIFF, acting on this realization, resolved to make the wearing of boots mandatory for Indian players. This step, albeit much delayed, was a momentous measure in the history of Indian football and seemed to pay immediate dividends. India reached the semi-final of the Olympic soccer as the first Asian nation and earned the fourth place in the tournament in 1956.[23] A distinguished contemporary soccer critic, thus, wrote:

> The surprise of the tournament, however, was India. At one time it was touch and go whether or not they decided to send a team, but once in Melbourne the Indians proved that with their ancient background of physical and traditional facility in ball games they will soon make their mark in Asian and, later, world soccer.[24]

India's win against Australia (4–2) in the quarter-final, in which Neville D'Souza scored a hat-trick, remains her only win in the Olympic soccer. Although India once again lost to mighty Yugoslavia (1–4) in the semi-final, her stirring performance in the match certainly

elevated the status of Indian football. As the *Hindustan Times* correspondent Lloyd Clarke observed:

> India today won herself a place in the ranks of the world soccer players.
> In a fast and open game with the highly rated Yugoslavia, who are equal
> favourites with Russia for the Olympic gold medal, she was defeated 1–4
> in match that gave the Yugoslavs the toughest work out.
>   The match was regarded as a pushover for the massive Slavs, but India
> gave a performance that convinced the crowd that the Australian victory
> was not a matter of chance and that they deserved a thunderous applause
> that they got for their performance.
>   India indeed emerged from the uneven struggle the moral victors so far
> as the thousands of spectators lining the stands of the main stadium arena
> were concerned.[25]

The Statesman, too, noted that 'the sole topic of discussion' after
the match was 'superb ball control and positional play of Indians.' It
concluded thus:

> But it was India who received the ovation at the end of match which vin-
> dicated the AIFF's persistence in sending a team in the teeth of opposi-
> tion by Indian Olympic Association. Several foreign critics including Dr.
> Wille Meisl, the famous soccer expert, said India had a great soccer future
> and felt amazement that there should have been even a though of not par-
> ticipating in the Olympic.[26]

In the 1958 Tokyo Asian Games, India finished a modest fourth.
In the Rome Olympic of 1960, India again put up a spirited display of stylish soccer and fought neck and neck with much stronger teams.[27] Although India made an early exit at the group league
stages, its overall performance seemed to impress European spectators. Incidentally, India's best display came in the 1960 tournament
when it held France to a 1–1 draw. Jaydeep Basu has lively narrated
the aftermath of the match:

> After watching them operate in great speed for 90 minutes, the spectators
> and the world media instantly fell in love with the Indians. The journal-
> ists and photographers created such a rush in the Indian dressing room
> immediately after the encounter that Rahim had to close the door finally.
> The Indian team boarded the same train with France to return to Rome.
> The entire French team came to Indian compartment to pose for a group

photograph. 'The match has been drawn, but you are the moral victors,' one of the French players said.[28]

While India could manage only a draw from its four-group league matches in the tournament, the exposure and experience the players gained from the tournament was to prove handy in Jakarta Asian Games two years later.

In the 1962 Asian Games, India staged her performance of the century and went on to win the soccer gold by beating South Korea in the final. This success can be attributed to a well-knit combination of some creative and skilled players, as well as to the guidance of the team's coach S.A. Rahim. The victory at Jakarta was expected to raise Indian football to new heights. As Jaydeep Basu argues:

> The victory in Jakarta could have been the turning point of Indian football. India had a dream team, capable of playing quality soccer against any opponent. It was a golden opportunity to use the success as a launching pad for the future of the game in the country and to get into the mainstream of world football.[29]

Yet the fervour in the wake of the victory proved ephemeral and the performance of the national team went steadily downhill in the 1960s. The death of Rahim was a major blow to the trend of progress, while retirement of key players, such as Chuni Goswami and Tulsidas Balaram, without immediate suitable replacements destroyed the balance of the team to a large extent. It was, however, the internal politics of AIFF that really aggravated the healthy flow of the game by reducing 'the post of national coach into a contest of musical chairs'.[30] While India was runners-up to Israel in the second Asia Cup at Tel Aviv in 1964, it failed to qualify for the Olympics. In the 1966 Bangkok Asian Games, India failed to cross the hurdle of the group league. Matters reached a rock bottom when India went to Rangoon in 1968 to play in the Tehran Asia Cup Qualifiers without a coach. The result was obvious: India even failed to qualify for the final stage.

The Indian soccer tiger roared for the last time in the Bangkok Asian Games of 1970. Winning the bronze in the games was what may justly be called the swansong of the Indian national team at the Asian circuit. The same year, India earned the third place in the Merdeka Tournament at Kuala Lumpur. These performances certainly gave a ray of hope for a rejuvenation of Indian football. But the momentum could not be sustained. In the 1970s, India produced dismal results in the international tournaments she had participated in. The series of shameful defeats began with an unprecedented rout at the hands of Burma by 1–9 in the 1971 Merdeka Tournament. Although India staged a slight recovery by emerging joint champions with South Vietnam in the Pesta Sukan Tournament at Singapore in 1971, she tasted ignominy in the Tehran Asian Games of 1974 when she again got routed 1–7 by China. In the next games at Bangkok, India maintained the trend of suffering humiliation by conceding a huge defeat against Kuwait, the scoreline reading 1–6. The decline, thus, had begun to continue unabated through the 1980s with rare flurries of excellence in sporadic matches and tournaments.[31] In her pre-Olympic campaign before the 1984 Los Angeles Olympics, India lost to Saudi Arabia 0–5. In fact, India never qualified for the Olympics after 1960.

India's poor performance in the pre-World Cup encounters also reflected this downswing of Indian soccer. The 1990s proved no better for Indian football as the union government decided against the nation's participation in the consecutive Asian Games in Seoul (1990) and Hiroshima (1994). In the pre-World Cup Qualifiers for the USA World Cup 1994, South Korea thrashed India 7–0, while in the 1998 France Cup Qualifiers, India suffered humiliation at the hands of Qatar 0–6. In the 1996 Asia Cup Qualifiers, too, the Indian team was humiliated in both her matches. Indonesia routed her 7–1 and Malaysia beat her 5–2. India's decline in soccer becomes more evident if one considers her performance in South Asian tournaments, such as the South Asian Federation (SAF) Games or South Asian Football Federation (SAFF) Cup. Even while playing against much inferior teams and latecomers such as Nepal, Bangladesh, Pakistan or Sri Lanka, India won the SAF Games soccer gold only thrice in its nine editions till date while she performed a little better by winning the SAFF Cup four times in six occasions.

India in Olympic Soccer, 1948–2012: A Quantitative Reappraisal

While India put up a more or less spirited display of its soccer talent in the Olympics from 1948 to 1960, the rate of its success was not a very upbeat one even during that period. India could win only one

Table 2.1

India's Match Results in the Olympic Soccer: 1948–1960

Year–Place	India's Match Results
1948–London	France 2 India 1
1952–Helsinki	Yugoslavia 10 India 1
1956–Melbourne	India got walkover against Hungary, India 4 Australia 2, Yugoslavia 4 India 2, Bulgaria 3 India 0
1960–Rome	Hungary 2 India 1, France 1 India 1, Peru 3 India 1

Source: Kumar Mukherjee. 2002. *The Story of Football*. New Delhi: Ministry of Information and Broadcasting, Government of India; *Historical Database*, www.indian-football.com; Jaydeep Basu. 2003. *Stories from Indian Football*. New Delhi: UBSPD.

Table 2.2

Indian Soccer Team's Overall Performance in the Olympics: 1948–1960

Year	Played	Won	Drawn	Lost	Goal Favour	Goal Against
1948	1	0	0	1	1	2
1952	1	0	0	1	1	10
1956	3	1	0	2	6	9
1960	3	0	1	2	3	6
Total	**8**	**1**	**1**	**6**	**11**	**27**

Source: Kumar Mukherjee. 2002. *The Story of Football*. New Delhi: Ministry of Information and Broadcasting, Government of India; *Historical Database*, www.indian-football.com; Jaydeep Basu. 2003. *Stories from Indian Football*. New Delhi: UBSPD.

and manage a draw out of the eight matches it played in the main rounds of the Olympics (Tables 2.1 and 2.2). And, as already mentioned, after 1960, Indian national football team never qualified for the Olympics. Its performance in the qualifying rounds too deteriorated steadily since the 1960s with rare good results, albeit mostly against other South Asian teams ranked lower than her (Table 2.3). To put it statistically, out of a total of 47 matches India played in the Olympic Qualifiers since 1960, it has won 15, drawn 7 and lost 25 matches (Table 2.4).

It is therefore of relevance here to look at how India performed in the main and qualifying rounds of the Olympics in order to have a better understanding of the status of Indian soccer in the Olympic

Table 2.3

India's Match Results in the Olympic Soccer Qualifiers: 1960–2012

Year	India's Match Results
1960	India 5 Afghanistan 2, India 4 Indonesia 2, India 2 Indonesia 0
1964	India 5 Ceylon 3, India 7 Ceylon 0, Iran 3 India 0, Iran 3 India 1
1968	Withdrew from the tournament
1972	Burma 4 India 3, Indonesia 4 India 2, Israel 1 India 0
1976	Did not participate
1980	China 1 India 0, Singapore 1 India 0, India 4 Sri Lanka 0, Iran 2 India 0, North Korea 2 India 1
1984	Saudi Arabia 2 India 1, Singapore 2 India 1, Indonesia 1 India 0, India 3 Malaysia 3, Saudi Arabia 5 India 0, India 1 Singapore 0, India 1 Indonesia 0, Malaysia 2 India 0
1988	Withdrew from the tournament
1992	India 1 Oman 1, Lebanon 3 India 1, Syria 1 India 0, Kuwait 2 India 1
1996	India 2 Pakistan 1, Oman 3 India 2, India 3 Pakistan 1, Oman 2 India 1
2000	Thailand 2 India 0, Thailand 0 India 0
2004	Turkmenistan 2 India 0, India 1 Turkmenistan 0
2008	India 1 Myanmar 1, India 1(4) Myanmar 1(1)
	Iraq 3 India 0, Thailand 1 India 0 (Thailand won the match 1–0, but points awarded to India as Thailand played suspended player), Iraq 1 India 1, Thailand 2 India 0, North Korea 2 India 0, North Korea 2 India 1
2012	India 1 Myanmar 1, India 2 Myanmar 1, India 1 Qatar 1, Qatar 3 India 1

Source: Kumar Mukherjee. 2002. *The Story of Football*. New Delhi: Ministry of Information and Broadcasting, Government of India; *Historical Database*, www.indian-football.com; Jaydeep Basu. 2003. *Stories from Indian Football*. New Delhi: UBSPD.

map. Tables 2.1–2.4 will give an idea of India's performance in the Olympic Qualifiers since 1964.

Tables 2.1–2.4 clearly show that India has never been able to assert her soccer power at the Olympic stage since 1960. This poor show has also been a part of India's overall dismal performance at the international level, including the World Cup Qualifiers. India's plight in the Olympic, alias international football, since the 1960s can be most meaningfully explained in terms of an unresolved dichotomy between the interests of the nation and the clubs as well as a long-term failure of the AIFF to appreciate the importance of professionalism and commercialism in Indian football.

Table 2.4

Indian Soccer Team's Overall Performance in the Olympic Qualifiers: 1960–2012

Year	Played	Won	Drawn	Lost	Goal Favour	Goal Against
1960	3	3	0	0	11	4
1964	4	2	0	2	13	9
1968	NA	NA	NA	NA	NA	NA
1972	3	0	0	3	5	9
1976	NA	NA	NA	NA	NA	NA
1980	5	1	0	4	5	6
1984	8	3	1	4	11	12
1988	NA	NA	NA	NA	NA	NA
1992	4	0	1	3	3	7
1996	4	2	0	2	8	7
2000	2	0	1	1	0	2
2004	2	1	0	1	1	2
2008	8	2	2	4	4	12
2012	4	1	2	1	5	6
Total	**47**	**15**	**7**	**25**	**66**	**76**

Source: Kumar Mukherjee. 2002. *The Story of Football*. New Delhi: Ministry of Information and Broadcasting, Government of India; *Historical Database*, www.indian-football.com; Jaydeep Basu. 2003. *Stories from Indian Football*. New Delhi: UBSPD.

Nation versus Club

With the 1970s drawing to a close, regional rivalry around the inter-provincial Santosh Trophy[32] began to lose importance as Bengal established its domination as a regional footballing force. It won the championship five times in a row from 1975 to 1979 and, with a gap of one year, again in 1981–1982. Bengal's dominance was also clearly discernible in the national squad where footballers from Bengal began to occupy the lion's share. This, however, did not bid well for Indian football. As Jaydeep Basu argues:

> The lack of challenge did hardly any good to Calcutta football either, as the feeling prevailed that it was in a position to dictate terms to the rest of the country and it started putting the club interest above the national

interest. While club football brought capacity crowd to all centres from Calcutta to Bombay and Delhi to Kannur in the 70s, the national team suffered defeat after defeat.[33]

During the 1960s and 1970s, regional rivalry reflected through performances in the Santosh Trophy seemed to merge with a more virulent one based on club loyalty. Clubs from different states became representatives of their regions in several national-level tournaments.[34] In Bengal, the situation came to acquire a rather different dimension as the players of the three big clubs, namely, Mohun Bagan, East Bengal and Mohammedan Sporting, started getting paid handsomely from the 1970s onwards. In the peculiar amateur set-up of Bengal/Indian football, most players were employed in public or private sector offices while obtaining healthy seasonal payments from their clubs. This 'sub-professional' football culture of Bengal made the nation–club clash inevitable.

The writing on the wall was, therefore, clear. Only a splinter was needed to set the barrel alight. And that was provided by the AIFF's decision to hold long preparatory camps before the 1982 Asian Games, which also involved a series of foreign tours.[35] Fulfilment of such an ambitious plan required top recruits of Calcutta's big clubs to remain with the national squad for nearly two seasons. Moreover, the AIFF did not take into consideration the players' financial liability and their contracts with respective clubs. As the transfer season was in the offing, the selected players requested the federation to consider the matter, which the latter scathingly turned down. This led 21 players[36] to walk away from the national camp on 19 February 1981. The point became crystal clear from this action: they were more loyal to their clubs than the nation.

The media, the government and others concerned took strong exception to the incident. Both the central government and the state government strongly condemned the players' action. Jyoti Basu, the chief minister of West Bengal, categorically stated: 'What is more distressing is that these players have placed their private consideration over the demands of the country.'[37] The players' image in the public eye was tarnished severely, thanks to critical newspaper reports:

They [sports desk of a leading vernacular daily] unwittingly drubbed the camp deserters as traitors to the country, albeit within quotes. Not only was the news item frontpaged, it was made the lead news. The mass circulation of the paper coupled with the notorious credibility of the printed word brought an immediate and sharp reaction from the people. Indignation ran rampant and condemnation of the players began to pour in from all possible quarters. It appeared that the country had been swept overnight by a surge of patriotism, somewhat comparable to that prevailing during the days of the Chinese aggression or the battles with Pakistan! The players were painted as black as possible. Short of physical violence, they had to suffer from all sorts of ignominy. The 'patriots' began to heckle them like anything in their places of work and public places too. One of them was even threatened with the withdrawal of the Arjuna award for which he had been named earlier.[38]

Confronted with a near social boycott, the footballers got apprehensive. In fact, they were victims of an unusual clash of interests between the nation and the clubs. Yet this was but inevitable given the AIFF's overall policy. Rather than attempting a long-term solution to the crisis, the federation took recourse to further coercion. In an emergency meeting of its working committee, it decided to recall the players, provided the latter agreed not to play for their clubs until their release from the camp.[39] Despite the players' submission to the gravity of the situation, the decision taken by the AIFF seemed totally unjustified as it completely sidetracked the important issue of compensation to the players in view of the bar imposed on them to play for their clubs. Finally, at the insistence of Field Marshal Manekshaw, head of the All India Sports Council, the AIFF declared a monthly remuneration of ₹2,000 to the players during their stay at the national camp.

Jaydeep Basu blames the AIFF for the fiasco:

> It was unfortunate that no attempt was made to solve the problem. The federation was aware of the under-the-table professionalism that existed at domestic level for a long time. The players, most of whom came from middle class background, were getting payments from their respective clubs. It was an open secret for many years, but the AIFF made no effort to check it or legalize the whole business. It was rather encouraging it. ... While the players could be accused for showing scant respect to the national feeling and the clubs for instigating them, the main blame should go to the federation for unimaginative handling of the whole situation. The controversy could have been easily avoided had the AIFF been a little more sensible in its approach.[40]

While Basu's point merits attention, the roots of the nation–club conflict lay elsewhere. The trajectory of the game's evolution in the first half of the twentieth century suggests that football as a metaphor for nationalism came out as part of a negative response against British imperialism. It was, beyond doubt, assertive yet negative in character. Even in the heydays of football's frequent appropriation as a nationalist tool, it was the club teams and mainly Mohun Bagan that represented the 'nation in the making'. While the annual Indians–Europeans matches evoked enthusiasm among Indians and attracted big crowds from the 1920s, these could hardly match the nationalist fervour expressed through a Mohun Bagan versus Calcutta Football Club League or Shield match in the same period. The flow of this unique club-based 'national' football culture got a further fillip in the 1930s when regional rivalries over the question of control and organization of the game and the start of an inter-provincial tournament under the aegis of the newly constituted AIFF added a new dimension to it. It continued unabated after Independence and even during the national team's glorious successes at the international stage, particularly in the Asian Games of 1951 and 1962. Rather, the ties of club loyalty got strengthened with a few clubs becoming signifiers of their respective regional sentiments from the 1960s. The governments—both central and state—never realized football's importance as a national emblem in independent India. Nor did they understand the game's potential as a commercial force. Hence, the AIFF remained an amateur organization throughout the twentieth century. This appalling failure of the Indian sports administration to adapt to the changing dimensions of the global game meaningfully explains the unresolved dichotomy between the nation and club in Indian football, which, even in the twenty-first century, continues to shape the future of soccer in India.

The Failures of Indian Soccer Administration

Corruption and lack of professionalism go hand in hand in Indian football. The sport's apex body in India—AIFF—has not played its expected role to perfection. The anomalies of the organization have ranged from pecuniary inconsistency[41] to administrative high-handedness. So far as the question of professionalism is concerned, it fares little better. Since its birth in 1937, the AIFF showed an utter lack of professional 'attitude' towards the game. It took 11 long years to get affiliated to the world apex body, FIFA. It played its flawed part in India's failure to participate in the 1950 World Cup. The unresolved dichotomy of national and club football has been, to a great extent, a result of its failure and amateurish duplicity. Moreover, factionalism, favouritism and infighting within the Federation are plain to see since its inception.[42] Jaydeep Basu elaborates this point further in his recent work on Indian football.[43]

As one of the better administrators of Indian soccer/AIFF argued in 1961:

> In our country, however, things are absolutely different. Whether it be in the All-India sphere or in the State sphere, you will find very few people in the administration who could claim to be players themselves. Unless this vital change is introduced in the selection of the administrative personnel, I am afraid, our football will never attain its rightful stature. I have travelled throughout the world and had an opportunity to see the football set-up in all those places ... There football is guided by *experts*; here by all sorts of people, and the difference is there for all to see.[44] (emphasis added)

If this conception of experts seems a bit drastic, then here are a few more radical updates:

> A spineless Federation, headed by a politician, can't do a thing. In fact, ever since Priya Ranjan Das Munshi, a high-profile Congressman, took over in 1988, the slump is all the more visible.[45]
> It may be a co-incidence that our football began to grow pale, to the point of no redemption, ever since P. R. Das Munshi got himself associated with the AIFF in the late 1970s. In the face of a series of disasters, a number of heads have rolled while he stays put in his chair. But then he is a politician, after all.[46]

Examples of comments like this are numerous. It is, however, unhistorical to put the entire onus on administrators and the like. In fact, one must acknowledge that it is Priya Ranjan Dasmunsi, the president, who, almost single-handedly, kept the National Football League (NFL) afloat during its years of extreme duress. It was his initiative that roped in financial giants, such as Oil and Natural Gas Corporation

(ONGC), as title sponsors before the National League in December 2004. In fact, it is rather the peculiarly amateur set-up of soccer that explains the deep-seated ills of Indian football. This is not to deny that the AIFF officialdom has been the major villain in this system. This tendentious amateurism has not only made footballers' status confusing, but has also given birth to a sizeable group of non-professional, non-technical officials, both at club and association levels, who allegedly reap personal gains by virtue of their lucrative positions in the sports bureaucracy. Even the top string of India's present soccer bureaucracy agree that amateurish management is the main hindrance towards ushering in professionalism in Indian football, be it NFL or any other meet. As Alberto Colaco, the AIFF secretary, once argued, 'What we need in India is professional and paid people to run the clubs as well as the federation. Then only can we achieve the target.'[47]

It has become evident by now that Indian footballers by themselves are no longer crowd-pullers as they used to be in the past. This reflects a growing aversion even among the genuine supporters of Indian football to watch domestic matches. With ample opportunity to watch high-quality European and Latin American games on satellite sports channels, such as ESPN-Star Sports, DD Sports or Ten Sports, watching Indian football has become a matter of disgust for many. In such a situation, as A. Vinod points out:

> [T]he AIFF has done precious little to stem the tide by chalking out meaningful programmes for the development of the game in this country. Instead, it has preferred to remain a silent spectator, caught in the cobwebs of the power struggles within itself, untouched by the consequences of its own ineffectiveness. Should it fail to get its act together without any further delay, it certainly would not take much time for the epitaph of Indian football to be written some day or other in the none-too-distant future.[48]

If there is any worthwhile boost the AIFF provided to Indian football, it was the introduction of the NFL in 1996 (now called the I-League).[49] The event certainly infused new vigour into Indian soccer. But the NFL is still found wanting in several key aspects: organization, marketing, publicity, itinerary and, above all, adequate sponsors. Soccer-wise, it proved to be a keenly competitive league in the last 20 years, with a lot of twists and turns till the end, but it left a lot to be desired on the organizational front. But the major hiccup that has only recently been solved—thanks to the efforts of

Dasmunsi—is the utter inadequacy of sponsorship. Many, however, hold AIFF responsible for the shortcomings of the National League. It has also been argued that some of its officials were responsible for 'the AIFF breaking up with the IMG, ESPN/STAR Sports and also for not finding a sponsor.'[50] It is also argued that the NFL itinerary and logistics have been a topic of ridicule, as teams have had to criss-cross the vast country with very little or no gap between matches.[51]

Also, while promoting the NFL, the AIFF has systematically under-mined the important and prestigious tournaments, such as the Durand Cup, DCM Trophy, Rovers Cup and IFA Shield, which used to act as breeding grounds for soccer talent in the country as well as to nour-ish a sound club culture. It is urgent to restore them to their erstwhile status and importance to broaden the base of the game throughout India. At present, regular football leagues take place only in a handful of states, including Kolkata, Mumbai, Goa, Bangalore, Kerala, Delhi, Hyderabad, Punjab and the Northeast. The rest of the AIFF units have nearly proved ineffectual. Even with FIFA support, the AIFF has not been able to implement to perfection the most rudimentary soccer development programme. For this, as Bill Adams points out, it is 'cronyism, ageism and amateur ineffectiveness' are much to blame.[52]

The AIFF has also shown its culpability in the organization of international tournaments in the recent past. Its millennium venture, the Millennium Sahara Cup which came off in January 2001, was much publicized as the biggest football show in Asia. However, its promise turned out to be superficial. In fact, it promised much but delivered nothing for Indian football. The coordination between the AIFF and the organizers, Studio 2100, was so poor that they could not compensate for the last-minute withdrawals of teams from Iraq, Indonesia and Cameroon. Among the participants, only the team from Chile brought a few Olympians in their rank, while the remain-ing teams used the tournament to experiment with young players. It was alleged in some quarters that the AIFF did not provide adequate technical information and trained personnel to the organizers Studio 2100.[53] Henna Juneja, frustrated CEO of Studio 2100, was said to have remarked that the tournament was sabotaged due to factional-ism within the AIFF.[54] Novy Kapadia has argued that 'some officials used the build-up for this tournament as part of their election cam-paign and once their purpose was achieved, shirked all responsibility in organisation.'[55]

Finally, as regards the appointment of foreign coaches with the avowed aim of raising the standard of Indian football, AIFF has done little. In the last two decades or so, the AIFF experimented with at least seven foreign coaches for the senior Indian national team, most of who failed to deliver any long-term benefit for Indian football. The list includes Dietmar Pfiefer from East Germany, Ciric Milovan from Yugoslavia, Josef Gelei of Hungary, Jiri Pesek of Czech Republic, Rustam Akramov from Uzbekistan, Stephen Constantine from England and Dave Houghton from England. Except Milovan, none really looked impressive enough to transform India into a sound fighting combination. And even when they tasted occasional success, it was more due to the exceptional ability of some talented Indian players, such as I.M. Vijayan, Jo Paul Ancheri or Baichung Bhutia, than due to proper planning by the coaches. However, the foreign coaches too have had their points to offer. Novy Kapadia argues: 'Inadequate foreign exposure, limited opportunity with the national team and interference in team selection [by the so-called soccer bureaucrats] dampened the enthusiasm of the foreign coaches and they did not devote adequate time with either the senior team or the age group teams.'[56] What India requires from a foreign coach is a sensible approach towards the anomalies of the Indian game as it is played right now. As Mario Rodrigues points out, 'a dedicated foreign coach who understands the Indian psyche (as John Wright is said to have done in Indian cricket) can help Indian football take the much-needed strides in the strategic department.'[57] The AIFF needs to rope in the likes of Guus Hiddink, who played a pivotal role in South Korea's remarkable success in the 2002 World Cup or Russia's re-rise as a soccer force in the 2008 Euro Cup, as coach of the national team. In fact, lack of a long-term perspective has been a hallmark of the organization's long history.

Wake-up calls to AIFF from various concerns of sport became common since the 1980s. Some of these sincere voices even found a place in souvenirs of international tournaments conducted by the AIFF itself. To that extent, perhaps, the organization deserves some applause. An instance is befitting in this context:

India has proved time and again that the talent is there. It has rarely been harnessed properly. The AIFF had, in the past, announced grandiose plans but they never could be implemented, petty bickerings, parochialism and perpetuating oneself in the high offices are the present state of affairs in our soccer set up. The casual attitude of the 'super stars', and the growing indiscipline among them are the aspects that the AIFF must address itself now.

Let us hope the AIFF wakes up now. The talent is there to spot. But it has to be groomed properly and if it is done methodically, starting from schools, India can re-establish itself at least in the Asian scene, in the near future.[58]

Danny McLennan, the veteran football coach of Churchill Brothers, once offered some suggestions for the rejuvenation of Indian football that may be of contextual value here:

Indian football is like a racing car with damaged engine and flat tyres. I can only pray and hope that it repairs itself and tries to keep pace at least with the Asian countries. It's better not to talk about world football.

The whole infrastructure, if it exists at all, should be updated and the All India Football Federation should be manned by professional people having sound technical background. In other words, it is better if former National level footballers adorn top posts. A country's football should not be run like this. There must be a well-thought out calendar, which should be followed till the end. There should be good leadership. The leader should be backed by eager and knowledgeable committee, which is keen to improve. If you are a proper leader you should know how to delegate powers. AIFF President could be seen in the inaugural match of the National league and then, perhaps we only in the last match or at the prize distribution ceremony. On a number of occasions it has been observed that the President announces something but the secretary denies it. There must be more harmony at the top.[59]

The big question, therefore, is: Will the Indian football administration be able to rise to the occasion by redefining its old priorities? Or will the AIFF be able to shake off its age-old amateur status and wear the global apparel of professionalism?

From Amateurism to Professionalism

In November 2000, on the eve of the fifth National League, nine leading Indian clubs,[60] aggrieved over the AIFF's faulty role in the management of the game, set up the Indian Premier Football Association (IPFA) under the presidentship of 'liquor baron' Vijay Mallya, the chief of the United Breweries Group, and announced a boycott of the high-profile NFL. Having failed to make the AIFF president, Mr Priya Ranjan Dasmunsi, see reason and bring him around to the negotiating table, the IPFA decided upon direct confrontation with football's governing body. A shoddy itinerary, which left players gasping for breathing space, partial payment of dues coupled with a disastrous administration added fuel to the simmering fire raging in the minds of players for quite some time. The IPFA, whose demands included greater autonomy for the clubs, a proper calendar and revival of the Federation Cup, wanted football to be made more 'spectator-friendly, television-friendly and sponsor-friendly'. Accordingly, everyone had an excuse to rebel. Mallya also questioned the closure of the Nehru and DCM Cups, and cited misappropriation of funds as the main reason for an abandoning of these prestigious tournaments.[61]

AIFF, which till then had been stubbornly declaring that the fifth edition would go on even if IPFA clubs did not participate, suddenly changed track. The president, in view of the forthcoming AIFF office-bearers election, understandably changed his rigid stance and conceded to the infant institution's demands. Clouds cleared and IPFA immediately responded by announcing its participation in both the League and Millennium soccer championships.

Although the onus was put mostly on the manoeuvres of administrators in action—the AIFF president, the Punjab Football Association chief and joint managing director of JCT Industries and UB Group, sponsors of three leading clubs of India, for this entire jigsaw—the core of the problem still lay in the failure of the government to adopt a viable sports policy specific to football and thereby putting an end to the existing semi-professional institutional approach aimed at developing the game.

The agreement between the Federation and the IPFA, which represented a conglomeration of some of the clubs involved in the National League but in the main those controlled or floated by influential business houses, had the ingredients to revitalize the game in the country. It was even hoped in some quarters that if in the next three to four years' time Indian football took a turn for the better, 'the two sides could well sit back and pat themselves for having regenerated the game in the country.'[62] Some of the points on which an agreement was reached could and should have been implemented years ago, particularly the one relating to making a clear-cut difference between amateur and professional status. Ramu Sharma made the point amply clear:

> For years together Indian footballers, particularly those associated with the big clubs, have been allowed to wear the mask of amateurs and enjoying all the benefits despite bargaining for financial returns during the transfers. It was and is not their fault. It was the fault of the system which sought to mix priorities because of economic necessities. One could not fault a football player for earning extra money during the season even though, often enough, he had been given a job on the basis of his playing skill. And employed sportspersons in India are not expected to observe full time or duty. But clearly the money earned and demanded during transfers did violate the principles of amateurism.[63]

The transition from amateurism to professionalism looked an imminent possibility in the aftermath of the agreement between the two associations. As Sharma maintained:

> But if the agreement arrived at between the federation and the IPFA is any guide then India will at last have a set of professional players. They may lose out at playing in the Olympic Games qualifying rounds and other such meets at amateur levels but it certainly will go a long way in clearing the air and separate the amateurs from the professionals. This two-tier classification, however, does not mean that there should be two separate bodies of administration.[64]

Looking Ahead: Vision India and the Example of Manipur

The transition seems to have begun with the AIFF undertaking the Vision Asia[65] project offered by the AFC. Two Indian states—Manipur and Delhi—were initially taken under the Vision India project in 2004, an ambitious project under the aegis of the grand Vision Asia project of the AFC, envisaging the fulfilment of AFC's latest motto 'The Future is Asia',[66] a holistic approach towards the development of Asian soccer. Dato Peter Velappan, general secretary of AFC, launched the Vision India on 26 April 2004. Manipur and Delhi, as already mentioned, were chosen as the two sites for the implementation of the pilot projects of Vision India in the initial stage. In AIFF General Secretary Alberto Colaso's words:

> For a while Manipur has become a powerhouse of Indian football as they have already produced some of the finest players in the present Indian soccer. Football has a great mass appeal in the state. But unlike West Bengal, Goa and Kerala, absence of any premier soccer club has been a hindrance to the uplift-ment of soccer in the state. Through Vision India, AIFF hopes that soccer in Manipur will receive a big impetus, as they will restructure the entire soccer system in the state apart from conducting a thorough-professional talent hunt scheme and evolving out a good club soccer system.[67]

More importantly, Velappan, along with his fellow Vision Asia offi-cials, later visited Manipur to have a first-hand assessment of the soccer infrastructure in the state. Pleased with the enthusiastic approach of the AMFA, he declared that the AFC would put Manipur 'on the fast track of development'.[68] After discussions on Project Manipur, it was decided to start the Manipur district school league as well as the State League in 12 months' time with 12 strong clubs, which would have proper administration and other key facilities. It was also decided to intensify the grassroots and youth development programme in schools, including a competition structure for girls since Manipur is a stronghold of women's football in India. The AMFA studied Vision Asia's proposals, came up with their own action plan forming a task force and began implementation with the appointment of representa-tives responsible for coaches and referees' education.[69]

As part of the Vision India plan, two workshops were held at Imphal in May and July 2006, respectively, in preparation for the launch of a Districts' Schools League and for the development of the 12 clubs[70] that would figure in the State League.[71] The School League, the first step in implementation of AFC's Vision Asia— Project Manipur, was launched in September 2006. This was fol-lowed by the launch of the State League on 2 November 2006. Velappan, general secretary of AFC, and Priya Ranjan Dasmunsi, president, AIFF, attended the latter event. Dasmunsi, in his message, praised Manipur for its coordinated approach to the project:

> It is a great joy for all of us that Manipur shall be figuring in the history of Indian football, to be the first state to implement Vision India Programme in line with Vision Asia, in due time. After several visits of AFC Vision

delegation and with the hardwork of All Manipur Football Association in cooperation with the Government, they found it possible to maintain this time schedule of this programme. I thank the great people of Manipur and Football fans for making this effort a great success. I also thank All Manipur Football Association and the Government of Manipur for their total cohesion in this matter. I am confident future of India will have a great, great support in the field of football from the State of Manipur.[72]

Although the Manipur Project did not have any viable sponsor from the beginning, the AMFA could implement it successfully with the constant and emphatic support from the state government.[73] The AFC President Mohamed Bin Hammam's note of appreciation on Manipur's road to success seems to be more relevant here:

Manipur was selected by AIFF in 2005 as a pilot project for Vision India because of its enthusiasm for football, passion, leadership and commitment to progress and change. In a short span of just one and a half years, Manipur has made huge strides towards strengthening its core football activities: administration and management, clubs and competitions, grassroots and youth programmes, coaches and referees education. The most important element and key focus of Vision India Project Manipur is the Manipur State League, a League which provide a high-performance platform for the players, clubs, coaches, referees and officials. I am confident that this League will work as a catalyst towards football development in North East India. I urge other states in India to follow the lead of Manipur in embracing the Vision India programme, and thereby commit the goal of making India a formidable force in international football.[74]

Manipur's progress under the project assumes more significance in the context of Delhi's lamentable performance in the same even with much better infrastructural and resource prowess. As Brandon Menton, AFC director of National Association and Clubs Development, rightly argued, 'Delhi don't have to look too far for inspiration. Manipur would be a great example for them to follow. The sense of purpose and the professional manner in which Manipur conduct their events is really heartwarming.'[75] If Velappan's prophetic vision is to be believed, then 'The future is Asia' and 'India is the sleeping giant of Asian soccer who will one day wake up to become the spearhead of Asian football.'[76] But Velappan also warned: 'This is the last chance for India. If India don't take advantage of Vision India project, then God help Indian football.'[77] If India at all wakes up from its football slumber to catch up with the international standard, then it will certainly be the state of Manipur, complemented by its neighbours Mizoram and Meghalaya, which will lead the road to that renaissance.

The introduction of the State League under Vision India should have far-reaching implications for Manipuri society and economy. Apart from providing a high-performance platform for the players, clubs, coaches, referees and officials, the league would definitely help transform football as a viable economic force in Manipur. The young footballers would now be able to pursue football as a career for earning their livelihood. With a tangible process of professionalization already set in the AMFA and the clubs, paid jobs as support stuff should open up another option for employment. Besides generating employment opportunities, once the league and the clubs begin to attract sponsors, Manipur might be able to host major national/international tournaments, thereby giving fillip to its tourism prospects and raising its economic infrastructure. And if the state could succeed in sending one or two club teams to the I-League, football might thrive as an industry in Manipur. The example of Manipur quite naturally should inspire other states of the Vision India project, selected in 2007, namely, Tamil Nadu and Kerala, to realize the sport's potential as an economic force.

The success of Vision India is significantly related to the future of India's qualification for the Olympic football. At present, any national football team in the Olympic is permitted to field only three players who are above 21 years of age. So the preparation to the qualification for the Olympics requires building up basically a team of quality under-21 players. The objective of the Vision project too insists upon creating a viable pool of quality young talents who would be groomed professionally to become professional footballers of the future to be able to serve the national team as well as the club sides.

Conclusion: Will the Slumber Cease?

AFC Secretary General Peter Velappan, who has closely been monitoring AIFF's functioning, warned a few years back: 'As the "Vision" is a tailor-made programme, the future of Indian football totally lies in the hands of Indians. Some goals have been proposed, but the Vision India team has to agree upon it.'[78] In fact, the lead must come from the AIFF. What Korea and Japan had done in the recent past to attain soccer excellence and host the World Cup was no mere sporting venture; rather, it was more a politico-economic project to raise their international status and strengthen national/economic muscle. Sport, especially soccer, in the twenty-first century, it can be justly claimed, is a thriving industry. Indians, from the sports minister to a lay spectator, urgently need to realize this truth. Baichung Bhutia, the only Indian footballing icon in the new century, puts it thus:

> The way India is going it might never become a football force to be reckoned within Asia; it may just continue the way it is. The above can only damage the outlook of the sport in India and endanger its future development. For football to survive and thrive in India, the right environment must be created. It must attract peoples from all classes, not just the lower and middle classes. It must attract, and keep, the interest of future generations that will ensure the success of Indian football for generations to come. Football can only improve if it is well managed, well marketed and run in a very professional way. ... Something must be done to put India on the football map. Who will give the helping hand? If no one does then, may be God should!!![79]

In fact, the future of Indian prospects in the Olympic, alias international soccer, depends largely on the ability of the government, the AIFF and the leading clubs to adapt to the changing terms of the game: commercialization and professionalization of football, the most crucial challenges Indian football confronts in the new millennium.

However, one needs to understand and analyze India's failure to make a mark in the Olympic soccer in the wider context of her failure to perform well in all other Olympic sports. The utter failure of the nation to develop an Olympic culture emanates from the Indian government's flawed or rather lack of approach towards the global Olympic Movement. The sports associations of the country, which have never shown any worthy coordination among themselves and the media, which offer a very marginal space to Olympic sports, have also been major culprits in the process. All these actors in Indian sports arena urgently need to appreciate the importance of a holistic sports/Olympic policy in order to arrest India's downward trend in the Olympics. In the last two Olympics, a beginning seems to have been made in this direction. And soccer cannot remain for long an aberration in this process.

Notes and References

1. Keith Cooper, 'Foreword', in Paul Dimeo and James Mills, eds. *Soccer in South Asia: Empire, Nation, Diaspora* (London: Frank Cass, 2002), p. ix.
2. 'Report on the Conference of Indian Football', in *Proceedings of the All India Football Federation Annual General Meeting*, 10 January 2004 (New Delhi: AIFF), p. 86, housed in IFA Archives. I am grateful to the IFA officials for access to this document.
3. Ibid., p. 85.
4. Ibid.
5. Shamya Dasgupta, 'India is loser, AIFF scoring the own-goal of corruption. Football: FIFA official slams unprofessional, corrupt system', *The Indian Express*, 13 January 2004.
6. Ibid.
7. For a useful history of India's place in international football through the ages, see Jaydeep Basu, *Stories from Indian Football* (New Delhi: UBSPD, 2003), especially Chapters 3–6, 8–11 and 13; and Kumar Mukherjee, *The Story of Football* (New Delhi: Ministry of Information and Broadcasting, Government of India, 2002), Chapter 11.
8. India defeated the strong Metropolitan Police side 3–1, Pinner Club 9–1, Hayes Club 4–1 and Alexandra Park 8–2. For details on these matches, see *Amrita Bazar Patrika*, 19 July (p. 6), 25 July (p. 12), 28 July (p. 6) and 30 July 1948. Interestingly enough, in some of these matches, most Indian players played with boots.
9. *Amrita Bazar Patrika*, 19 July 1948, p. 6.
10. *The Statesman*, 2 August 1948, p. 6. Sailen Manna and Mahavir Prasad missed the opportunities to score.
11. Cited in Mukherjee, *The Story of Football*, p. 132.
12. After Indian side defeated the Isthmian league team, a strong amateur combination, by a convincing margin of 3–1.
13. Cited in *Amrita Bazar Patrika*, 24 August 1948, p. 6.
14. Basu, *Stories from Indian football*, p. 39.
15. Ibid.
16. *The Statesman*, 17 July 1952, p. 6.
17. *Amrita Bazar Patrika*, 17 July 1952, p. 6.
18. *The Statesman*, 18 July 1952, p. 6.
19. Ibid.
20. Ibid.
21. Ibid.
22. Basu, *Stories from Indian Football*, p. 50.
23. India went down to Yugoslavia 1–4 in the semi-final while it lost to Bulgaria 0–3 in the match to decide third place.
24. Cited in Anthony De Mello, *Portrait of Indian Sport* (London: P.R. Macmillan Ltd/ D.B. Taraporevala Sons & Co., 1959), pp. 197–198.

25. Cited in Basu, *Stories from Indian Football*, pp. 59–60.
26. *The Statesman*, 5 December 1956, p. 10.
27. India lost to mighty Hungary 1–2, drew with France 1–1 and went down to Peru 1–3.
28. Basu, *Stories from Indian Football*, p. 66.
29. Ibid., p. 99.
30. Ibid.
31. India's improved performance in the early 1980s was due mainly to the able guidance of its Yugoslav coach Ciric Milovan. Under his coaching, India did well in 1984 Asia Cup Qualifiers and reached the finals, while at home, it put up some spirited fights against world-class sides in the Jawaharlal Nehru Invitational Gold Cup.
32. Santosh Trophy, the inter-provincial tournament, was instituted in 1941 by the AIFF.
33. Basu, *Stories from Indian Football*, p. 133.
34. Such tournaments include the IFA Shield, Durand Cup, Rovers Cup and DCM Trophy.
35. The foreign tours included the Merdeka Tournament at Kuala Lumpur as well as the King's Cup in Bangkok apart from other invitation tournaments in different parts of Asia.
36. Of these players, 19 were from Bengal while one each came from Kerala and Andhra Pradesh.
37. Quoted in Basu, *Stories from Indian Football*, p. 134.
38. Ranjit Kumar Ghose, 'Club versus Country?' *93rd IFA Shield Tournament Souvenir* (Calcutta: IFA, 1985).
39. In fact, the players were asked to give a voluntary declaration to that effect. For details, see *Amrita Bazar Patrika* and *Ananda Bazar Patrika*, 20 February 1981.
40. Basu, *Stories from Indian Football*, pp. 136–137.
41. For a detailed discussion of the AIFF's pecuniary anomalies, see Boria Majumdar and Kausik Bandyopadhyay, *Goalless! The Story of a Unique Footballing Nation* (New Delhi: Penguin/Viking, 2006), pp. 172–174.
42. To give one instance of such trends of factionalism within the AIFF, the row between Pankaj Gupta on the one hand, and Manindra Dutta Ray and Ziauddin on the other, over the selection of the coach and some players assumed a ugly proportion, affecting the integrity and balance of the side during the 1952 Helsinki Olympic tour.
43. For details on this point, see Basu, *Stories from Indian Football*, pp. 46–49.
44. Dutta Ray, 'Playing Experience Needed in Our Football Administration', *WIFA Golden Jubilee Souvenir* (Bombay: WIFA, 1961). Incidentally, Dutta Ray was the president of AIFF at that time.
45. Shyam Sundar Ghosh, 'A Messy Affair', *The Statesman*, 25 November 1998.
46. Gautam Roy, 'No Hopers on a Sinking Boat', *The Statesman*, 25 November 1998.
47. Jaydeep Basu, 'Visionless NFL clubs ignore long-term development', *Hindustan Times*, 7 December 2003.
48. A. Vinod, 'Football is groping in the dark, and the AIFF couldn't care less', *The Hindu*, 29 April 2000.
49. In the early 1980s, the introduction of the Nehru Cup at the initiative of Ashok Ghosh was considered a major step in providing Indian football a major booster. The tournament featured world-class teams from European and Latin American countries and provided Indian players an opportunity to compete and gain experience at the international level. Unfortunately, within a decade the tournament lost its importance, with the organization and standard both falling sharply.

50. Qaiser Mohammad Ali, 'National soccer league found wanting' from the India Abroad News Service, in www.indianfootball.com, accessed on 24 November 2004.
51. Ibid.
52. Bill Adams, 'Saving Soccer in India', www.indianfootball.com
53. Novy Kapadia, 'The Millennium Cup Flop', *indya.com football diary*, January 2001.
54. Ibid.
55. Ibid.
56. Novy Kapadia, 'A Short History', *Sahara Times*, 30 August 2003, p. 36.
57. Mario Rodrigues, 'Hope and Hoopla', *The Statesman*, 23 May 2001.
58. M. Madhavan, 'Wake Up, A.I.F.F.!' *Souvenir of VIIth Jawaharlal Nehru Invitation International Gold Cup Football Tournament* (Siliguri: AIFF and IFA, 1988).
59. Arnab Ghosh, 'Indians should keep pace at least with the Asians', *The Hindu*, 15 April 2000.
60. The trouble that started in Bengal spread not to the states, but to the senior clubs: Mohun Bagan, East Bengal, Mohammedan Sporting and Tollygunge Agragami from Calcutta, Salgaocar, Churchill Brothers from Goa, Mahindra United from Mumbai, F.C. Kochin from Kerala and JCT Mills Phagwara from Punjab, most of them being owned or sponsored by industrialists.
61. For a detailed understanding of the episode, see 'Off-field dribbles kept football in the news', *PTI*, 28 December 2000, featured in *indianfootball.com*. Also see Amardeep Bhattal, 'IPFA on a Collision Course with AIFF', *Sports Tribune*, 2 December 2000.
62. Ramu Sharma, 'Wake-up Call to Indian Football', *Sports Tribune*, 16 December 2000.
63. Ibid.
64. Ibid.
65. Vision Asia is the AFC's grand plan for a continent-wide programme to raise the standards of Asian football at all levels, be it on the field of play, administration or sports science. This is the brainchild of AFC President Mohamed Bin Hammam, who launched the programme in January 2003. Nine months later, after much fine-tuning, Hammam unveiled Vision Asia as a well-defined blueprint to international delegates and VIPs during the FIFA Congress in Doha, Qatar. The president firmly believes that Asia, with its 3.7 billion population, has the potential to produce many world-class footballing nations. His ultimate goal is for an Asian team to win the FIFA World Cup someday. Hammam has identified 11 disciplines—akin to 11 players on the football field—that Vision Asia must address if Asian countries are to catch up with their counterparts in Europe and the rest of the world. They are: national associations (goalkeeper); marketing, grassroots, coach education, referees, sports medicine (defenders); men's competitions, women's competitions, futsal (midfielders); media, fans (forwards). AFC has already recruited experts with specialist skills in each discipline. These consultants are being assisted by development officers, one for each of the four zones—West Asia, Central/South Asia, South East Asia and East Asia (gathered from www.the-aiff.com/vision_India.php).
66. FIFA President Sepp Blatter initially told the world that 'The future is Asia.' The AFC, since then, adopted the phrase as its motto.
67. Colaso revealed this in a personal communication to Suvam Pal, then a sports journalist with the *Sahara Time*. For details, see Suvam Pal, 'Guts, Grits and Glory', unpublished paper, 2005. I am grateful to Suvam Pal for giving me the opportunity to go through this paper.

68. 'Development of Manipur to be fast-tracked', 22 July 2005, available at www. the-afc.com, accessed on 21 September 2006. Incidentally, the AFC delegation could find to their surprise as many as 200 fields and 296 clubs in Manipur.

69. Ibid.

70. These 12 clubs are SAIRC, NEROCA, TRAU, Eastern Sporting Union, MPSC, Southern Sporting Union, YMC (all from Imphal), RACC (Churachandpur), Kakching FC (Kakching), AMOFA (Moirang), PYC (Thoubal) and YWO (Bishnupur).

71. 'Successful workshop held in Manipur to prepare the ground for schools league', 28 May 2006; 'Club development workshop held in Manipur', 11 July 2006, available at www.the-afc.com, accessed on 21 September 2006.

72. Available at www.the-aiff.com/news_details, posted on 28 October 2006, accessed on 20 December 2006.

73. Shaji Prabhakaran, Director of Vision India, admitted this in 'Delhi to launch school football league Wednesday', available at www.indianmuslims.info, 2 September 2006, accessed on 20 December 2006.

74. 'India could become major football power: Bin Hammam', available at www.the-afc. com, 3 November 2006.

75. 'Delhi "Vision India" project slower than expected', available at http://footballdy-namicsasia.blogspot.com/search/label/Vision%20Asia, accessed on 10 April 2007.

76. Velappan reiterated during the launch to the media. Cited in Pal, 'Guts, Grits and Glory'.

77. '"Vision India" goes practical', *Times of India*, 21 July 2006.

78. Nilanjan Datta, 'The future lies in the hands of the Indians', *Times of India*, 13 May 2004.

79. Baichung Bhutia, 'Slow Death', in Game Plan, reproduced in www.indianfootball. com, accessed on 24 November 2004.

3

Towards a Professional Identity: Soccer as a Career Option in Contemporary Manipur

Manipur has been excelling in the recent past in the field of sports. Many do not know that polo has been played here for centuries—much before the British introduced it in the rest of India Manipur has been excelling in most sports ranging from football and hockey to weightlifting Manipur sportspersons are household names across the country. I hope that continues to produce world-class sportsmen and women who will bring glory to our nation.

Given the diversity of culture and traditions in Manipur and the strong bonds that like Manipuris with their fellow citizens, I believe that Manipur should benefit from the economic growth processes which are transforming our country.[1]

Introduction

Arguably, for development from within, a state or a group of states need, along with governmental support, peoples' urge to develop by appropriating and utilizing the available natural and human resources in the best possible way. A dispassionate look at the contemporary political, social and economic situations in the north-eastern states of India suggests, however, that the Northeast has internalized over the years a state of political insurgency, economic dependence and cultural isolation not conducive to integrated development strategies

at all. In the age of globalization, commercialism and professionalism are the two most crucial weapons by which the underdeveloped
states of the region could cope with political instability (insurgency
and counter-insurgency), economic backwardness (infrastructural
debilities and unemployment) and social anomalies (drug abuse and
spread of AIDS). It is in this context that sports, such as soccer, can
be looked upon as a lucrative career option generating new avenues
of employment as well as sources of livelihood to the youth of the
region. This chapter takes up the case of Manipur, where soccer has
done wonders to provide the young generation with a viable professional alternative to political instability and social maladies.
Women's soccer in Manipur, on the other hand, creates a powerful
space for gender empowerment,[2] although this has been left out of the
purview of the present discussion.

Problems Facing the Manipuri Society

Since its merger with India in 1949 and even after its attainment of
state status in 1972, Manipur remained a hotbed of ethnic clashes
and insurgent activities.[3] Sanjoy Hazarika explains the roots of ethnic
clashes in Manipur in the following terms:

> Manipur's slide into anarchy has been sure and steady. The hills of the
> state, where a majority of Nagas live, are dominated by one faction or
> another of the National Socialist Council of Nagaland (NSCN). Other
> groups active there include the Kuki National Army. In the plains—
> essentially, the small and fertile Imphal valley—live the majority com-
> munity, the Meiteis. For all purposes, the Meiteis are hemmed in on all
> sides by the hill groups. But here too ethnic disparities are reflected in the
> insurgencies as well: the Meiteis have their own fighting groups which
> demand independence, including the United National Libertaion Front
> (UNLF) and the People's Liberation Army (PLA). The dominant Naga
> group accuses the UNLF of trying to intimidate Nagas and apparently
> has its own Meitei front which has targeted supporters of the UNLF.
> Unending ethnic divisions and bitter rivalries have brought Manipur to the
> brink of unmitigated disaster. The longstanding feuds between the Kukis
> and Tangkhul Nagas resulted in killings and counter killings in the early
> Nineties, with the active participation of militants from both sides.[4]

The state also faced the imposition of the draconian Armed Forces Special Power Act (AFSPA)[5] in 1958 by the Government of India in a desperate attempt to curb the unrest. The fierce combat between the insurgents and armed forces saw thousands of youths falling victims to the bloody turmoil. At the height of the turbulence in the 1980s and early 1990s, the Manipuri society felt crippled by unrest, frustration and uncertainty. As increase in population was not complemented by a comparable increase in the number of jobs, unemployment became the order of the day, breeding a deep sense of despair and insecurity among the Manipuri youths, who were left with two vicious options—either to take up guns or to fall prey to the menace of drug abuse. As one writer elaborates, 'Thousands of jaded youth joined insurgent groups and a few more thousands sought 'heaven' in opium, heroine and LSD.'[6] Subtly describing the appalling pervasiveness of Manipur being an oasis of drug abuse, another commentator stated:

> Brothers acquainting you with opium, a peddler aunt giving you a treat of heroin, or access to heroin that your father peddles to other youngsters, a habit that your husband shares with you, quick money your neighbourhood unemployed uncle makes—whoever your source, howsoever your induction, the bottom line here is neglect.[7]

While analyzing the crux of the problem, she argued:

> The neglect of the north-eastern states by the Centre has manifested in Manipur as a drug problem, thanks to easy access to the 'high stuff' through the porous border with Myanmar. A fairly literate population, high unemployment and social unrest have resulted in the Manipuris resorting to substance abuse, and more specifically intravenous heroin addiction.[8]

Related to this evil is the spread of AIDS. This deadly disease began to flex its muscle since the 1980s. Sharing of syringes among addicts is the most common reason for the spread of this disease. While the pattern of HIV infection through sexual transmission route is as high as 86 per cent in other regions in India, in Manipur, about 72 per cent of HIV infection is through sharing of needles and syringes by drug addicts.[9] At present, Manipur has one of the highest per capita HIV-positive patients in India.

Thus, Manipuri society is infested with a plethora of political, social and economic problems: armed insurgency and ethnic clashes, long-term unemployment and economic insecurity, drug abuse and HIV infection. The masses of the state have become weary of this situation for quite some time now. Given such perilous social situation, most of the families in Manipur, who can afford, prefer to send away their sons and daughters to other states. For the majority, who cannot afford to do so, one way out to save their young children from social as well as political ills has been to encourage them to embrace different sports much more dearly than ever.

Sporting Traditions of Manipur

Incidentally, Manipuris are sports-loving people to the core and the state enjoys one of the most glorious sporting traditions and heritages in the world. Since the ancient days, numerous indigenous sports and games originated in the state. In fact, the game of polo originated in this state a few centuries back as it was conceptualized and incepted in Manipur as *Sagol Kangjei* in the ancient times. The game on the horseback, which embodies regal gallantry, later on, underwent changes in rule under the British regiment officers posted in that area in the nineteenth century, who were readily enticed by the game and transplanted it to the international sporting commune as polo. As Peter Parkes points out, 'The curious story of polo's imperial reinvention and metropolitan reprocessing, its raw retrieval from Manipur to Hurlingham and its re-export as a finished product to the subcontinent, offers an instructive paradigm for the historical anthropology of other colonially appropriated sports.'[10]

Apart from Sagol Kangjei, there are a few other indigenous sports, such as *Thang Ta* and *Sarit Sarak* (Manipuri martial arts), *Khong Kangjei* (Manipuri hockey), *Yubi Lakpi* (Manipuri-style rugby), *Hiyang Tanaba* (boat race), *Mukna* (Manipuri wrestling) and *Kang*. All these sports originated in Manipur and were widely played in the state, which thus manifest the local people's profound passion and love for sports and games. The people of Manipur comprise 29 communities, which predominantly include three distinct groups of people with different cultural, social and religious backgrounds, namely, *Meiteis*,[11] *Kukis*[12] and *Nagas*.[13] These three tribes with their Mongoloid warrior lineage inherently perform and excel in various martial arts and endurance sports with their physical fitness and acrobatic skill.

The Government of India, in its drive to normalize the ongoing grim situation, initiated several welfare activities in Manipur. In that process, SAI—the nodal sports promotion body of India—came to play an important role in the rehabilitation of the youth energy in Manipur, as it once again rekindled the passion for sports among the Manipuri youths. In the 1980s, the SAI started conducting several sports development programmes, especially among the youths and the school children. This ushered a new era in Manipuri sports as the small state for the first time started making foray into the apex league of Indian sport, and the sportspersons started carving niche for themselves in the national sporting arena.

Inspirational Role of Sportspersons from Hockey to Football

In the early 1980s, it was P. Neelkamal, the prolific hockey goalkeeper, who became a trendsetter of a sort for the 'golden generation of Manipuri sportspersons'.[14] With his acrobatic penalty save in the 1984 Los Angeles Olympics, Neelkamal became a household name in the panic-stricken state and acquired an iconic status among the youngsters. Neelkamal's success at the international level triggered off a new beginning as thousands of youngsters charged up to fulfil their dream to represent the country in the sport. Within a couple of years, Indian hockey witnessed the meteoric rise of two of the most gifted hockey stars from Manipur—Brojen Singh and Thoiba Singh.

The late 1990s marked a watershed in the history of modern sports in Manipur as several sportspersons in different sporting fields came into prominence in the national and international sporting arena. It was in the Sixth National Games, held at Imphal, the capital of Manipur in 1999 that Manipur emerged as the overall team champion surpassing the giants like Punjab or Kerala. The success of Manipuri sportspersons could be attributed to the dedication, devotion and, above all, obsession for sports among the people. Since the late 1990s, Manipur had the distinction of producing international- and national-level sportspersons in various sports. The illustrious list of internationally successful Manipuri sportspersons included women weightlifters N. Kunjarani Devi[15] and Sanamacha Chanu, prolific boxer N. Dingko Singh[16] and couple of mainstays of national women's hockey team like ace game-maker Suraj Lata Devi[17] and bustling forward Sanggai Chanu, and most importantly the prodigious woman boxer Olympic medalist Mary Com.[18] The prominence of such internationally successful sportsmen and women was complemented by a steady rise of Manipuri footballers at the national level. The list included Somatai Shaiza, Renedy Singh, Bijen Singh, Manitombi Singh, Tomba Singh, Surkumar Singh, Dharamjit Singh, Rajesh Meetei, Raju Singh, Ratan Singh, Shanta Singh, Bungo Singh, Lolendro Singh, Santosh Singh, Samson Singh, Tiken Singh, James Singh, Gouramangi Singh, Momocha Singh, Napoleon Singh, Akbar Singh and many others. Thus, Manipur has become a nursery of most sports sans cricket in India. In the words of a journalist: 'These days it seems all a Manipuri has to do is to kick a ball, lift a baseball, shoot an arrow, throw a punch and he/she will win a medal.'[19]

Rise of Manipur as the New Powerhouse of Indian Soccer

Amidst the changing balance of power in contemporary Indian football, new forces are clearly on the ascendance. If the lead in this regard initially came from Goa, Manipur—a rather young entrant from the Northeast into the national football theatre—has most successfully followed it up. Manipur won the 34th National Championship for the Santosh Trophy in 2002, displacing the traditional bastions of Indian soccer, signalling the arrival of a new soccer power centre in India, namely, the Northeast. The victory of Manipur, so long considered as a minnow in Indian football, opened up possibilities for the game to flourish in the region. Moreover, the successful hosting of the tournament by the AMFA pointed to its professional approach towards the game,[20] lacking in many other state units of AIFF.

It is a bit surprising that Manipur has taken so long to strike at the National Championship. For the one decade preceding it, the state provided a steady stream of classy players like Gunbir Singh, Kiran Khongsai, Renedy Singh, Bijen Singh, Khemtang Paite, James Singh, Lolendro Singh, Manitombi Singh, Tomba Singh and Dharamjit Singh to both national and club sides. It is now common to find Manipuri players in almost all the leading club teams of the country. As Animul Islam wrote a decade back:

> Browse through the names of the national squad, Manipur have representatives in the senior, junior and sub-junior teams. There is no denying the fact that Kolkata and Goa have the best of clubs at their disposal but Manipur possess the players. Today, most club officials make the trek to the North-East state to hire their footballers.... After Manipur's historic win (in the last edition of the Santosh Trophy), Bengal cannot claim to be the sole bastion of Indian soccer. Except a few of their home grown players, club officials in Kolkata rely on outstation players; the Singhs have outpaced the Chatterjees and Banerjees ...[21]

It is interesting to understand how Manipur came all the way to confirm its new status as a soccer force in India. Renedy Singh, a key member of the national squad and a member of the victorious Manipur team of 2002, noted: 'There are no academies or institutions that can nurture talent. There's nobody to guide us, yet we have done it. It is a story of hard work and dedication.'[22] Manitombi, another rising Manipuri footballer of the time, explained the overwhelming Manipuri presence in clubs of other states: 'There is no money in Manipur. The leagues are not very popular, unlike those in Bengal or Goa. So naturally players like us would always want to move to a better place where we can earn a better living.'[23] In nourishing the talent of Manipuri footballers, Tata Football Academy (TFA) of Jamshedpur and SAI's Special Area Games Programme have played a fruitful part.[24]

Lack of exposure, scarcity of talent scouts and recruiters and ethno-cultural differences with the other parts of India played as hindrance to the Manipuri soccer players and made them confined to the state, while the mainstream India remained unaware of their soccer skills. Way back in the early 1990s, it was one self-made individual who broke all the shackles to catapult Manipuri soccer to the national level. Former Indian midfielder Kiran Khongsai—a *Kuki* by descent—surpassed all odds to move out of the state and pursued soccer as a profession as he started playing for East Bengal Club of

Kolkata, one of the top soccer clubs of India. Sooner, a few more players such as Gunabir Singh, Gumpe Rime and Khemtang Paite, from *Paitei* community,[25] too joined the fray, joining East Bengal, Salgaonkar Sports Club and Air India, respectively.

Till late 1990s, thanks to various initiatives of the SAI and the AMFA, Manipur registered some landmark performances in several all-India sub-junior and junior tournaments, but the state failed to transmit that to the senior level. Social instability and financial insecurity prevented them from pursuing a career in soccer. The emergence of Khongsai, Gunabir and Paite into national soccer actually propelled Manipuri soccer to the Indian soccer horizon, as a diligent band of bustling soccer players followed the trend to make it to the highest level of Indian soccer. The success of the troika had also generated a massive interest in soccer in the state. More importantly, the successful Manipuri soccer players set a trend of acting as recruiters-cum-promoters for the budding soccer stars from the home state. Except for the TFA[26] products, who are readily promoted by the academy itself after passing out, nearly all the present and former Manipuri soccer stars were brought to their respective clubs by their state predecessors or seniors. For example, former Air India player Khambiton Singh played a crucial role to rope in three of the talented players—Tomba Singh, Manitombi Singh and Bungo Singh—for his club.[27]

Nevertheless, it was Somatai Shaiza, more popularly known as 'Soso' by his teammates and fans, who became the first Manipuri star of Indian soccer. While Soso flourished in national soccer, other players from Manipur such as Ratan Singh, Khambiton Singh and Sanaton Singh also made themselves quite indispensable to their respective club sides.

The TFA played a crucial role in bringing this 'golden generation of Manipuri soccer stars' into the limelight. With its policy of spotting and picking of some of the raw and young soccer talents in the remote parts of the country and subsequently nurturing them for the highest level of national soccer, the TFA made a significant contribution to the sudden surge of Manipuri players as it endorsed and then brought into focus a list of star players, such as Renedy Singh, Lolendro Singh and L. James Singh to the national level. This band of players played a pivotal role in the giant leap the state's soccer has made in recent times. The number of Manipuris in the cadets of TFA has registered a significant leap since 2002. The percentage of

Figure 3.1

Ratio of Manipuri Cadets in Tata Football Academy

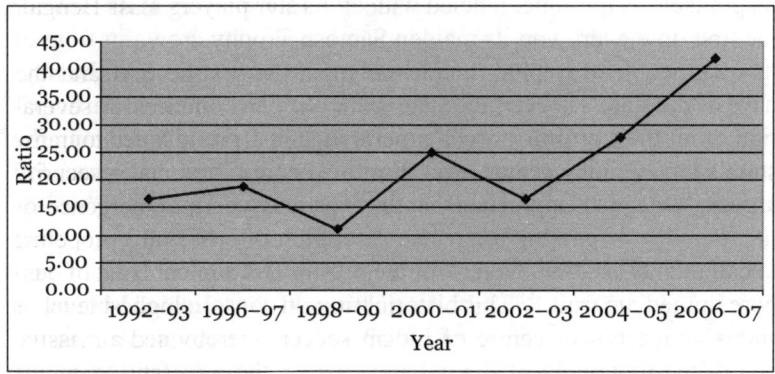

Source: http://www.tatafootballacademy.com/ex_cadets_batch.asp

Manipuri footballers in the outgoing cadets from TFA increased from 16 per cent in 2002 to 42 per cent in 2006 (see Figure 3.1). The same trend continued with the next two batches of TFA cadets (2008–2009 and 2010–2011).

Alongside Renedy, it was Bijen Singh who also gave a boost to Manipur's young generation to absorb soccer as a career. However, unlike Renedy, Bijen was a home-grown player as he had begun his soccer career with the National Sports Talent Contest, a national scheme of SAI to spot young talent in various sports. After representing his home state and subsequently the country in the junior-level tournaments, he joined East Bengal in 1997.[28] Another most exciting Manipuri player was Tomba Singh, who earned the rare honour of the 'Best Player of the Year 2003' by AIFF by dint of his stellar performance in the NFL.

Despite establishing themselves as one of the supreme powers at the national stage throughout the 1990s, players from Manipur had failed to win their elusive title of Santosh Trophy,[29] which could have strengthened the state's position as the most powerful state in Indian soccer. Interestingly, before 1999, Manipur had never even reached the quarter-finals of the inter-state championship, mostly dominated by Bengal and on a few occasions by only Kerala and Goa. In 1999 in Ooty in Tamil Nadu, Manipur made it to the quarter-finals before losing to formidable Bengal and thus registered their best ever performance till that time.[30] But three years later, Manipuri soccer reached its pinnacle as the state, fancied with all its star players in its rank for the first time ever, won its maiden Santosh Trophy crown in front of its own people at Imphal. Incidentally, for the first time in the heydays of the state's soccer, the state witnessed the combined participation of all their prolific soccer experts together, proudly donning the state's jersey in the senior level. For this historic first, as Suvam Pal argues, 'One must appreciate that the ever-idiosyncratic AIFF's creditable policy of passing the recent resolution of ensuring every state to call their outstation players for the prestigious Santosh Trophy as it bore immediate fruit.'[31] This historic triumph consolidated Manipur's status as the power centre of Indian soccer, thereby signalling the end of the monopoly of Bengal and Goa. In the past few years, the success of Goa, Mumbai and Bengal soccer giants, such as Dempo Sports Club, Mahindra United, Churchill Bothers, Mohun Bagan and East Bengal, can be attributed to the important role of players from other states, in which Manipur figures prominently, not to speak of the foreign recruits.

The AMFA was established in 1976 under the aegis of the Government of Manipur. Earlier, the All Manipur Sports Association (AMSA) was in charge of football in the state. It was with the directive of the AIFF and on the principle of 'one game one association' that the AMFA got separated from AMSA. Till 1992, AMFA was directly responsible for all activities, including inter-club leagues, inter-districts, state/national championships, preparation of state teams and other soccer development programmes. However, realizing the necessity of propagating the game in the state with great potential, the AMFA directly assigned the inter-club leagues to the district associations—which were divided into 12 district units, namely, Imphal West District Football Association, Imphal East District Football Association, District Sports Association, Bishnupur District Sports Association, Kakching District Sports Association, Churachandpur District Sports Association, Sadar Hills District Sports Association, Ukhrul District Sports Association, Senapati District Sports Association, Tamenglong District Sports Association, Chandel District Football Association, and Thoubal and All Jiribam Sports Association. All these district associations have boasted of a few, good number of local clubs, divided into four categories:

Super Division, First Division, Second Division and Third Division. However, unlike most of the sporting organizations of India, with all its handicaps, AMFA played a decent role towards the uplift of the game of soccer, at least at the junior level. Manipur's glittering track record of producing as many as 200 internationals in both men and women categories is quite largely attributed to the modus operandi of the nodal organization, which tried its best for a holistic development. Though Manipur is located in the extreme north-eastern part of the country, the AIFF, giving due recognition to its recent performances, has been trying to entrust a good number of national championships to the Association every year. In fact, the Association has now emerged as one of the most successful and well-organized state-level sports organizations in the Northeast with its fully computerized office, permanent staff and other modern amenities. Words about the association's achievements have reached such proportions that FIFA, the world's governing body in football, and the International Olympic Committee had listed the honorary secretary of the association in the list of volunteers honoured in connection with the commemoration of the International Year of Volunteers.[32]

Even after the initiation of a tangible process of professionalization and commercialization in the domestic circuit, Indian football with its attractive paraphernalia of mass spectatorship is far away from adapting to the contemporary trends of the game's global culture.[33] When India as a footballing power of some worth flexes its muscle at the Asian stage, it is again a particular club, and not a national side, which gives us a toast of national victory and instils a sense of national pride.[34] India needs more Manipuris to attain the status of a developing footballing nation because Manipur does not represent club syndromes, but provides a viable pool of young promising footballers who can serve the national team. The number of new registrations of Manipuri footballers in National League teams since 2002 reiterates this point. The number increased from three in 2002–2003 to 14 in 2006–2007 (see Figure 3.2).

The inter-state transfers' list of AIFF in 2006 shows that out of 452 transfers, 103 players (about 23 per cent) came from the north-eastern states, of which 65 (about 14 per cent) were Manipuris. On the other hand, among the players from the Northeast, Manipuris represented 63 per cent.[35] Since 2006, the rise in the number of registration has almost galloped. More importantly, the 20-member Indian senior

Figure 3.2

Number of Players Registered in National League Teams: Manipur

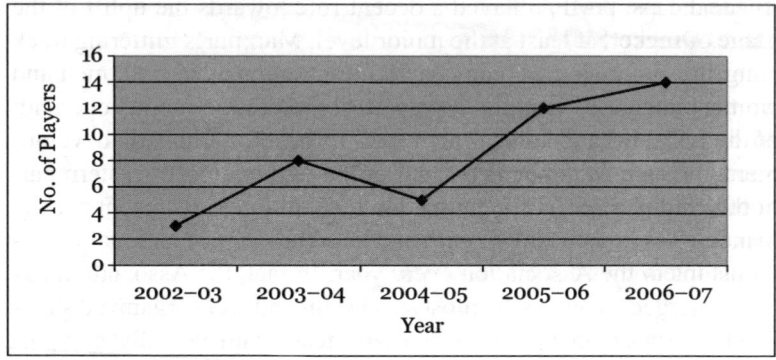

Source: National League Registration Files, All India Football Federation.

national soccer squad that took part in the Doha Asian Games, 2006 comprised as many as seven players (35 per cent) from the Northeast, including four Manipuris. More importantly, the 22-men under-20 Indian team that participated in the AFC Championship 2006 had 14 players (63 per cent) from the Northeast in their rank.[36] This trend has continued to prosper in the last nine years, as Manipuri representation has strengthened its mark in the national squad at all age levels.

Soccer as a Career Option and Professional Identity

Thus, men's soccer in the state has attained such a standard in the last one decade, thanks mostly to the efforts of the AMFA and the SAI, that young football players from Manipur have opted for playing outside Manipur in different club teams throughout India, thereby creating for themselves alternative career options and earning a decent living. Tomba Singh described football to be 'our passport to success in life.'[37] The veteran Renedy Singh puts the prospect on a high pitch: 'Watch out for some more names [in the national squad] in the next couple of years. Soon, Manipur will be - all and end-all- for Indian football.'[38]

Instead of destroying their ethnic identity by some or other means, this has given wider recognition to their professional expertise and has enhanced the prestige and status of their community at the national stage. Dingko Singh, who sparked off a sporting revolution by winning the Asian Games gold medal in boxing in 1998, neatly sums up the essence of the situation: 'There's nothing else for youngsters to do here; no money, no business. So they get hooked onto some sport because that's the only way they'll find a job.'[39] In the case of football, this became apparent at the turn of the century. Bijen Singh talked about the prospect of carving out an independent career in one of his interviews a few years back:

> Now Manipur has a lot of good footballers. Why now, even in the past, when I was young, Manipur had good crop of footballers. But Manipur does not have clubs of the stature of East Bengal and Mohun Bagan. So, for survival, we have to go outside. There are so many players from Manipur who are playing for the top clubs across the country. We cannot go back and play for Manipur at senior level. If one considers all these players, then Manipur will be a very strong side in the se3nior level, at par with the best. Even the junior players who Manipur win the BC Roy Trophy for the second consecutive year, will now move outside Manipur to enhance their career.[40]

The young Manipuri cadets of the TFA also argued that playing the game in right earnest could give them a tangible option of earning a decent and respectable living outside Manipur, thereby putting an end to the increasing anxiety of their parents and families in the state.[41] However, it is important that the AMFA should utilize the experience and support of these soccer stars to boost up the infrastructure and quality of football in the home state.

Vision India and Manipur: Soccer as an Employment Opportunity within the State

In 2000, Manipuri soccer star Somatai Shaiza lamented that 'there are not enough scopes for the Manipuris to show their talent to the outside world.'[42] He also noted that no one could think of making football a career living in Manipur at that time. He attributed this state of affairs to lack of infrastructure and apathy of the officials towards football. And to put an end to all these possibilities, he was determined to start his academy after his retirement.[43] Things, however, began to change radically, particularly since 2002, after AMFA's successful hosting of the Santosh Trophy as well as Manipur's victory in the tournament. Still, there was not much scope for the young Manipuri footballers either to find a job through sport or to take up the game as a profession within the state itself. This was mainly because no leagues like Kolkata or Goa or no major tournaments were staged in Manipur to make the players economically viable for the Manipuri clubs.

Manipur finally got an opportunity to mine out its incredible talent pool in a systematic and organized way when Manipur along with Delhi was taken under the Vision India project, an ambitious project under the aegis of the grand Vision Asia[44] project of AFC, envisaging the fulfilment of AFC's latest motto 'The Future is Asia'[45]—a holistic approach towards the development of Asian soccer. The Vision India was launched by Dato Peter Velappan, general secretary of AFC, on 26 April 2004. As already mentioned in Chapter 2, Manipur and Delhi were chosen as the two sites for the implementation of the pilot projects of Vision India at the initial stage. In AIFF General Secretary Alberto Colaso's words:

> For a while Manipur has become a powerhouse of Indian football as they have already produced some of the finest players in the present Indian soccer. Football has a great mass appeal in the state. But unlike West Bengal, Goa and Kerala, absence of any premier soccer club has been a hindrance to the upliftment of soccer in the state. Through Vision India, AIFF hopes that soccer in Manipur will receive a big impetus, as they will restructure the entire soccer system in the state apart from conducting a thorough-professional talent hunt scheme and evolving out a good club soccer system.[46]

As discussed in details in Chapter 2, Manipur's progress in the field of soccer has been accelerated by the fruitful implementation of the Vision India programme since 2004. The introduction of the State League under Vision India has made a deep impact on the Manipuri society and economy as it has provided a high-performance platform for the players, clubs, coaches, referees and officials. In other words, the league has transformed football as a viable career option in Manipur. The young footballers have become able to pursue football as a career living. With a tangible process of professionalization already set in the AMFA and the clubs, paid jobs as support staff have also opened up another option for employment. Manipur seems to have a great future ahead with potentials for attracting sponsorship deals, sending club teams to the I-League and hosting national/ international tournaments, which might help materialize its tourism prospects and raising its economic infrastructure. Other states of the Northeast have already been inspired by Manipur's example.

Soccer as a Social Opiate: Sport, Youth and Sociopolitical Stability in the Northeast

As Manipur has been under the shadow of insurgency and counter-insurgency for decades now, the viability of both is being questioned from different quarters. For the insurgents, their desired goal, that is, secession and independence, comes first and peace and development second, while the Government of India justifies counter-insurgency in terms of restoration of peace and development in society. However, it might not be too impressionistic to argue that common people of the state are also becoming tired of this stream of insurgent/counter-insurgent activities as well as the ethnic clashes.[47] In view of this tendency, restoration of peace and stability can be the prime requisite to lead the society and economy of Manipur into a road to development.[48] With the Manipuri youth in large numbers being attracted to football in the last one and a half decade, the game can play a positive role in this process of sociopolitical stabilization.

A new tinge of colour may be added here to understand the ground realities of sports situation in Manipur. Sports, such as football, in the last decade or so have become more than a mere pastime for on-field entertainment in this state of north-eastern India. Rather, in the turbulent north-eastern states like Manipur continually struck by insurgency and terrorism, sport assumes the dimension of a partial opiate. As Animul Islam observes: 'Deprived of creature comforts and saddled with insurgency, drugs and AIDS, they turned to the one thing they knew best: sport.'[49] In fact, sport can be one powerful medium through which the restless energies of the north-eastern youth can be appropriated to serve their respective states and the nation. Manipur has started developing a sports policy,

> which aims to win younger people away from the pursuit of insurgency and the frustration of searching for government jobs or opting, at least for those who can afford it, paying out at all levels to capture contracts and assignments, and become wealthy and well-known.[50]

But, to implement this policy fruitfully, the government and the concerned authorities should consult and listen to the trained sportspersons, including players and professionals, in the field. As one commentator argued, 'they know better than others what is needed to make sports an attractive avenue of channeling the energies of the young and a real alternative for employment.'[51]

Stan Rayan wrote about football in contemporary Manipur: 'Football is now fast becoming *a way of life* for the Manipuris. With insurgency, drugs and AIDS turning many lives into a nightmare, and with many young falling prey, parents heave a big sigh of relief when their children take to sport.'[52] That is why even continuous socio-political unrest could hardly hinder the game to flourish. As one young Manipuri cadet of the TFA says:

> We want to play the game as it provides us an opportunity to become professionals. Our parents have taken the pain of sending us to this training centre in the hope that we would do well to earn our living. It's our turn to fulfil their dreams and make them happy by becoming self-sufficient. Both the young generation and their guardians in Manipur have the belief that football can achieve this end.[53]

Another Manipuri cadet of the same academy argues:

> Sports like football can certainly be one way out to the political turmoil and social instability in contemporary Manipur. Since the game has become a profession by itself, it has become synonymous with employment. Moreover, by showing *our* worth as good footballers and contributing to the success of the *national* team, we wish to raise the status of our state and rebuild its image in the eyes of Indian public.[54]

At times, the game has been used as a therapy for drug addicts. For example, an NGO called 'Sahara' runs a treatment centre for HIV-positives in New Delhi, where football has been used in this way with great success. As one of its programme managers commented, 'The game helps our inmates not only to gain fitness but also acts as an instrument of empowerment. It has helped them boost their morale and lead a healthy life.'[55] Most players on the Sahara teams come from north-eastern India in general and Manipur in particular, and many of them have made it to Delhi's A Division League.[56] One such player, Diosiam, remarked, 'I was fed up with life but could not get out of drugs. During rehabilitation, football gave me a zest for life and I now play in Delhi's A Division League.'[57]

Conclusion

Broadly speaking, this chapter intends to put emphasis on two objectives: first, to devise peaceful cultural means and constructive social strategies to provide the youth in the Northeast with wider and diversified economic opportunities in order to overcome political instability and social anomalies, and second, to explore, locate and earmark the fruitful areas of professional expertise of the north-eastern people, so that the outcome might be useful in utilizing both the specialized skill and professional expertise for the development of the region from within as well as relocating such skilled human resources of the region to other states of India where such expertise may be meaningfully deployed. As I have tried to show, soccer can be fruitfully appropriated as a novel cultural means to realize this double strategy of generating alternative employment opportunities and achieving socio-political stabilization. However, this could be successful only if the central and state governments, state- and central-level soccer associations, the media and the people of the Northeast appreciate the importance of an integrated developmental approach and move together to fulfil that purpose. However, one pertinent question remains to be answered in this context: how do the insurgent groups view this attempted and partially successful integration through sports? Given the history of inter-ethnic clashes and inter-tribal feuds in the state as well as interdiction of Indian goods, Hindi cinema and other matters for a long time, it must be said that football has been largely successful in not eliciting any adverse reaction from insurgent groups, thereby breaking the jinx of isolation.

I will wind up my discussion with another excerpt from the prime minister's speech I began with:

I have already said we want to improve Manipur's connectivity to the region around. We would like to invest in the creation of modern infrastructure to enable this. However, for this to happen, we need peace, security and political stability. If we can work together to bring normalcy back I can assure you that Manipur will become Jewel of India.[58]

There are definitely government-earmarked areas where Manipur could make a lot of progress. The Government of India has started to take small steps in the right direction[59] in order to regain the confidence of the population, which is no easy task. However, creating viable employment opportunities would be a more effective way in making the state a worthy contributor to the nation's progress as a fast developing economy. With soccer, Manipur has the great potential to achieve this end, as it has already become a jewel in the crown of Indian soccer.

Notes and References

1. Prime minister's speech on 20 November 2004 at the handing over of the Kangla Fort to the Government of Manipur, available at http://pmindia.nic.in/speech/content.asp?id=50, accessed on 21 September 2006.
2. One interesting essay that deals with this theme, albeit in a somewhat misconstrued way, is: James Mills, '"Nupilal": Women's War, Football and the History of Modern Manipur', in James Mills, ed. *Subaltern Sports: Politics and Sport in South Asia* (London: Anthem, 2005).
3. For wider historical discussion on the roots, evolution and discourses of insurgency movements in Manipur, see S.C. Sharma, *Insurgency, or, Ethnic Conflict: With Reference to Manipur* (New Delhi: Magnum Business Associates, 2000). Also see: G. Kabui et al., *Modern Manipur* (Imphal: Modern Book, 1991); P. Roychowdhury, *The North East: Roots of Insurgency* (Calcutta: Firma KLM, 1986); Sajal Nag, *Contesting Marginality: Ethnicity, Insurgency and Subnationalism in North-East India* (New Delhi: Manohar, 2002); N. Sanajaoba, *Manipur: Past and Present* (Delhi: Mittal, 1990); K.M. Singh, *Hijam Irabot Singh and Political Movement in Manipur* (Delhi: B.R. Publishing, 1989); N.J. Singh, *Social Movements in Manipur* (Delhi: Mittal, 1992); *Colonialism to Democracy: A history of Manipur 1819–1972* (Delhi: Spectrum, 1992); Lokendra N. Singh, *Unquiet Valley: Society, Economy and Politics in Manipur 1891–1950* (Delhi: Mittal, 1998); B.K. Ahluwalia and S. Ahluwalia, eds. *Social Change in Manipur* (Delhi: Cultural Publishing House, 1984); G. Phukon, *Ethnicization of Politics in Northeast India* (Delhi: South Asian, 2003); L. Zehol,

Ethnicity in Manipur: Experiences, Issues and Perspectives (New Delhi: Regency. 1998); and P. Tarapot, *Bleeding Manipur* (New Delhi: Har-Anand, 2003).

4. Sanjoy Hazarika, 'Manipur Lost', in 'A Route Map to the North East', *The Asian Age*, 10 January 2001.

5. The Armed Forces (Special Powers) Act (AFSPA), 1958, was first imposed in some parts of the state as it was hit by the Naga rebellion. Later in 1980, the act was imposed in the entire state towards the height of insurgency in the Northeast.

6. Suvam Pal, 'Guts, Grits and Glory: The Manipur Soccer Story', unpublished paper, 2005.

7. Vani Saraswathi, 'Educated and jobless, youth here seek "heaven" in heroin', *The Indian Express*, 17 November 1998.

8. Ibid.

9. Rasheeda Bhagat, 'HIV/AIDS in Manipur: In the "state" of despair', *The Hindu Business Line*, 7 October 2002.

10. Peter Parkes, 'Indigenous Polo in Northern Pakistan: Game and Power on the Periphery', in Mills, ed. *Subaltern Sports*.

11. *Meiteis*, who inhabit in the planes of Manipur, comprise 70 per cent of the total population of the state. They have a grand history as Meitei kings were rulers of Manipur state till the British took over its administration towards the end of the nineteenth century. Meiteis are Vaishnavite (who worships Vishnu) Hindus. For further details, see V.P. Kaur, 'The Manipur Minefield', *The Indian Express*, 26 June 2001.

12. The *Kukis* are Christian, but quite distinct from *Nagas*, and reside primarily in southern hills of Manipur. *Kukis* have a significant place in the history of Manipur as they initiated the historical Kuki Rebellion against the British in (1917–1919) Manipur.

13. Though Manipur have a significant *Naga* population, majority of the *Nagas* are inhabitants of Manipur's neighbouring state Nagaland. The *Nagas* are overwhelmingly Christians and live in the surrounding hills in the west, north and east of Manipur.

14. Suvam Pal has used this phrase in his paper.

15. She won medals in various international competitions, including Commonwealth Games and Asian Games, apart from finding a place in the hall of fame of top 100 international weightlifting legends of the century.

16. He won a gold in boxing in the 2002 Busan Asian Games.

17. Prolific hockey midfielder Suraj Lata has so far led the Indian team to two its most memorable triumphs till date—Commonwealth Games gold at Manchester in 2002 and Asia Cup triumph in New Delhi in 2004.

18. Chanu was the top scorer for India in their Asia Cup victory in 2004.

19. Animul Islam, 'Jewel in the crown', *The Indian Express*, 10 October 2002.

20. The tournament's successful hosting bears witness to AMFA's long-term commercial and professional planning. The title sponsor of the tournament was LG India. More importantly, the Association launched its official website on the occasion of its hosting the tournament.

21. Islam, 'Jewel in the Crown'.

22. Quoted in ibid.

23. Ibid.

24. While Manipuri players have always made their presence felt among the top string of TFA graduates since the mid-1990s, SAI offered its sponsorship to a few institutions like the Army Boys School, thereby helping a great deal to locate and nourish the budding talent.

25. *Paitei*s, an ethnic clan of Mizo origin, comprise a meagre portion of Manipur's population.

26. Tata Football Academy (TFA) is a venture solely undertaken by Indian corporate giant Tata Group of Companies for the upliftment of Indian soccer. The soccer academy, situated at Jamshedpur, has already produced a long list of soccer players who have been successfully playing for various top-level clubs of the country, apart from representing the national team.

27. Islam, 'Jewel in the Crown'.

28. Incidentally, Bijen was also the youngest ever captain of East Bengal Club at the age of 21 in the 87-year-old history of the glamour outfit.

29. Santosh Trophy is the apex and most prestigious interstate soccer championships in India and was started by the All India Football Federation in 1941.

30. Islam, 'Jewel in the Crown'.

31. Pal, 'Guts, Grits and Glory'.

32. I have collected these pieces of information on the AMFA from the official website of the Santosh Trophy 2002. For details, see www.santoshtrophy2002.nic.in/news.htm, accessed on 21 September 2006.

33. For football's changing global dimension through the ages, see Richard Giulianotti, *Football: A Sociology of the Global Game* (Cambridge: Polity Press, 1999). For considerations on the variegated pattern of contemporary global culture of football, see Gerry P.T. Finn and Richard Giulianotti, eds. *Football Culture: Local Contests, Global Visions* (London and Portland, OR: Frank Cass, 2000).

34. For example, East Bengal Club's victory (July 2003) in the ASEAN Cup at Jakarta, Indonesia, by beating the top club teams from Southeast Asia was perceived as an emblem of national spirit.

35. All India Football Federation Inter-State Transfers 2006, available at www.the-aiff.com/interstate.php, accessed on 10 April 2007.

36. All India Football Federation National Team Profile, available at www.the-aiff.com/Team.php, accessed on 10 April 2007.

37. Stan Rayan, 'Football, a way of life for Manipuris', *The Hindu*, 15 November 2005.

38. Ibid.

39. Quoted in Islam, 'Jewel in the Crown'.

40. 'Bijen Singh: A Whiff of Fresh Air', available at www.calonline.com/cal/alaap/bijensingh.html, n.d., accessed on 21 September 2006.

41. The author had a discussion with two of the Manipuri footballers of the 2006–2008 batch of Tata Football Academy cadets, Henry Gangte and Jibon Singh. Both expressed this view in confidence.

42. 'Sosho wants to start football academy in Manipur', *Oriental Times*, Vol. 3, Nos. 27–28, 22 November–6 December 2000.

43. Ibid.

44. Vision Asia is the AFC's grand plan for a continent-wide programme to raise the standards of Asian football at all levels, be it on the field of play, administration or sports science. This is the brainchild of AFC President Mohamed Bin Hammam, who launched the programme in January 2003. Nine months later, after much fine-tuning, Hammam unveiled Vision Asia as a well-defined blueprint to international delegates and VIPs during the FIFA Congress in Doha, Qatar. The president firmly believes that Asia, with its 3.7 billion population, has the potential to produce many world-class footballing nations. His ultimate goal is for an Asian team to one day win the

FIFA World Cup. Hammam has identified 11 disciplines—akin to 11 players on the football field—that Vision Asia must address if Asian countries are to catch up with their counterparts in Europe and the rest of the world. They are: national associations (goalkeeper); marketing, grassroots, coach education, referees, sports medicine (defenders); men's competitions, women's competitions, futsal (midfielders); media, fans (forwards). AFC has already recruited experts with specialist skills in each discipline. These consultants are being assisted by development officers, one for each of the four zones—West Asia, Central/South Asia, South East Asia and East Asia (gathered from www.the-aiff.com/vision_India.php).

45. FIFA President Sepp Blatter initially told the world that 'The future is Asia'. The AFC, since then, adopted the phrase as its motto.

46. Colaso revealed this in a personal communication to Suvam Pal, then a sports journalist with the *Sahara Time*. For details, see Pal, 'Guts, Grits and Glory'.

47. That the people of the Northeast could even compromise with the ultimate goal 'independence' in lieu of autonomy for the sake of peace is amply illustrated by the case of Nagaland. As Sajal Nag rightly points out, 'The event (the granting of statehood by the Indian Government to the Naga Hills) was all the more meaningful because it signified the polarization of the mass base. The moderates had control over a large section of these polarized masses who, caught between the violence of the Indian Army and the faction-ridden underground insurgents and traumatized by the bloodshed and harassment, were willing to settle for little less than complete freedom for the sake of peace.' Nag, *Contesting Marginality*, p. 313.

48. This is probably one of the reasons why the Government and the National Socialist Council of Nagaland (Nagalim) (NSCN-IM) are going to considerable lengths to accommodate each other. As Hiranmay Karlekar has argued, 'The latter, as well as the NSCN (K) are under tremendous pressure in Nagaland where ceasefire has not only made the demand for peace to snowball but has also enabled the emergence of a civil society—comprising church, tribal and clan leaders, educationists and so on—which is articulating it vigorously.' Hiranmay Karlekar, 'Nagaland: Intimations of Peace?' *The Pioneer*, 6 May 2007.

49. Islam, 'Jewel in the Crown'.

50. Namaram Kishalaya, 'Beyond Santosh Trophy: Big Bucks Must Back Manipur Sports', Manipuronline.com/Opinions, 13 September 2002, accessed on 21 September 2006.

51. Ibid.

52. Rayan, 'Football, a way of life for Manipuris' (emphasis added).

53. Interview with Henry Gangte, 2 May 2007.

54. Interview with Jibon Singh, 2 May 2007.

55. See www.breitbart.com/news/na/060729052913.1q9deia7.html, accessed on 21 September 2006.

56. Ibid.

57. Ibid.

58. PM's speech on 20 November 2004 at the handing over of the Kangla Fort to the Government of Manipur. Available at http://pmindia.nic.in/speech/content. asp?id=50, accessed on 21 September 2006.

59. Such steps include the handing over the Kangla Fort to the State Government of Manipur, upgradation of the Manipur University into a central university or the new Jiribam–Imphal rail project.

4

Cricket, Politics and Diplomacy: A Study of India's Friendship Tour of Pakistan, 2004

Introduction

Cricket is the de facto national game in India, if not her only secular religion of late. Indians, it is often suggested, like talking, reading and writing on cricket. Indians love to watch their national cricket team play. They worship their cricketing icons. They also invest safely in the 'cricket industry'. Such pre-eminence of cricket in Indian life has also led to its construction and interpretation in terms of political transition, social tension, economic transformation, diplomatic relations or cultural development. And when it comes to India's cricketing relations with Pakistan, it begins to signify different meanings and convey different messages to different people in India: nationalism, communalism, war, infiltration, insurgency, terrorism, diplomacy, peace, election, cultural exchange, commercial boom, cricketing conflict and so on. The Indian team's tour to Pakistan in March–April 2004 is an excellent case in point here. The tour evoked a plethora of responses in Indian public life. From the learned to the laity, people began to consider cricket as a means to various ends: a diplomatic ploy to accelerate peace process, a political instrument to generate electoral confidence, an economic means to ameliorate the nation's pecuniary distress, a cultural arena to assert cricketing muscle, an emotional tool to soothe traditional enmity and so on. For example, the apparent popular perception of a political tension between the two countries stood in striking contrast to the friendly ties between the two cricket boards at the international level till 2008, while the game still remains one major and viable confidence-building arena in the long-term process of normalization of diplomatic relations between the two neighbouring states. This chapter seeks to explore, understand and analyze such varied representations of the tour as evidenced in popular media in the wider context of domestic political debates, subcontinental diplomatic relations and purely cricketing arch-rivalry.

Indo-Pak Cricket and Cricketing Nationalism

The Partition of 1947 and the resultant turmoil triggered off hatred, distrust and prejudice in almost every sphere of activity in the subcontinent.[1] Interestingly, it was cricket that formed the first bilateral exchange in 1952, when Pakistan led by Abdul Hafeez Kardar toured India, evoking spontaneous, albeit tense, response. It was reciprocated two years later when India paid the first official visit under Vinoo Mankad, generating equally sensitive response. Yet since 1947, a 'cricket conflict' brewed simultaneously between the two countries, based on the nationalist antagonism between the two teams and backed by passionate fans on both sides. This nationalist fervour perpetuated by the history of hostility cuts across class, caste, ethnicity and gender, and leads to unanimous support for the national team. For the millions of Indians and Pakistanis, cricket has become the ultimate test of patriotic zeal and loyalty. On and off the pitches, cricket fans vent their passions against the 'other' country in forms which range from the funny to the grotesque. Those among 'us' who may happen to support 'them' for their sportsmanship usually get rebuked for their suspected sense of nationalism, citizenship and loyalty. As one sportswriter has commented:

> Today Indo-Pak cricket offers a striking case study to see how a political conflict between two states has trickled down to the mass level and saturated the mass psyche to such an extent, that political hostilities are not only played on the Line of Control but also on the cricket field. This mass psyche of a purported nationalist conflict has been also revved by years of

state propaganda against the enemy country, which permeated in all forms of interaction and exchange with the enemy—be it sports or war.[2]

Sport, particularly cricket, between these two countries has, thus, always been played with nationalist fervour, and even fear. Many of the early tests between India and Pakistan were drawn, both teams showing an excess of caution, petrified of losing to their neighbour. A loss against any other team did not matter—both teams were habitual losers until the 1970s—but a defeat to their neighbour rankled deeply. Abbas Ali Baig's promising career is said to have been derailed because of an average run of scores against Pakistan, when a similar streak against any other side would not have mattered. Javed Miandad's last-ball six off Chetan Sharma still rankles in the Indian psyche as a low point for the 'nation'. In every World Cup, Indians and Pakistanis treated their game against the other with as much importance as the tournament itself, not caring if they lost the Cup, as long as they beat their immediate opponent. When Pakistan lost the 1996 World Cup match to India in Bangalore, the house of their captain, Wasim Akram, was stoned. In fact, this typical brand of 'cricketing nationalism' could be discernible during all the India–Pakistan matches in the four World Cups between 1992 and 2003. The importance of India–Pakistan match in the Cup and its impact on the psyche of the Indian and Pakistani public in every case, as revealed in the contemporary media coverage, pointed to the fact that the victory or defeat in such a match came to be looked upon as a test of national superiority.

Sport has always been described in terms of war. Games are often described as 'battles', teams are often said to have been 'routed', 'slaughtered' or 'demolished', in a vocabulary of alpha-male aggression. 'Sport is an unfailing cause of ill-will', thus said George Orwell. In a celebrated essay written in 1945, Orwell argued:

> I am always amazed when I hear people saying that sport creates goodwill between the nations, and that if only the common peoples of the world could meet one another at football or cricket, they would have no inclination to meet on the battlefield. Even if one didn't know from concrete examples (the 1936 Olympic Games, for instance) that international sporting contests lead to orgies of hatred, one could deduce it from general principles.[3]

The point Orwell went on to make was that all sport was competitive, and involved winning or losing, and thus pride. A sport between nations thus took on bigger proportions, as it involved national pride—as much as war would. Indeed, Orwell was bold enough to question the very act of playing and following sport that is representational: 'as soon as the question of prestige arises, as soon as you feel that you and some larger unit will be disgraced if you lose, the most savage combative instincts are aroused.'[4] He did not of course suggest that 'sport is one of the main causes of international rivalry; big scale sport is itself, I think, merely another effect of the causes that have produced nationalism.'[5] Sport, thus remains to Orwell, 'a mimic warfare', 'bound up with hatred, jealousy, boastfulness, disregard of all rules and sadistic pleasure in witnessing violence.'[6] While many other bi-national rivalries exist in sport—the Ashes in cricket and Brazil–Argentina in soccer, for example—none are quite so fierce and filled with 'ill will' as that between India and Pakistan. As Kapil Dev, the legendary Indian all-rounder, argues:

There's no place for sentiment when India meets Pakistan in cricket. My very first experience in Pakistan makes it amply clear that the political differences between these two countries get translated into this game. If you are batting, you feel that even the fielders are hostile. I wish they played more with a spirit of competition than hostility. I must have played about 20 matches against them. It's the spectators who make it so electrifying because people are so tense. No politician can understand the level of this hostility until and unless they go and play on the ground.[7]

Media in the twenty-first century, perhaps, plays the most important role in representing sport as a metaphor for war. Whenever India and Pakistan play cricket against each other, the media talks of the game as a metaphor for war, and perversely with a sense of glee and anticipation. The feelings that India–Pakistan cricket inspires are extreme, and sentiments like pride and honour 'are' affected by victory or defeat, much as they would be in a war.[8] Naturally, when India prepared for a full tour of Pakistan in March–April 2004, media representations began to mould the public imagining of the same in more ways than one.

The 2003 World Cup Experience

The 2003 World Cup may be said to have triggered off, and given full fruition to, the new brand of 'cricketing nationalism' in India. A brief analysis of the importance of India–Pakistan match in the Cup and its impact on the psyche of the Indian public at that time may serve as a useful exemplar in this context.

Although it has been argued quite rightly by one historian that the communal character of cricket sometimes enhances its commercial prospects,[9] in the light of past 20 years' experience of turbulence and instability in Indian politics, the desirability of such a development is a questionable proposition. In the context of present political equation where the lines between nationalism and communalism sometimes seem to be extremely blurred and ambiguous in the post-Godhra age,[10] as well as the rising heat of Indo-Pak foreign relations over the Kashmir issue after Pokhran[11] and Kargil,[12] an India–Pakistan cricket match in a World Cup specially in its public appeal cannot be isolated from its overtly political/communal overtones.[13] The victory or defeat in such a match is looked upon as a test of national superiority. Let me give a few instances from the 2003 World Cup experience that would hopefully substantiate my point.

Immediately after India's victory over Pakistan in the World Cup group league match on 1 March, the streets and lanes of Kolkata reverberated with the sound of blowing conches, bursting crackers and the chanting of slogans. At Kalighat,[14] many were seen waving national flags with pictures of Sachin Tendulkar struck in the middle of the *Ashoka Chakra*. Cries of 'Sachin! Sachin!' rent the night, alternating the shouts of 'Pakistan hai hai!'[15] Gujarat, on the other hand, witnessed incidents of Muslims being stopped from celebrating the occasion.[16] Celebrations led to rioting, injuries and one death in Ahmedabad.[17] Violence also followed in Bangalore during the post-victory celebrations.[18] In all these places, prohibitory orders were to be imposed and security to be tightened in the face of such incidents. More importantly, the reaction of Indian politicians to the victory requires careful notice. Prime Minister Atal Bihari Vajpayee and his deputy, L.K. Advani, too watched the game on television back home. Advani promptly called up the team in the hotel to congratulate the players.[19] Next morning, Finance Minister Jaswant Singh sent a congratulatory message to the team and consequently announced tax concessions on World Cup prize money.[20] Army Chief N.C. Vij, too, congratulated the boys over the telephone for their thumping win.[21] Considering all this, it seems, it did not matter to them if India could not make it to the super six, semis or final. Many sensible Indians became critical of this irresponsible behaviour of Indian politicians, and even the general public did not seem to have agreed to Jaswant Singh's offer of tax sops to India's extraordinarily well-off cricketers. Here is one voice that furnishes a logical touch to this sentiment:

> While the entire nation salutes Sachin and his men for their epoch-making win against Pakistan, likening it to a victory in war or raising high-voltage jingoistic cries—as our politicians and military brass did—does not augur well for the rapprochement we seek so eagerly with our neighbour. And then to have Jaswant Singh declaring that it did not matter if we won the World Cup or not, and offering tax sops! No wonder our country is in the financial mess it is in. If our cricketers have any sense, they should refuse the Finance Minister's offer in the interest of the nation.[22]

However, amidst the general trend of escalating belligerence over the victory, the best antidote came from the man who creatively and aggressively marshalled this new-look Indian team, Sourav Ganguly. 'Beating Pakistan does not mean we have won the World Cup,' said the Indian captain. 'A lot of works remains to be done and we don't want to be caught napping.'[23]

The question that really surfaces as a result of this incidental communalization and politicization of cricket (which is, of course, neither a universal phenomenon in India nor universally endorsed by the learned or the laity) is whether it is possible to resolve or dissolve these relational complexities between sport and politics in this era of 'hyper-nationalism', where an Indo-Pak match becomes a war by other means. Cricket historian Ramachandra Guha addresses the question more succinctly, 'As society and politics became more polarized, cricket was drawn into the vortex.'[24] In this specific context of communal polarization on the rise, the successes of India's two young guns, Zaheer Khan and Mohammad Kaif, became an emblem of both solace and hope for the Indian Muslims. Ashis Nandy makes the point more clear:

> For Muslim youth, the presence of Zaheer and Kaif represents an area open to them. If these two can make it, so can they … nationalism is

getting to be a headache in India. ... Muslims all over are as paranoid as those living in the riot-prone states of western India. They know India is their country and they will fight it out here, which is why the achievements of Muslim player make them feel good.[25]

The subsequent sections of this chapter will try to show how such imagining or imaging of cricket performances could be appropriated by the state as well as its representatives to better effect in order to serve presumed cause of the nation.

'Peace Tour', 'Feel Good' and Electoral Politics

Despite the enormous media hype on the tour, representing it as a diplomatic tool or a confidence-building measure in the normalization of relations between the two countries, it is important to keep in mind the confusion and hesitancy, speculation and sensationalism that preceded it. With the escalation of militancy in Kashmir in the mid-1990s, culminating in the Kargil War in 1999 just after the conclusion of the Pakistan tour to India, the Indian government imposed an embargo on Indo-Pak cricket series for a while. Interestingly enough, as Kingshuk Chatterjee has argued, the government seemed to manufacture a semi-consensus on the issue with relative ease 'as part of its nation-building project based on the premise of aggressive nationalism.'[26] All through 2003, the debate, or what Chatterjee calls 'the lack of it', on the advisability of playing a series in Pakistan in 2004 recurred on the pages of newspapers and magazines, and on TV channels. Even when the political and diplomatic relationships between the two countries improved enough to suggest a resumption of cricketing relations towards the end of 2003, the actual decision to clear India's tour of Pakistan, albeit again manufactured smoothly by the government, was fraught with many dilemmas.

The media tirelessly speculated during the months preceding the actual official decision to clear the tour[27] that the tour was in serious doubt. Although security reasons were cited in a media campaign pressing for postponement, the real fear was that any 'untoward incident' during the series would spoil the 'feel-good' factor before the polls.[28] There were several arguments both in favour of and against the proposed tour.[29] Some held that the risk was simply not worth it: an attack or assault on the team by motivated parties would in a stroke destroy the peace process and set off a series of calamities.[30] Some reasoned that not touring would be the real sabotage of the peace process, preventing, as it would, the rare opportunity of thousands of people meeting thousands of people across the border and watching a game.[31] Yet, some others argued that it was precisely because of the danger posed by thousands of people meeting thousands of people and watching a game that the tour must not proceed.[32] More prudent politicians, such as L.K. Advani, the influential home minister and the veteran leader of the Bharatiya Janata Party (BJP), was in favour of shelving the tour until after the general elections slated to begin on 20 April. He sensed—but definitely not the people, as the polls would later show—this heavy ephemeral buzz, a 'feel-good' factor sweeping through the nation and what might a possible cricket loss to Pakistan on the eve of polls do to that. And would such friendly overtures towards Pakistan before elections make the party look too soft in the eyes of the voters?[33]

The Ministry of External Affairs, on the other hand, was in favour of the tour because it feared that a postponement of the tour, a key confidence-building measure, would hit the peace process and expose Vajpayee's peace initiative as hollow. As one newspaper correspondent reported:

> It would have vitiated the atmosphere ahead of the official level dialogue between the two countries, beginning on Monday. Calling off the tour would have also taken away the current diplomatic advantage that Delhi has over Islamabad, the foreign office held. ... Going back on any confidence-building measure would have invited questions about India's intentions of improving relations, it believed.[34]

Another commentator suggested,

> had India cancelled the tour, Pakistan would have raised the issue in the UN and scored diplomatic brownie points in the process. The cancellation might have been used as a ploy to engage international attention to the fact that it is India, after all, that is delaying the peace process in the subcontinent.[35]

Naturally therefore, Vajpayee's success in clearing the tour despite Advani's reservations about the same was seen as 'a loss of face for the home ministry'.[36]

More importantly, it was widely argued that when Atal Bihari Vajpayee, the Indian prime minister, ahead of his government's re-election, cleared the Pakistan tour, despite objections from several quarters, including those by Advani, he was trying to utilize cricket as a tool for forthcoming election propaganda against his political rival Sonia Gandhi, the Congress leader. As Sachidananda Murthy pointed out:

> The cricket tour has much at stake for Vajpayee. If Sachin Tendulkar and company overcome the nasty surprises readied by Javed Miandad, the BJP will tout it as another shining example of the feel-good factor. Even if the result is disappointing, the success of the tour would be touted as vindication of the friendly hand extended to Pervez Musharraf.[37]

Boria Majumdar emphasizes this fruitful marriage between sport and politics rather interestingly: 'India's Pak tour will surely go down in history as a googly that stamped the jingoists, albeit the debate will go on about how much the tour was about keeping "India shining". But then, politics and sports have always had a love-hate relation.'[38] That it was Vajpayee's political strategy to clear the tour, however, occasionally got vehemently critiqued by a few in the media on purely cricketing grounds. As Ashok V. Desai maintained:

> Before the boys in blue left, I thought it made no sense as cricket, and all sense as Vajpeyan politics. It was crazy to send our best cricketers to play in April, when the temperature in Multan would be touching forty. They had just returned from an exciting tour of Australia; only an election-crazy politician would send them into another grueling series even before they had unpacked their bags.[39]

Yet, others argued that postponing the series for the time being would mean having to play in May, 'in the most hellishly searing innards of summer, where cricketers and spectators alike would have fallen like flies.'[40] Moreover, both teams had a packed schedule of cricketing commitments beyond the summer. Some among the political circles therefore hinted at 'splitting the tour into two, holding only the Tests—"less excitable for the masses"—before the elections.'[41]

Some others smelt a bane at the way expectations and preparations gathered momentum around the tour:

> At the best of times, a tour to Pakistan is difficult because of the emotions involved. The pressures are political, diplomatic, emotional, and that's even before you get to the cricket. There is more the ruling coalition's hope that a successful tour will convert the electoral gains. That is a dangerous game to play given its glorious uncertainties.[42]

When the players met the prime minister before their departure for the tour, Vajpayee urged the Indian cricketers straightaway 'to not only win the matches in Pakistan but also win the hearts of the people there.'[43] He presented a bat to skipper Sourav Ganguly, on which was written 'Khel hi nahin, dil bhi jitiye' (Win not only the game, but also win hearts). The placards waved around while Vajpayee met the team featuring messages such as 'Best of Luck' and 'Atal ne diya cricket ka uphaar, India-Pakistan sadbhavana ka prachar' (Atal's cricket gift spreads harmony in India and Pakistan).[44] On the other hand, Priyanka Gandhi and Rahul Gandhi, representing the Congress outfit at the National Stadium in Karachi to watch India play, emphasized the need to develop people-to-people contact and cricket's potential role in the process.[45]

Many Indians were aware that the series might have major repercussions on the forthcoming elections. India's stirring performances in the one-day series led to animated discussion on whether the BJP would be back with a significant majority. As one commentator argued, 'It was as if every four or six hit by Ganguly's men counted for one more vote for the BJP. *India* was certainly *shining* and the "feel good" mood escalated no end.'[46] While the economic consequences of the tour were well understood, many also appreciated the government's decision to send the team, ignoring electoral considerations. On the other hand, it was quite rightly pointed out that the decision was 'a well thought out electoral strategy'.[47] 'With three Muslims spearheading the Indian challenge in Pathan, Zaheer and Kaif, the liberal image of the BJP government was bolstered no end, a political masterstroke in election hour.'[48] However, the point that often begs attention is that Vajpayee's decision might have been precipitated by purely cricketing counsels. Given India's consistently better performance on the field since the World Cup in February–March 2003, the team seemed to have a bright chance of beating the

Pakistani team on their own soil. As Krishnamachari Srikkanth, the former Indian captain, confidently argued on the eve of the tour, 'We are the favourites to win the series. Both batsmen and bowlers are at a higher confidence level having proved themselves in Australia.'[49]

When India won the first one-dayer, hectic appropriation followed within the political parties of India. Priyanka and Rahul Gandhi spent time in the Indian dressing room. Soon SMSes beeped to mobile phones in India: 'Bharat ko jitney ki sahi aas thi, Rahul aur Priyanka team ke paas the!' (India was in right mood to win as Rahul and Priyanka were with the team).'[50] The sender was 'Congress', though the party later claimed it to be a hoax. The BJP retaliated with its own SMS: 'Khel bhi jeeta, dil bhi jeeta. Shabash India!' (The match is won, hearts are won too. Hail India!).'[51] And Vajpayee got on to the phone to Ganguly. Vajpayee rang him again on India's miraculous victory in the fourth one-dayer, thanks to brilliant innings by Rahul Dravid and Mohammad Kaif. The prime minister, on the campaign trail, wooed Muslim voters in Uttar Pradesh by praising the 'splendid work done by one of your sons, Kaif.'[52]

It is beyond doubt that the series presented a great opportunity for people on both sides of the border to interact one-on-one. Everybody understood on the eve of the tour that there were bridges to be built, hearts to be won. In fact, it was a great chance for both nations to capitalize on the prevailing feel-good atmosphere. For example, Indian cricketers launched a polio eradication campaign in Pakistan and joined hands with the Ministry of Health to send a message across the country to that effect. Surely, the victory in Pakistan made the average Indian feel 'better'. In fact, it was a lot more successful than the 'India Shining' campaign of the BJP. Yet it did not probably have much to matter for the party in the subsequent election.

Diplomacy, Peace Process and the 'Goodwill' Series

It is axiomatic that over the years, cricketing exchanges between India and Pakistan have been kept to minimum, primarily because of everlasting strained foreign relations. The two countries did not play any series twice for long—between 1961 and 1978, and between

1990 and 1999—due to political bad blood. More than anything else, it has had a detrimental effect on the quality of cricket the two countries put on display on the rare occasions they play each other. The rarity of the occasion leads to an unusual hype, and the pressure builds up to such an unrealistic extent that both teams approach the game in a completely negative frame of mind. As Asif Iqbal, a former Pakistani cricketer, has noted, 'Avoiding defeat becomes the primary and overwhelming objective. The result is that both teams play at a level considerably below their full potential and in an atmosphere where fear of defeat is such a major component that often dull draws are the only outcome.'[53] With the progress in cricketing relations from the close of 1970s, some improvement took place in the 1980s, as more matches were played and the approach to the game became more result oriented. Yet, thanks to another dry spell of series encounters in the 1990s, a fallout of sensitive political relations, cricketing rivalry between the two became confined mostly to a few tri-series tournaments, face-to-face Toronto meet in Canada for a few years and a match in the World Cup in every four years. Hence, the on-field tensions and off-field perceptions around the Indo-Pak match became not only stiff but complex, particularly in the wider context of Indo-Pak diplomatic conflict over the Kashmir and associated infiltration issue as well as the unhealthy nuclear power rivalry in the late 1990s. This complex cricketing jinx seems to be resolved with the decision of the Indian government to send its cricket team to Pakistan for a full tour in February 2004, albeit with numerous security conditions sorted out between the two cricket boards.

The departure for the tour was preceded by two major briefings for the entire team: Ministry of External Affairs briefing and security briefing. While the ministry spokesman reminded the members of the touring team that the tour was 'an important part of this Indo-Pakistan revival',[54] John Wright recollected nicely how the head of the VIP security division in the Ministry of Home Affairs, Yashovardhan Azad, who had made an inspection visit to Pakistan, briefed the team on security arrangements:

> We were given a 16-point list of do's and don'ts which included not discussing plans, programmes and engagements in public, not having a routine of going to the same place at the same time every day (bad news for those with regular toilet habits), and taking precautions before opening unidentified mail.[55]

As the Indian team reached Lahore, recounts Rahul Bhattacharya, one of the few journalists who visited Pakistan during the much-publicized cricket tour of Pakistan in March–April 2004:

> Entering the luxurious spick white premises of the Pearl Continental entailed, at the main gate, the boot and undercarriage scan, and past that, at the portico, the three-step check which over the next six weeks, at the grounds, at the team hotels and at the airports, would become like a bodily function: metal detector, body frisk, bag inspection. There was no point grumbling: this was India's condition for touring.[56]

Wright's description of the presidential-level security provided to the Indians on tour confirmed the rigidities as depicted earlier:

> Our convoy from Lahore Airport included an ambulance and 'jammer' cars to block radio frequencies in case of remote-controlled bombs along the route. There was also a decoy bus that took a different route to our hotel. The security arrangements meant that there was no dead time. When we went to practice, they simply blocked off the route so that what was normally a 30-minute stop-start chug through traffic became a ten-minute dash. It was the same on the return trip, and it didn't matter whether we finished practice 20 minutes earlier or later than we'd indicated: when we were ready to go, they closed the roads and we went. We were surrounded by tough-looking hombres from the Punjab Police's Elite Squad; they carried machine guns and wore black T-shirts with the 'No Fear' logo on them.[57]

The apex of this high-level security at times turned bizarre. As Bhattacharya shares one unique experience in that context:

> There were, reportedly, 250 security guards manning the hotel—that is, about fifteen per player. No access was available, naturally, to the players' floors; and no other guest was permitted to occupy a room on those floors. Any envelopes addressed to the team, it was said, were to be scanned by a bomb-disposal unit. All food for them was to be prepared under the strict-est supervision. Still, it did come as a shock when one of the commandos encircling the table in the lobby coffee-shop where Ganguly sat briefly with a few journalists asked that the tea be tasted before it passes the lips of the captain. A journalist obliged. Yes, we know our place in the world, we lot.[58]

Given such earnest efforts on the part of Pakistan to respond to India's decision to send its cricket team by giving them highest possible security along with warmest welcome and hospitality, should we make the point that cricket has the capacity to break the political jinx? Rohit Brijnath puts it prudently: 'Cricket will not heal wounds. But perhaps it can play a minor role. Perhaps this experiment can only work if we remember it is just cricket, that no nation is a lesser one for losing or a superior one for winning.'[59] Yet, in most circles, the resumption of cricket ties was seen as a political breakthrough, elevating cricket to one of the confidence-building measures that the two countries have gingerly embarked upon. The most glaring example of this attitude was Shaharyar M. Khan, the then Chairman of the Pakistan Cricket Board (PCB). Khan, while writing his classic *Cricket: A Bridge of Peace*, which throws light on his experiences as manager of Pakistan cricket team's tour of India (January–April 1999) and of South Africa (January–March 2003) acknowledged at the outset:

> I had not intended to publish my impressions until the unexpectedly warm welcome by the people of India to the 'enemy' team. Their enthusiastic response planted the seed in my mind that cricket's vast untapped energy could be harnessed for understanding and tolerance. ... After a lifetime in diplomacy, attempting, most unsuccessfully, to overcome tension, hostility and conflict, I realized that cricket could act as bridge of peace.[60]

And reflecting on overall impressions of the tour, he felt that 'its primary success had been at the political and public relations level.'[61] His continuous attempt to directly relate cricket to issues of politics and diplomacy was quite obvious:

> As the tour progressed, the groundswell of public acclaim provided the ideal stage in both countries for Mr. Vajpayee's bus journey to Lahore. The 40,000 strong crowd in Chennai giving a standing ovation to the victorious Pakistan team, ordinary people lined deep in Gwalior to wave the team good bye, the remarkable warmth shown to Pakistani visitors in Mohali where Sikh girls painted both Indian and Pakistani flags on their cheeks, the spontaneous chants of 'Pakistan-Hindustan *dosti Zindabad*' by the Pakistani element of the crowd, were images that seemed unbelievable when seen against the backdrop of the Shiv Sena threat to the team before the tour began and the daily vitriol exchanged between the two governments. The Indian public's response seemed to carry a clear message. It was, that though the two countries had been to war three times in fifty years, faced off, eyeball to eyeball, across the Line of Control in

Kashmir and had exploded nuclear devices to intimidate each other, the time had come for peace and mutual respect, so that poverty, violence and despair could be turned back. This message was as clear as the minarets of the Taj Mahal on a sunny day.[62]

In 2004, when people on both sides yarned for peace, the cricket tour, it was argued, after all the hype of uncertainty and security concerns, 'should pave a new road to constructive friendship and understanding.'[63] While the tour provided a great opportunity to the Pakistan government to demonstrate to the rest of the world its willingness to shake off its bad image that had grown up since the demolition of World Tower on 9/11, it could also help re-educate the minds of India and Pakistan, conditioned to think in traditional ways about each other. As Asif Iqbal rightly put it:

> It is good to see politicians of India and Pakistan finally batting together for the cause of peace and cricket in the sub-continent. I mention both peace and cricket in the same sentence advisedly, for here is a situation in which both can feed off each other, each enhancing and enriching the other. If nothing else the tour will show the leaders of the two countries how much genuine affection there is between people on either side of the great divide and that, hopefully, will cause many to stop and ponder.[64]

Imran Khan, the legendary Pakistani cricketer, too argued: 'When the two countries are trying to become friendly, cricket plays a healing role, cricket becomes a cement in bonding the countries together.'[65] Saba Karim's comment is perhaps most revealing in this context: 'When the relation between the two nations is strained, sportspersons can act as ambassadors and go a long way to heal the rifts.'[66] It was, thus, obvious that the tour had had a political dimension as the teams played in an emerging climate of rapprochement and peace. Even Colin Powell, the US foreign secretary, on his visit to India during the series in March expressed hope that the enthusiasm generated by the revival of cricketing ties would certainly have a positive impact on bilateral peace process.[67]

For Indians and Pakistanis, the people of the other nationality have been dehumanized through decades of mutual distrust and nationalistic propaganda. That is why intellectuals in both countries stress the importance of people-to-people contact, so that the other can be seen as human again, and one can feel empathy with them. Cricket can definitely play a part in this process. It has been argued with some conviction that 'the more we see our opponents, the more we are exposed to their humanness, and the less the mythic differences seem.'[68] The Indo-Pak series promised and provided a unique opportunity to 'humanize', if 'not normalize' the strained relations between the two nations. The cricketing skills on display, the emotions on the field—all draw people on one side towards the other side—and the appreciation can sometimes go beyond national pride. The spontaneous applause that the Pakistan team got from the Chennai crowds when they won the enthralling Test there in 1999 is a great example of this spirit. The cordial and hearty reception of the Indian team on their arrival to each city of Pakistan, the presence of sporting crowds at every venue cheering with passion on the occasion of every Indian victory with true sportsmanlike spirit and the overall attitude of friendliness and hospitality during the 2004 tour also provided a series of such desired occasions.[69] In a unique humanitarian gesture, the Indian cricket team appealed to doctors back home to treat a young Pakistani girl afflicted with cancer.[70] More importantly, Indian and Pakistani players wore symbolic red ribbons, reiterating international cricket's commitment to increase AIDS awareness during the series-deciding third Test in Rawalpindi. As part of the UNAIDS–ICC initiative, an HIV-positive person accompanied rival skippers Sourav Ganguly and Inzamam-ul-Haq out into the middle during the toss.[71] In a congratulatory message to the teams, UN Secretary General Kofi Annan said:

> AIDS is a common enemy that both India and Pakistan have to fight together. ... As cricketers you can win the hearts of your people. As role models, you can encourage young people to protect themselves, and urge your leaders to pay more attention to the epidemic. And by wearing the red ribbon, you show that you care deeply about AIDS and about people living with HIV/AIDS, and so help to remove stigma and discrimination, a major obstacle in the fight against the epidemic.[72]

That exposure to cricketers and ex-cricketers from the other country can also help foster an ambience of mutual benefit was perfectly illustrated by *The Shaz and Waz Show*, jointly hosted by Ravi Shastri and Wasim Akram, two most popular Indian and Pakistani ex-cricketers on ESPN-Star Sports. If the two nations could play cricket regularly, it seemed, then perhaps the game can move from being a metaphor for war to a vehicle of peace.

Economic Ramifications of the 'Friendship' Series

India's cricket tour of Pakistan 2004 was unique on more counts than one. The tour came against the backdrop of sincere quest on the part of India and Pakistan to forget the past and make a serious attempt to resolve their differences. While it was politics that couched the rhetoric of the tour, its economic dimension was no less significant. To give one example, the tour, a 37-day affair, involved the spending of ₹250 crore in advertising only. Given its huge economic potential, Pakistan therefore could not let the opportunity slip by simply raising fingers at India's intentions. That is why the Pakistani president was expected to reassure the Indian Prime Minster about the security of the cricketers. Thus, suggests Boria Majumdar,

> side-stepping the tour's political potential, foremost in the Pakistan's mind was the moolah it would bring in its wake—moolah that would help alleviate the nation's impending economic crisis. The threat of an economic catastrophe ensured, even if for a fleeting moment, that political differences be swept under the carpet. India, a sworn enemy, was suddenly the saviour, whose cricket team could help alleviate the economic disaster.[73]

For Pakistan, let alone, the hope and hoopla on the tour had multifarious dimensions. As Muralidhar Reddy argued:

> The tour is a bonanza for Pakistan for more than one way. It provides a great opportunity to the government to demonstrate to the rest of the world that Pakistan is certainly not about people merrily firing from kalashnikovs and scientists proliferating from nuclear secrets. It is no small gain considering the bad publicity Pakistan has got since the twin-towers in New York came down.[74]

Rameez Raza, the CEO, too, argued on the eve of the tour:

> On our side we realise that we have a lot to gain from India coming here. While it is a huge financial boost, there are other intangible gains by way of credibility for future games. The nation knows that the world is watching and we will have to show them that we can host any team at any venue without a hitch.[75]

Of course, the economic dimension of the tour was much more significant for the PCB. The PCB had been in dire straits in the years preceding the tour as several scheduled tours, including those of Australia, West Indies and England, got cancelled on security grounds. India's tour could have mended all the previous losses to a substantial extent for the PCB. It struck deals worth ₹120 crores while it expected ₹4.5 crores from ticket sales. Such was the response from the Indian companies that it had to reserve some deals for the Pakistani companies. Even the TV slots became four times costlier than they had been during the World Cup in 2003.[76] Sponsorship and commercial transactions reached a new high on the eve of the tour. Ten Sports paid a hooping ₹59.85 crore for the telecast rights and was expected to make close to ₹130 crore.[77] Hero Honda spent ₹7 crore on the sponsorship rights and later more on advertisements.[78] Samsung paid ₹20 crore for the title rights, while Samsung and Pepsi combined were expected to spend around ₹80 crore on the series.[79] Pepsi bought 150 ten-second TV slots ₹5 lakh each, while Samsung earmarked ₹60 crore for advertisements.[80]

Indo-Pak Arch-rivalry and the Cricketing Factor

With a new season of hope beginning to unravel with India's tour, cricket was primarily looked upon as more a diplomatic ploy to redress the domestic and foreign political priorities on the part of the Indian Government than as a game that pits against each other two of world's most fascinating cricketing nations with temperamental cricketing skill and peerlessly passionate fanfare. As Sambit Bal, in a befitting editorial to *Wisden Asia Cricket*, argued:

> Given the bitter history these two nations share, every little thing that promotes goodwill is worth clutching at, but there is a danger here of overestimating the power of cricket. ... But cricket is only a sport; it cannot be mistaken for diplomacy. The essence of sport is contest. Sportsmen cannot be expected to win and carry the candle of reconciliation at the same time. The life of an international cricketer is stressful enough; to burden him with national missions is stretching expectations. ... Diplomacy should not hijack the main agenda of the tour, which is cricket.[81]

Specialist cricket commentators and experts became concerned about the overemphasis on cricket as diplomacy, politics or peace. Harsha Bhogle, for example, warned his readers at the outset:

> I fear too many people are under delusion that India are going to Pakistan on a political tour. If that feeling persists, India will lose. There is far too much talk about the business of cricket and the politics of the sub-continent and far too little about playing cricket. ... The presence of our cricketers can be a political statement, but they must play cricket first. They can be ambassadors of peace they must be cricketers first. Merely landing in Pakistan will not be a victory, that is for politicians and poets, doing well and winning a cricket match will be. ... And you certainly cannot have them (people) thinking that this is a tour where politics, diplomacy and the building of cultural bridges is paramount. It is not. It is about playing cricket first. Everything else must follow, it cannot lead.[82]

Bhogle's point has much to commend about it as it addressed the importance of the series in terms of purely cricketing skill and brain. The tour on the pitch was a time for the professionals and pragmatic people. It put before the agenda the uniqueness of preparation of an Indian team touring Pakistan. Indian XI had to prepare well to contend with odds in Pakistan: the pace and bounce of the pitch, the reverse swing of the Pakistani pacers, the fierce spells of Shoaib Akhtar, oppressive security and many more.[83] The technical aspects of the game, therefore, should not be overlooked in the course of the apparent media hype of elevating sport to a diplomatic/political status. As S. Dinakar pointed out:

> An India-Pakistan clash is as much a test of nerves as skills. Mental strength or lack of it is often the decisive factor. India travels across the border with the confidence that it possesses a most accomplished batting line-up. And, Pakistan waits with what has often proved a destructive bowling outfit. ... Interestingly, while the sides' respective strengths could cancel each other out, how the supposed weak links—India's injury-hit bowling and Pakistan's largely inexperienced batting—fare could settle the issue.[84]

Even Sourav Ganguly, the Indian captain, categorically put his preference for the sporting aspect of the tour: 'I don't really agree with this *goodwill* issue—it's a cricket match and both teams are competing to win.'[85]

More importantly, this much-hyped blend of sport and diplomacy, cricket and goodwill, inevitably brought forth another important relational reality—cricket and match-fixing. That India won the one-day series by the narrowest margin of 3–2 with some closest finishes in at least three matches gave some critics to see the shadow of match-fixing under which the series was played. In Pakistan itself, it was reported, it was a worm of suspicion that slowly grew through the series, and on 24 March, the day of final one-dayer, it became a faith.[86] People were seriously engaged in deciphering the list of 'mysterious moments' in the series to lend credence to their argument that 'the governments have mutually fixed it'.[87]

When the one-day series was poised at 1–1, Raju Mukherji, a former Indian cricketer, had already become suspicious of the true cricketing competition of the series. He wrote a newspaper article which opened with these words: 'Was the result of the first one-day international of the India-Pakistan revival series in Karachi a gift to a guest? And that of the second at Rawalpindi a return gesture on the part of the visitors?'[88] His objections came on purely cricketing grounds:

> In the first one-dayer in Karachi, the way the Pakistani batsman, Moin Khan, moved away to the leg side and converted two wide balls into legitimate deliveries, was enough to raise a few questions. In that eventful last over, Pakistan was actually in the driver's seat and appeared to have the match in its grasp. But in that absorbing over, Khan seemed to have had other, farreaching ideas.[89]

Mukherji wondered whether it was a fallout of the 'goodwill' which both the Pakistani president and the Indian prime minister had been harping on. He concluded with a unique prayer:

> Now that the first two matches are over and the teams are at par, let us pray that the real cricket begins. Let us hope that from now on, the series is played in the spirit of competitive cricket and not in the spirit of gracious politics.[90]

Whether Mukherji's claim is justifiable or not is not really the important point here. Rather, that an ex-Indian cricketer could make such a claim in the midway of a tour certainly put a question mark on the integrity of the cricketing fraternity of the two countries.

It was over the result of fourth one-day international that cloud of suspect began to blossom. The ICC's anti-corruption unit rightly refused to say anything on the speculation, considering it unworthy of comment. A journalist asked Rahul Dravid, one of the heroes of the match, 'What do you have to say about the impression this match was fixed?' He uncharacteristically reacted: 'Somebody get this guy out of here.'[91] To a similar question from a television channel, Pakistan's captain Inzamam-ul-Haq was reported to have said, 'Shut up'.[92]

Cricket as a Confidence-building Measure

Given the entrenched differences between India and Pakistan over Jammu and Kashmir, and a history of four conventional wars and continuing hostilities in the Indian-administered part of Kashmir, the development of nuclear weapons as well as ballistic missiles by the two countries has heightened international concerns about peace and stability in that region. In this context, many proposals have been advanced regarding confidence- and security-building measures (CSBMs)[93] that could be considered or implemented between India and Pakistan. It has further been argued that 'people-to-people contact, free flow of information, economic cooperation, and use of appropriate technology to develop mutual confidence and verify cooperative agreements should be able to accomplish important breakthroughs in the normalizations of Indo-Pak relations.'[94] This approach, according to Suranjan Das,

> goes beyond the strategic or security studies paradigm and argues that an expansion of cultural, economic and technological cooperation could erode much of the mistrust and misgivings between India and Pakistan, creating a favourable climate for resolving pending military, political and strategic dichonomies in the region.[95]

In February 1999, the two sides agreed to a package of certain CSBMs; however, many crucial details and modalities remain to be worked out to this day.[96] Such a related measure would be to 'facilitate community-building and habits of dialogue involving the participation of various official and non-governmental sectors from India and Pakistan.'[97] People-to-people contacts should be encouraged to remove mistrust and create a congenial atmosphere for dialogue. Cultural exchanges are also prerequisites to CSBMs. Indian movies are popular in Pakistan, though there is a lot of restrictions on their screening. These need to be lifted. Certain organizations, such as the Jamaat-i-Islami in Pakistan and Shiv Sena in India, have issued threats to each other's cultural groups in the recent past. The Pakistani cultural group Junoon was threatened in India. The Shiv Sainiks were accused of disrupting singer Ghulam Ali's concert.[98] Similarly, the Pakistani government refused to give permission for the staging of a popular play *Tumhari Amrita* in Lahore, Karachi and Islamabad because of India's nuclear tests.[99] The function organized by the Indian Embassy on the eve of the 50 years of independence was disrupted by reactionary forces in Islamabad. However, the statements vowing not to allow the Pakistani cricket team to play in India were met with equally strong statements by the Indian government in 1999. Prime Minister Atal Bihari Vajpayee and Home Minister L.K. Advani assured safety and police protection to the Pakistani players during their stay in India. The statements were important, as Smruti S. Pattanaik points out, 'because they dispel doubt about the BJP government's sincerity about better Indo-Pak relations in spite of the political compulsions of the BJP which has an alliance with Shiv Sena, the party which had issued threats in Maharashtra.'[100] Such statements were not only reassuring, but also established a certain degree of confidence and created goodwill across the border. Wasim Akram, the captain of the Pakistan cricket team in 1999, shared this sentiment as well: 'We are going there to better the relations between the two countries, and I hope the Indian Government will not allow a handful of people to deprive cricket lovers of some action and tension packed cricket.'[101] Thus, both sides should include more programmes about each other's culture in their visual media to enhance friendship. In other words, rhetoric should be reduced and cultural exchanges should be encouraged. Arguing for cultural exchanges, a report said, 'Music lovers in Pakistan have said a public performance by Lata Mangeshkar in the city of Lahore may be more helpful to promote goodwill than the outcome of talks between the two foreign secretaries in Islamabad.'[102] K.S. Manjunath, Seema Sridhar and Beryl Anand, in an Institute of Peace Conflict Studies (IPCS) Report, pointed to the importance of the promotion of friendly exchanges in various fields in Indo-Pak composite dialogue during 2004–2005.[103]

In this report, they, however, failed to appreciate the role of other forms of popular cultural exchange such as cricket in the same process at crucial junctures of Indo-Pak relations.

It is suggested that playing against each other on a regular basis would definitely minimize the confrontational tension that usually accompanies rare occasions of cricket matches between the two countries. As Shaharyar Khan observed, of this 'most important, highly publicized and politically important cricket tour in Pakistan's cricketing history':

> The tour provided a memorable boost to bilateral relations and went a long way towards projecting Pakistan's image as a peaceful, moderate and progressive society. As the Indian High Commissioner, Shivshankar Menon, remarked, 20,000 Indian fans had gone back to India acting as Pakistan's ambassadors. Despite my anxiety at the beginning of the tour, cricket had acted as a genuine bridge of peace.[104]

It was however left to the policy makers, diplomats and politicians of both countries to toe the line set by cricket, when it comes to resolving outstanding issues in foreign relations.

Concluding Remarks

Thus, a greater introspection into the potential of cricket as a cultural tool for confidence building and as a medium for promoting reciprocally viable relationships between Pakistan and India is something that scholars need to take serious care of. Indo-Pakistan cricket, whatever be its incidental nature or contextual relevance at one time or other, is, at least, in part a celebration of a common cricket culture. It takes on its political and commercial importance as much because of this common culture as because of the history of conflict. The knowledge, appreciation and enthusiasm for cricket are the preconditions for the eminence of this tie among global sporting rivalries. The media, however, are certainly not the only responsible parties. For broadcasters, sponsors and advertisers, the easiest way to maximize the return on their investment in cricket was to inflate its value by infusing it with extraneous emotional value. They were, therefore, tempted to hype the series as the ultimate confrontation, a contest of unique importance to the nation, as 'war minus the shooting', in George Orwell's words. That was where the cricket-loving public of both nations had a responsibility: 'to discipline the private sector super patriots, to insist on a sense of proportion.'[105] Manifestly, emotions run high in cricketing encounters between India and Pakistan. But the fund of mutual 'goodwill' and 'friendship' out there in 2004 proved sufficient to handle these emotions, ensuring that mutual trust and reciprocal faith came back at least in Indo-Pak cricketing relations. In the midst of continuous tension in Indo-Pak relations, cricket might therefore be looked upon as a confidence-building measure in the new century. The tour of 2004 bears testimony to this point. The tour and its proceedings clearly showed that cricket has the potential to soothe some issues in bilateral relations in South Asia. However, cricket's role in this regard need not be exaggerated either. It can go some way forward to create an ambience of fraternity to normalize relations but could not resolve the outstanding issues that continue to puzzle the Indo-Pak relations. As Mike Marqusee has rightly remarked:

> Cricket will not be the agent of an enduring peace between India and Pakistan. And if we assign it too much significance we make it easier for political leaders to evade their responsibilities. The spectacle becomes a substitute for the deeper discussion that is necessary to build such a peace. The cricket series should therefore be seen as one among many confidence-building measures that must run alongside political negotiations that are bound to be protracted.[106]

Notes and References

1. Pakistan and India emerged as independent nation states on 14 and 15 August 1947, respectively, as the British left India.
2. Muralidhar Reddy, 'Pakistan has a lot to gain', *The Sportstar* (Chennai), 28 February 2004, p. 19.
3. George Orwell, 'The Sporting Spirit', quoted in Amit Verma, 'The Humanising Factor', *Wisden Asia Cricket*, Vol. 3, No. 4, March 2004: 46.
4. George Orwell, 'The Sporting Spirit', quoted in Rahul Bhattacharya, *Pundits from Pakistan: On Tour with India, 2003–04* (London: Picador, 2005), p. 16.
5. Ibid.
6. Ibid.
7. Kapil Dev, *Straight from the Heart*, quoted in Kapil Dev, 'Beginner's pluck', *India Today*, Collector's Edition (New Delhi), March 2004, pp. 28–34.

8. Amit Verma, 'The Humanising Factor', *Wisden Asia Cricket*, Vol. 3, No. 4, March 2004, p. 46.

9. For details, see Boria Majumdar, 'Communalism to Commercialism: Study of Anti-Pentangular Movement', *Economic and Political Weekly*, 15 February 2003, pp. 656–664.

10. In 2002, at a railway station in Godhra, Gujarat, two train compartments packed with Hindu political activists caught fire, killing almost all the passengers in those compartments. This incident triggered off a series of communal clashes in different parts of India, particularly in Gujarat, where the ruling BJP-led state government was held responsible for inaction to prevent this heightened communal assault on the Muslims, thereby hardening socio-political relations between the two communities and defaming India's secular face.

11. In early 1999, India's successful nuclear test at Pokhran reciprocated shortly by similar tests by Pakistan led to heightened political tension in South Asian diplomatic relations.

12. Cross-border infiltration into Indian Kashmir reached a peak in the late 1990s, culminating in a war between India and Pakistan in the mountainous range of Kargil adjacent to the Line of Control in mid-1999. The Indian army fought successfully to combat the infiltration and push back the Pak-sponsored army.

13. For an interesting discussion on the complex interplay of identities—Hindu, Muslim or Indian—during an Indo-Pak cricket match in a World Cup, see Jishnu Dasgupta, 'Manufacturing Unison: Muslims, Hindus and Indians during the India-Pakistan Match', in Boria Majumdar and J.A. Mangan, eds. *Sport in South Asian Society: Past and Present* (London: Routledge, 2005, pp. 239–248).

14. In Kalighat, a locality on the bank of Ganga in south Kolkata, is situated one of the most famous *Kali* temples of India, where thousands of devotees visit and pray to the mother goddess every day.

15. 'Down with Pakistan'.

16. *Outlook*, 31 March 2003, p. 32.

17. *The Statesman* (Kolkata), 5 March 2003.

18. *The Statesman* (Kolkata), 3 March 2003.

19. Ibid.

20. Ibid.

21. *The Statesman*, 5 March 2003.

22. D.V. Madhav Rao, Chennai, Letters to the Editor, *Outlook*, 31 March 2003.

23. *The Statesman*, 3 March 2003.

24. Quoted in Saba Naqbi Bhowmik and Priyanka Kakodkar, 'Keeping the Faith', *Outlook*, 31 March 2003, p. 32.

25. Ibid.

26. Kingshuk Chatterjee, 'To Play or Not To Play: Fabricating Consent over the Indo-Pak Cricket Series', in Majumdar and Mangan, eds. *Sport in South Asian Society*, pp. 277–294.

27. The decision to go ahead with the series, which surprised many, came after a confidential meeting at the residence of the prime minister, Atal Bihari Vajpayee, on 14 February. The meeting was attended by Deputy Prime Minister, L.K. Advani, external affairs minister, Yashwant Sinha, finance minister, Jaswant Singh, and national security adviser, Brajesh Mishra.

28. *The Telegraph* (Kolkata), 15 February 2004, p. 1.

29. These arguments have been briefly but eloquently dealt in Bhattacharya, *Pundits in Pakistan*, pp. 9, 13–14.

30. Ibid.
31. Ibid.
32. Ibid.
33. Ibid.
34. *The Telegraph*, 15 February 2004, p. 1.
35. Boria Majumdar, 'Willow Talk: Moolah and Mediation', *Sahara Times*, 13 March 2004, p. 22.
36. *The Telegraph*, 15 February 2004, p. 1.
37. Sachidananda Murthy, 'Icing on the feel-good cake', *The Week*, 14 March 2004, p. 34.
38. Majumdar, 'Willow Talk', pp. 22–23.
39. Ashok V. Desai, 'How sweet is my carrot', *The Telegraph*, 27 April 2004, p. 12.
40. Bhattacharya, *Pundits from Pakistan*, p. 9.
41. Ibid. The hint at this possibility was given by the newspapers on the day the official decision to go ahead with the tour was declared. For details, see *The Statesman*, 15 February 2004, p. 1; *The Telegraph*, 15 February 2004, p. 1.
42. *Sahara Times*, 13 March 2004, p. 3.
43. *The Statesman*, 11 March 2004, p. 1.
44. Ibid.
45. 'Pakistan Notebook', *The Sportstar*, 27 March, p. 22.
46. Boria Majumdar, 'Cricket turns global', *Sahara Times*, 3 April 2004, p. 17.
47. Ibid.
48. Ibid.
49. K. Srikkanth, 'India can deliver the goods', *The Statesman*, 25 February 2004, p. 13.
50. Bhattacharya, *Pundits from Pakistan*, p. 141. Also see, *Ananda Bazar Patrika*, 26 March 2004.
51. Bhattacharya, *Pundits from Pakistan*, p. 141.
52. Ibid.
53. Asif Iqbal, 'Change of pace', *India Today* (March 2004), p. 36.
54. John Wright, *John Wright's Indian Summers* (New Delhi: Penguin Books, 2006), p. 173.
55. Ibid.
56. Bhattacharya, *Pundits from Pakistan*, p. 32.
57. Wright, *John Wright's Indian Summers*, p. 174.
58. Bhattacharya, *Pundits from Pakistan*, p. 33.
59. Rohit Brijnath, 'India-Pakistan: Why we need to remember this is just sport', *The Sportstar*, 28 February 2004, p. 9.
60. Shaharyar Khan, *Cricket: A Bridge of Peace* (Oxford: Oxford University Press, 2005), p. vii.
61. Ibid., p. 92.
62. Ibid.
63. S. Thyagarajan, 'The tour should pave a new road to constructive friendship', *The Sportstar*, 28 February 2004, p. 29.
64. Iqbal, 'Change of Pace', p. 36.
65. *The Statesman*, 11 March 2004, p. 12.
66. Saba Karim, 'The soothing balm that sports can be', *The Statesman*, 25 February 2004, p. 13.
67. *Ananda Bazar Patrika* (Kolkata), 18 March 2004.

68. Verma, 'The Humanising Factor', p. 47.
69. Rameez Raja, CEO of the Pakistan Cricket Board, told *Wisden Asia Cricket* that the crowds for this series were the most sporting he had seen for any series in Pakistan, let alone one against India: 'I mean, I have never in my experience seen Indian and Pakistani flags stitched together.' Indian vice-captain, Rahul Dravid also maintained: 'Everywhere we went we have been cheered. The guys who fielded at the boundary kept saying how appreciative the crowd have been.' For further details on this aspect, see Rahul Bhattacharya, 'A glow of warm feeling', *Wisden Asia Cricket* 4, No. 5 (April 2004), p. 31.
70. The team issued an appeal asking its country's doctors back home to come forward to save life of 10-year-old Huba Shahid, who was diagnosed with rhabdomyosarcoma, or facial cancer.
71. 'Pakistan Notebook', *The Sportstar*, 24 April 2004, p. 17.
72. Ibid.
73. Majumdar, 'Willow talk', pp. 22–23.
74. Reddy, 'Pakistan has a lot to gain', p. 18.
75. Rameez Raza, 'Board games', *India Today*, March 2004, p. 48.
76. Neeru Bhatia, 'The Scent of Money', *The Week*, 14 March 2004, p. 32.
77. Ibid.
78. Ibid.
79. Ibid.
80. Ibid.
81. Sambit Bal, 'It's Just a Game', *Wisden Asia Cricket*, Vol. 3, No. 4, March 2004, p. 5.
82. Harsha Bhogle, 'It's a cricket tour, not a political one', *The Sportstar*, 6 March 2004, p. 16.
83. Ibid.
84. S. Dinakar, 'Indian batting and Pakistan bowling hold the key', *The Sportstar*, 13 March 2004, p. 11.
85. Quoted in Bhattacharya, *Pundits from Pakistan*, p. 35.
86. Manu Joseph, 'La Horde!' *Outlook*, 5 April 2004, p. 50.
87. Ibid., p. 51.
88. Raju Mukherji, 'Cricket killed with goodwill', *The Telegraph*, 18 March 2004, p. 13.
89. Ibid.
90. Ibid.
91. Joseph, 'La Horde!' p. 48.
92. Ibid.
93. Confidence- and security-building measures (CSBMs) are 'those steps or arrangements on which the states agree with mutual benefit in mind, and states have faith that such agreement shall be obeyed by all the concerned. It could include diverse arrangements—such as hotlines, people-to-people exchanges, and prior notifications of military exercises—that can help reduce tensions and promote good neighbourly relations. These steps or agreements ultimately develop trust between the states and help in having peace and stability in the region.' Muhammad Irshad, 'Indo-Pak Confidence-Building Measures', www.defencejournal.com/2002/august/confidence.htm, accessed on 10 May 2006.
94. Suranjan Das, 'Regional Security through Constructive Bilateralism: Prospects for Indo-Pak Cooperation and South Asian Stability', in Bhaskar Chakraborty, ed. *Exploring Regional Security: South and Central Asia* (Kolkata: K.P. Bagchi, 2003), p. 193.

95. Ibid.
96. Tariq Rauf, 'Confidence-Building and Security-Building Measures in the Nuclear Area with Relevance for South Asia', *Contemporary South Asia*, Vol. 14, No. 2, June 2005, p. 176.
97. Ibid., p. 188.
98. *Hindustan Times* (New Delhi), 30 April 1998, referred to in Smruti S. Pattanaik, 'Indo-Pak Relations: Need for a Pragmatic Approach', *Strategic Analysis*, Vol. XXIII, No. 1 (April 1999), file://A:/Strategic Analysis Indo-Pak Relations.htm, accessed on 8 June 2006.
99. *The Indian Express* (New Delhi), 27 May 1998, referred to in Pattanaik, 'Indo-Pak Relations'.
100. Pattanaik, 'Indo-Pak Relations'.
101. Wasim Akram, the Pakistani captain on tour to India in 1998–1999 is reported to have said this. Quoted in Bhattacharya, *Pundits from Pakistan*, p. 11.
102. Moonis Ahmar, 'War Avoidance between India and Pakistan: A Model of Conflict Resolution and Confidence-Building in the Post-Cold War Era', *Strategic Studies*, Vol. 24, Nos. 1–2, 1993, p. 23.
103. K.S. Manjunath, Seema Sridhar and Beryl Anand, 'Indo-Pak Composite Dialogue 2004–05: A Profile', *IPCS Special Report 12* (February 2006).
104. Khan, *Cricket: A Bridge of Peace*, p. 187.
105. Mike Marqusee, 'Border crossings', *India Today*, March 2004, p. 68.
106. Mike Marqusee, 'Make cricket, not war?', *The Indian Express* (New Delhi), 25 February 2004.

5

Cricketing Politics or Political Cricket: Politics, Power and Cricket Board Elections in India, 2004–2006

Introduction

'Sport is no sanctuary from the real world because sport is part of the real world, and the liberation and the oppression are inextricably bound', thus said Robert Lipsyte in his introduction to C.L.R. James' *Beyond a Boundary*.[1] In India today, too, cricket is not a mere sport; its implications have moved far beyond the rubric of leisure or entertainment. Rather, cricket is more about politics, about economy. In other words, as one cricket historian concludes, 'Indian cricket makes sense today, when it is placed in the broader politico-economic context.'[2] While cricket has always been represented as a vector of forces like imperialism, nationalism, communalism, regionalism, commercialism and professionalism in twentieth-century India, its importance as a political tool has rarely attracted that much attention. In its early days of promotion, princely patronage of cricket had a definite political dimension in colonial India.[3] Throughout the last century, regional politics, power play and personality conflicts affected the development of the game in India.[4] However, this cultural politics of cricket did by no means amount to either politicization of cricket or political appropriation of cricket. Political influence in cricket administration also remained minimal in this period. However, the new century has seen the beginning of a new trend. Cricket is now intricately linked to politics, intrigue and business. The recent trends of operation and development in the organization and control of the game in India at both central and regional levels are clear proof of this argument. The elections of the BCCI in 2004 and 2005 marked the steady intrusion of mainstream politics into the fold of cricket, thereby making it 'political cricket', while the CAB election of 2006 provided an occasion for not only the clash of this new trend with traditional 'cricketing politics' but also a serious rift within mainstream politics on the desirability of political intervention in sport. The present chapter intends to explore the intricate relationship between cricket, power and politics in the context of the BCCI elections of 2004–2005 and the CAB elections of 2006.

The First Battle: BCCI Elections, 2004

The recent chapter of political intervention in cricket administration started in 2004 when Sharad Pawar, a cabinet minister of the United Progressive Alliance (UPA) government and the chief of the Nationalist Congress Party (NCP), decided to contest for the post of president of the BCCI against Ranbir Singh Mahendra, the protégé of Jagmohan Dalmiya, the reigning president. The powerful BCCI presidential chair used to go on a rotational basis among the five zones. The coming term in 2004 was North Zone's turn, but Pawar decided to contest based on a nomination from one of the North Zone's member states, namely, Punjab.[5] It was reported that 'his motive to contest for the coveted post in Indian sports was to thwart the election of the BJP leader Mr. Arun Jaitley, who was to be North Zone's first choice nominee.'[6] Thus, political considerations began to play an important role in the BCCI electoral battle of 2004 from the very beginning. As one newspaper correspondent rightly remarked:

> Much as we want sport and politics to be as far apart as one-day cricket is from Tests, the lead-up to the Board of Control for Cricket in India (BCCI) elections in its platinum jubilee year has seen an extraordinary marriage between the two.
> From heads of national parties to Chief Ministers to influential politicians (some even out of 'active' affairs), everybody has been approached

either by Union minister Sharad Pawar, who is challenging Jagmohan Dalmiya's hold, or the acclaimed administrator himself.[7]

The Pawar camp calculated a possible victory, mostly on political strength. It believed that 'the many states where the Congress is in power will vote for an important ally in the centre.'[8] Pawar also expected to get the votes of institutional members—Railways, Services and Indian universities—through directives from respective ministries.[9] However, sources in New Delhi maintained, 'only one will actually go his way. The top reason being two ministries are headed by gentlemen who aren't on back-slapping terms with Pawar.'[10] The Pawar camp, however, realized that in case of close contest, every vote was going to be crucial. This explains why 'Pawar's backers requested Samajwadi Janata Party leader and Uttar Pradesh Chief Minister Mulayam Singh Yadav to try and ensure a high-profile MP from his party represented the state at the Annual General Meeting (AGM) and not Dalmiya confidant Jyoti Bajpai.'[11]

On the eve of the election, Pawar had said that he would contest only if he was sure of a victory: 'I have not taken a decision myself. Some of my well wishers have been asking me to contest. But I will contest only I am sure of a win.'[12] BJP leader Arun Jaitley, who was initially expected to emerge as a consensus candidate, decided to steer clear of the electoral battle at this stage, thus keeping himself in the reckoning for the future. Jaitley's initial attempt at candidature was also wrought with political calculations. As it was the turn of the North for presidentship of BCCI in 2004, he was considered one of the best candidates for the job. BJP leaders had reportedly told him that 'it was all right till he could manage a consensus. Mr. Jaitley even courted both Mrs Priyanka Vadra and Mr Rahul Gandhi who are said to have concurred with his candidature.'[13] Even Lalu Prasad Yadav, the Railway Minister, had indicated 'he would not mind voting for him.'[14]

In fact, the Pawar group tried to woo the regional and local cricket bosses through the chief ministers of the states ruled by the Congress or the Left. The Communist Party of India-Marxist (CPI-M), the ruling political party of West Bengal, supported Pawar's candidature. As Mr Anil Biswas, the party secretary, said, 'The CPI-M will be happy if Mr. Pawar succeeds Mr. Dalmiya.'[15] So far as the involvement of Indian National Congress in this electoral contest was concerned, the initial impression that one gets from the newspaper reports was encouraging Pawar to lobby:

> Despite its signal that it would steer clear of the BCCI presidential election slated for tomorrow, the Congress central leadership is likely not to oppose Mr. Pawar's bid for the post. A minor Congress leader from Haryana, Mr. Ranbir Singh Mahendra has also thrown his hat into the ring. The AICC, however, does not gain much from supporting Mr. Mahendra who is backed by Mr. Jagmohan Dalmiya. On the other hand, Mr. Pawar is a crucial ally whose role will have a bearing on the Congress-NCP alliance's prospects in the 13 October Maharashtra elections. This explains why Mr. Pawar is expected to squeeze through the BCCI poll.[16]

Dalmiya, too, did not sit idle and approached Mr Pranab Mukherjee, the veteran Congress leader and the defence minister, to secure the vote of services.[17] Mukherjee, however, made it explicitly clear that since it was an election of the cricket board and not of any political body, there was no question of interfering in the matter by the Congress high command and that the latter would by no means instruct any of its political affiliates to vote for any particular candidate.[18] The press, too, did not seem to support this political orientation of the BCCI election. As one newspaper editorial on the day of the election argued:

> Various politicians are fighting for the BCCI president's post he (Dalmiya) is vacating. Some of them, Arun Jaitley and Sharad Pawar, for example, should be too busy fighting the Maharashtra elections to spare time for cricket politics. There is nothing healthy about a BJP-Congress fight in BCCI elections. For one, and given that cricket's popularity often means it raises question governments have to deal with, A BCCI chief who's been elected after a proxy political fight, can become too close to the ruling dispensation or too disfavoured by it, depending on his political affiliations. On first principles, politicians can aspire to administer cricket as much as anyone else. But since politicians' aspirations are inspired by wrong reasons, it is time we have professional cricket administrators. Otherwise, what has happened in Pakistan, where heads of government have been known to express opinion on team selection, can happen in India. Surely, that is enough reason for someone to do something.[19]

The result of the election was revealing on more counts than one. Pawar was defeated in a close contest by the casting vote of the reigning president, Jagmohan Dalmiya. After the election, Pawar was said to have remarked to the media: 'It was a cricket match in which the bowler and the umpire are the same person.'[20] In fact, the way Dalmiya manoeuvred the voting process on the day of election in favour of his protégé Ranbir Singh Mahendra was an example of masterly cricketing politics quite Greek to political heavyweights, such as Pawar. First, just before the election, the Dalmiya faction obtained an interim order from the Madras High Court, which withdrew an earlier order appointing retired Justice S. Mohan of the Supreme Court as commissioner to conduct elections to all BCCI posts. Then, in the AGM, with the legal help of retired Justice Bhagwati Prasad Banerjee, Dalmiya could nullify the claim of D. Agashe, a Pawar confidant, to vote for the Maharashtra Cricket Association while at the same time allowed Kishore Rungta, a Dalmiya loyalist, in place of the Pawar loyalist Lalit Modi, to cast the vote of the Rajasthan Cricket Association. This made the result tie up on even numbers (15–15) as Dalmiya's casting vote as the reigning president turned it in favour of Mahendra. On the one hand, the election gave Sharad Pawar a stern lesson that 'politics—especially of the cricketing kind—just isn't, well, cricket.'[21] Omar Abdullah, the representative of Jammu and Kashmir, made the point more clear: 'Coming to the cricket election for the first time, I realize that there is a greater *politics* even outside our politics.'[22] One newspaper editorial put it more sarcastically:

> Pawar is an influential politician. He has a number of aficionados even outside Maharashtra. Still, as fish is not comfortable outside water, Pawar too is not at ease outside Maharashtra.... Sources from some quarters have claimed that if Sonia Gandhi would have issued clear instructions, Pawar could have had it easy with at least nine votes of Congress-led state associations. But Pranab Mukhopadhyay made it absolutely clear before the election that there was no question of the Congress High Command getting involved in the matter as it was an election of cricket organization and not of a political one. The CPI-M state secretary, on the other hand, openly advocated their support to Pawar. Thus cricket is now living with politics.[23]

It also maintained that while Dalmiya and his colleagues used to run cricket administration keeping it more or less away from direct politics, Pawar's efforts to grab power in the BCCI clearly set the trend of direct political intervention in cricket. Hinting at another political reality, the editorial argued,

> This defeat could be a bane to Pawar's political career. It might affect the Congress-NCP alliance in Maharashtra on the eve of assembly elections there. Moreover, with the myth of Pawar's invincibility shattered in the BCCI election in public, it would be interesting to see how the Maratha voters respond to this distraction in the forthcoming election.[24]

Dalmiya, too, was taken completely by surprise when he had to save his candidate only by his casting vote in the closest possible electoral battle. He was quite confident of victory by a comfortable margin before the election. But in reality, some of his confirmed vote banks defected and betrayed on the floor. The defection was mainly due to political trick and influence exercised by Pawar, whose political stature stretched the Dalmiya camp to the utmost and took him to the 15–15 stage. As one Dalmiya aficionado argued: 'It's difficult identifying everybody who defected, but we do have a reasonable idea.... Pawar used his connections in the world of politics to influence voters who would normally have gone with Dalmiya.'[25] This also explains why the other candidates of the Dalmiya camp, Secretary S.K. Nair, Treasurer Jyoti Bajpai and Joint Secretary Goutam Dasgupta, won comfortably as they did not have to contend with persons of high political stature. Dalmiya also complained of underhand monetary transactions apart from political influence, hooliganism and legal petition in explaining the strong bid of his opposition to power.[26] However, the electoral battle through frantic lobbying, intense networking and clever politicking visible in the BCCI election 2004 signalled the beginning of a deepening conflict between Dalmiya's 'cricketing politics' and Pawar's 'political cricket'.

Turn to 'Political Cricket': BCCI Elections, 2005

Taking lessons from the BCCI elections 2004, Pawar realized that Dalmiya was a master of cricket politics, which was an entirely different ball game compared to mainstream politics in which the likes of Pawar excel.[27] It made him more resolute to stage a powerful fightback in the next year's elections, albeit with an entirely different strategy. Yet, Pawar was initially hesitant about treading again 'on the mine-infested fields of BCCI politics' or 'the treacherous territory of cricketing politics.'[28] Moreover, Pawar was aware that in the last election, although it had overtly assumed political tones as it was held between the parliamentary elections and the Maharashtra assembly polls, he, despite being a key Congress ally, could not secure the support of many BCCI affiliates controlled by Congress leaders. Hence, Pawar was determined to ensure this time that all those state associations controlled by the Congress should vote for him. That was why he met Sonia Gandhi, the Congress supremo, before boarding his flight to Kolkata to attend the AGM. This indicated that Pawar might actually be better placed in 2005 'in mobilizing votes of states where the Congress is in power or where the units are headed by Congressmen.'[29] In West Bengal, too, Pawar could find enough favour in political circles, including both the CPI-M and the Trinamool Congress, albeit due to different reasons. The CPI-M did not like Dalmiya because of his 'tardy work' at the Calcutta Leather Complex, while the Trinamool Congress alleged that Dalmiya had been 'running a coterie' in the BCCI to suit his interests.[30] As one newspaper correspondent remarked:

> It is, therefore, a vulnerable Mr. Dalmiya—an unusual position for him to be in—who's fighting to retain his now tenuous hold over the BCCI. The fact that the BCCI is a house divided and political big-hitters have entered the arena to oust the ruling faction have made the battle even more acrimonious this year.[31]

Yet Dalmiya did not accept the compromise formula offered by the Pawar camp that entailed 'allowing incumbent Ranbir Singh Mahendra to continue as the BCCI president this year on condition that Mr Pawar would not be opposed next year.'[32] Dalmiya, on the other hand, insisted on a third term for Mahendra. This act naturally incensed the anti-Dalmiya lobby.

The 2005 BCCI election had also a major cricketing dimension to it. It was preceded by an unprecedented spat between Greg Chappell, the newly appointed Indian coach, and Sourav Ganguly, the Indian captain. Sourav's outburst at Chappell's suggestion to step down from captaincy during the Zimbabwe tour of 2005 which was made public by Sourav himself; Chappell's email to the BCCI president expressing strong views against Sourav's actions as a captain and cricketer, which was leaked to the press mysteriously; the decision of the BCCI to resolve the controversy by making a truce between Chappell and Ganguly and by imposing a ban on cricketers on talking to press about cricket and subsequent removal of Ganguly from captaincy and from the one-day squad—all this took Indian cricket to a boiling point on the eve of the election. Two former BCCI chiefs, Inderjit Singh Bindra and Raj Singh Dungarpur, both supporters of Pawar, held Dalmiya and the ruling administration entirely responsible for this series of controversies.[33] As Dungarpur said, 'What happened in Zimbabwe is unparalleled (in the history of Indian cricket). It reveals the failure of the ruling group in handling situations both on and off the ground. But these things, though unfortunate, are going to help us.'[34]

More importantly, the election was wrought with legal battle and debate from the very beginning. On 21 September, the day before the meeting, the Calcutta High Court appointed Suhash Chandra Sen, a former Supreme Court judge, as an observer to ensure the elections were held in a free and fair manner.[35] This move was followed by a civil suit filed by the Netaji Cricket Club at the Madras High Court, seeking appointment of a neutral authority to conduct the elections and the eligibility of voters and contestants.[36] This legal wrangling resulted in the sine die adjournment of the AGM by the reigning Board President Ranbir Singh Mahendra on the scheduled day of the election. It was followed by another legal move by the Rajasthan Cricket Association to the Calcutta High Court which appointed two more observers, namely, K.N. Singh and M.M. Poonchi, both former chief justices, to oversee the BCCI elections.[37] However, on the challenge of the ruling faction, the order was revoked the very next day by a division bench of the Calcutta High Court.[38] Yet, at the end of the day, the AGM was adjourned to be reconvened before 30 November. It was expected that the reconvened AGM won't see any action then as both the factions seemed to be on their way to find 'a more civilized way of holding elections'.[39] Moreover, the fact that Sharad Pawar, the candidate for the post of BCCI president of the dissident faction, was inducted into the marketing committee of the Dalmiya-controlled BCCI, along with his supporter N. Srinivasan of Chennai, pointed to the fact that 'the two factions have perhaps decided to share the spoils that come from control over the world's richest cricket body.'[40] Dalmiya was himself optimistic that all the matters would be sorted out amicably:

> We needed to stop the process of acrimony that was going on for the past two days. True it was a waste of money and time, but whatever was happening was not right. Going to court for everything shows bankruptcy for cricket administration. The meeting ended in the right spirit. I have been saying that a consensus must be reached.[41]

I.S. Bindra, a heavyweight in the rival faction, considered it to be a good beginning: 'We will have to build on it. We have arrived at a consensus and now we need to find a transparent method of holding elections and in the matter of running the BCCI.'[42]

However, as it turned out, the efforts to reach a compromise ultimately went in vain. In that context, the Supreme Court appointed former Chief Election Commissioner T.S. Krishnamurthy as the observer to the elections to be held on the reconvened days of the AGM, that is, 29–30 November 2005.[43] The apex court also urged an immediate clarification of the controversial issue of eligibility of members for casting vote in the elections. In fact, while appointing the observer, it clearly stated that after the elections the observer would send his report with brief reasons for his ruling on voting rights and on eligibility/disqualification to the Supreme Court within a week.[44] Krishnamurthy issued a circular formulating the guidelines for the election to make it 'free for anyone to contest from any association'.[45] When the BCCI moved the Supreme Court alleging that Krishnamurthy had overstepped his jurisdiction in issuing such guidelines, the court declined to entertain the petition before the elections.[46] Dalmiya, of course, made an attempt to convince Krishnamurthy about the legal justification of his views on rulings given by the latter. Krishnamurthy had also heard representations from other disputing parties and associations. On the basis of these discussions, the observer released a list of authorized representatives of the affiliate units and agreed to allow the BCCI president to vote by virtue of being the chairman of the AGM. He also gave the right to vote to the Jharkhand State Cricket Association at the expense of Bihar. He also cleared the representatives of the cricket associations of Uttar Pradesh, Delhi, Himachal Pradesh and National Cricket Club to vote.[47] However, at the end of his declaration, Krishnamurthy expressed deep 'surprise' at the level of factionalism within the BCCI. He pointed out that while the Election Commission had successfully conducted elections countrywide in 800,000 polling booths, 'there are multiple factions for such a small poll (in the BCCI).'[48]

As Pawar and his men thrashed the Dalmiya faction by a whooping margin (20–11) in the election, the intimate link between sport and politics once again came to the fore as the guiding force behind the election. As already mentioned, in the BCCI presidential and office-bearers' election, the representatives of all the affiliated state associations cast votes. It has been argued that Pawar, equipped with the blessings of Sonia Gandhi, the Congress supremo, managed to draw on the votes of nearly all those states in his favour, which had Congress-led governments.[49] This was because, as the media represented, Sonia Gandhi issued strong instruction to all Congress-controlled state governments to ensure so that the votes of their respective associations were cast in favour of Pawar:

> Ever since the last Assembly poll in Maharashtra. Mrs Sonia Gandhi had been looking for a way to placate Mr Sharad Pawar, given the fact that the latter had given up his party's claim to chiefministership of the state despite having more seats than his ally, the Congress. The BCCI polls today provided her the opportunity to cozy up to the Maratha strongman by organizing a sizeable number of votes that enabled Mr Pawar to win comfortably.[50]

Pawar's victory by such a comfortable margin also strengthens this argument. When the AGM was adjourned in September, many in the BCCI considered it to be Dalmiya's masterstroke. But as it proved out to be, 'it simply allowed Pawar adequate time to set his house in order and explore his contacts in the Congress camp.'[51] Dalmiya's reaction in such context deserves mention: 'There's no problem if a politician fights. But, if the politician is in power, it's better to nationalize associations instead of interference from the ruling party.'[52] This was probably a unique instance when direct political pressure was applied to rest the BCCI authority from the hand of a cricket administrator and secure it for an influential political personality.

However, this trend seemed only natural in contemporary period, as given the commercial prospects, financial opportunities or popular emotion associated with the game, it is very difficult to set cricket asunder from politics. Thus, what remained 'cricketing politics' in the age of Dalmiya became 'political cricket' with the onset of Pawar to Indian cricket administration.

The CAB Election 2006: Politicization of Cricket and Power Play within Politics

With this backdrop in mind, we may approach the countdown, course and aftermath of the CAB elections that took place on 30 July 2006. In this election, an anti-Dalmiya panel led by Prasun Mukhopadhyay, the police commissioner of Calcutta, contested for the coveted posts at the CAB office. As in the last BCCI elections, Prasun Mukherjee was openly supported by Buddhadeb Bhattacharya, the chief minister of West Bengal. However, compared to the BCCI elections, this electoral battle had some unique dimensions. First, the voting pattern of CAB election is entirely different. Here, majority of the voters come from CAB's affiliated clubs, while others represent district associations and universities. Second, given this pattern of electoral representation, it becomes difficult for any political party even when in power for a long time to dictate terms in such an election as the clubs' interests are controlled more by intricate power politics and a kind of long-standing patron–client relationships, while the district associations are not always easy to control given the spatial and local control enjoyed by individuals or political factions. Third, in its support for Prasun, the CPI-M/Left Front leaders could not take a unanimous stand. While Buddhadeb Bhattacharya and some of his close associates, such as Asoke Bhattacharya wanted Dalmiya's removal from power, Subhas Chakraborty, the reigning sports minister, and Kshiti Goswami, another state minister, quite happy with Dalmiya at the helm of CAB, did not like this political interference in sport. Biman Bose, the CPI-M state committee secretary, and the veteran ex-Chief Minister Jyoti Basu sailed in the same boat, arguing that the party had nothing to do with their views as these were deemed to be their 'personal comments'. The only common cricketing issue in both the elections was probably the Sourav Ganguly controversy. In the CAB elections, one of the main electoral agendas of the anti-Dalmiya faction was the inclusion of Ganguly in the Indian team, which they believed could be done by ousting Dalmiya from power, thereby pleasing Pawar and using subsequent political connections. Sourav himself became involved in the electoral game as he sent an email on the eve of the elections, ventilating his grievances against the existing CAB establishment who, according to him, used to play with and spoil the career of many cricketers by their dirty tricks in order to satisfy their own vested interests. This email, taken at its face value by both the parties, seemed to suggest that Sourav was also very anxious of a change in the CAB power, thereby leaving his age-old cricketing patron to show unity with his political patrons with a final mission of drawing favour from Pawar. Moreover, in both cases, the fight took place between two contradictory approaches to the game: 'cricketing politics' championed by Dalmiya and 'political cricket' waged by Sharad Pawar or Prasun Mukherjee. In the BCCI, as we have seen, the former won in 2004 but tasted defeat in 2005, while at CAB, the former was to win the first battle in 2006.

Apart from the Sourav issue, the Prasun-led section had some relevant points to make to draw on support for their candidates such as continuous corruption of the present CAB administration, undemocratic mode of its operation and authoritarian attitude of Dalmiya in dealing with important administrative issues. But the most important point raised by them argued that as long as Dalmiya, the number one enemy of the then BCCI establishment, would remain at the helm of power, the BCCI would continue to deprive the CAB, alias Bengal, in respect of financial grants, holding of international matches at the Eden Gardens and inclusion of Bengal cricketers in the national teams. Sourav's email at a crucial juncture, they argued, also strengthened their cause. They also promised to bring back democratic ambience and transparency in CAB administration if they get elected to power. They also urged that Dalmiya should himself step down from power after enjoying so long a tenure at the CAB so that a new generation of people with new ideas could step in to inject fresh blood into the cricket's controlling body in Bengal. Dalmiya should also keep away from CAB until and unless he could be able to clear himself from the charges of corruption labelled against him by the BCCI.

It was with these arguments that Buddhadeb Bhattacharya asked his sports minister to persuade Dalmiya not to contest the election, albeit without success. However, the real motive, as many suspected, was to take CAB under the control of the party. When most arenas of life, including education, had already fallen into the fold of leftist hegemony, why cricket with a lucrative autonomous body like CAB should remain outside that fold? The open stand of Buddha and Asoke on the removal of Dalmiya from power met with equally strong opposition from Subhas and Kshiti. The former Chief Minister Jyoti Basu, too, seemed to concur with the latter's position. Thus, the rift in the upper echelons of the party became quite clear. As *The Statesman* wrote in its editorial:

> By far the most astonishing feature of the CAB election is that there are far too many backroom boys whose number keeps increasing each day, and is presently somewhat out of proportion to the singular vacancy the Cricket Association of Bengal on offer—the post of president. It must be astonishing no less that the election to the helm of a sportsbody has turned out to be an occasion for vigorous political shadow-boxing within the Communist Party of India (Marxist) and within the Left Front as well. Despite protestations to the contrary made at the level of state committee last year, the party has now intensely involved... Mr. (Subhas) Chakraborty's determination to contest has intensified intra-left bickering... This is politics fair and square, a diverting left slideshow of immense public interest that to an extent has deflected attention from the murkier travails of rural Bengal. The short point must be that this isn't cricket. The Club House is only incidental.[53]

The opposition political parties in West Bengal too criticized Buddha for interfering in sports. And once Dalmiya went ahead to contest despite Buddha's request (order!), a section of the CPI-M got involved in the election to ensure victory for Prasun. The question was whether the Subhas faction of the CPI-M would fight the battle in favour of Dalmiya or not. However, one thing became very clear over the election issue: the internal conflict within the CPI-M, so efficiently kept in check by its former Party Secretary Anil Biswas, came into open over an issue that became a serious source of rift in the rank and file of the party.

As expected, Dalmiya's support almost wholly came from a majority of the first and second division clubs, while the bulk of

Mukherjee's votes would have come from the districts and the institutional bodies. Obviously, he picked up some votes from the clubs as well. The result was a close shave in favour of Dalmiya (61–56). While the loss may not mean much to Mukherjee, that outcome would have finished Dalmiya not only in the state but within the BCCI in India. Dalmiya acknowledged the significance of the win when he told the media: 'This win gives me a platform to set the record straight.'[54] Thus, he earned the platform to fight on the external front against the 'personal' allegations which the Board had publicly levelled against him. He also added that he had to contest on the insistence of his colleagues: 'The Chief Minister had wanted me not to contest this election, but my companions insisted that I fight it. So I decided to fight.'[55] However, many felt that Dalmiya's win was made possible by the covert political support provided by Subhas Chakraborty and Lalu Prasad Yadav, Minister for Railways, Government of India.[56] On the other hand, some argued that the attempt of the leader of the government in power to defeat Dalmiya by exercising his political muscle created a widespread sympathy in favour of the latter:

> When the might of the state is turned against an individual, an underdog is created. And once created, it matters little that the dog was rabid and a menace to everyone; public sympathy is reserved for those who appear to be fighting uphill battles. That was an appearance that Mr. Dalmiya carefully nurtured in the days leading up to the elections for the Cricket Association of Bengal. It is not so much the battle that Mr. Dalmiya won at Eden Gardens that ought to detain us; it is the battle that Mr. Bhattacharjee lost outside the CAB that is of greater import, for this was a battle that the Chief Minister had to wage with his reason and self-control. And he lost it.[57]

Once Dalmiya emerged victorious in what was regarded as a fair election in CAB after a long time, Buddhadeb Bhattacharya came up with a stunning reaction:

> It is a victory of evil over good, over right-thinking people. This happens at times. Mr. Dalmiya should leave the organization in the interest of budding cricketers and sports enthusiasts. He has many vested interests outside cricket. No one can compromise with this end of an evil force. This war will continue.[58]

For many, this reaction came as unwarranted and unbelievable in a democratic society. May be it was a rare moment of rush of blood that made the otherwise gentlemanly chief minister to make such a comment! But it revealed that it was difficult even for a seasoned politician like Buddhadeb to believe or accept defeat sportingly once he becomes accustomed (addicted!) to tasting win only. And even if we take it for granted as the CPI-M officially declared that it was Buddha's personal comment, it was shocking to find a chief minister, working at the helm of a democratic government/administering democratic governance, speaking against the spirit of democracy by talking of removing a democratically elected person. Buddha's comment was greeted with shock and disbelief in the party and outside. Subhas and Kshiti as well as the oppositions condemned it. Jyoti Basu spoke disapprovingly of his comments, saying that the issue should be discussed in the CPI-M Secretariat, representing the highest state-level body. Basu's point is important: 'I must make it clear that the Left Front had no candidate for the CAB president's post. Mukherjee was the chief minister's candidate and the fact is that he lost.'[59] Biman Bose, the party secretary, cleverly stated: 'I have made it clear that the party will never interfere with sports. I don't know what the Chief Minister has said. I will talk to him.'[60] The state committee of the party at a subsequent meeting decided to hush up the issue and warned all concerned not to make any further moves on the same. As Biman Bose stated in a press conference, 'CPI-M members may be individually involved in sports. But as we are n't organizationally represented in sports, the party has no role to play in games or sports. No minister or party representative will henceforth talk about the CAB elections.'[61] Jyoti Basu too argued on the same line: 'Things have been amicably sorted out. Now no party leader or minister will talk about the CAB election. The injunction applies to me as well. The only person authorized to speak about it is our secretary Biman.'[62]

Why the chief minister gave such a shocking reaction is the point that baffles us. Subrata Mukherjee, a Congressman, said: 'Buddhababu has lost balance. He has no business asking Dalmiya to leave CAB. We want him and his party to leave government, will he do it?'[63] Those charitable to the chief minister said: 'He is an extremely emotional person.'[64] A CPI-M legislator argued: 'It is very difficult for him to stomach the humiliation he has suffered after

Dalmiya won the poll defying the chief minister's expressed instruction to step aside.' An editorial in *The Statesman* reflected this view more elaborately:

> ... characterizations on the basis of good and evil have no place in Indian public life. Who is good and who is evil? It is becoming increasingly evident that the Chief Minister is, in his second spell in office, no longer self-righteous as much as he is overbearing. Perhaps he has begun to believe the hype those sycophants within the media churn out. Perhaps he has begun to imagine that the Tatas and the Ambanis come calling on him because they think that he is a nice and honest man. Perhaps he sees himself as bigger than the system that created him. Perhaps he is beginning to believe that he alone represents good. These are dangerous signs, and can easily drive a man to megalomania. For his own good, and for that of the state, Mr. Bhattacharjee needs to pause, introspect. There is far too much good in him that can help West Bengal for him to allow the evil of arrogance to overwhelm it.[65]

Many, however, blamed some of Buddha's 'sports advisors' for egging him on.[66] Many regretted the absence of Anil Biswas, the former party secretary, as Biswas, adept at managing inner contradictions, they believed, 'would never have allowed the conflict to spin out of control.'[67]

An Academic Discussion on the Issue: Responses and Comments

Grasping the importance of the ever-rising socio-political debate on the CAB elections, the MAKAIAS, Kolkata, an autonomous research institute under the Ministry of Culture, Government of India, organized an academic discussion on 'Cricket and Politics in India: The CAB Elections 2006' on 23 August 2006, where the author initiated the discussion. The responses and comments the discussion generated were revealing. It is worthy to reproduce the most important comments and observations here:

> I don't agree that money is a motivating factor for the politicians to meddle into sports. If that be the case, then it should apply to people from all walks of life who interfere with sports like cricket. Rather, it is wider

social popularity and control that a highest place in the cricket administration can bring to one, which make politicians like Sharad Pawar interested in the administration of the game. In a cricket crazy country like India, this kind of social popularity and control could be safely invested as social capital during elections to impress upon the people at large about a person's social credibility.

So far as the interference of Buddhadeb Bhattacharya, the Chief Minister of West Bengal, in the CAB elections and his reaction after the victory of Dalmiya are concerned, it seems that the Chief Minister got involved in the electoral battle in order to ensure a transparent, democratic and efficient cricket administration in Bengal. However, another prime consideration for him was to remove a person from the CAB, who was supported by Subhas Chakraborty, the ever-troubling sports minister in the Left Front over the last five years. Despite Buddha's repeated requests, Subhas could not persuade Dalmiya not to contest the elections. Moreover, the factional politics in the rank and file of the CPI-M was clearly reflected during the days preceding the elections as Subhas openly contradicted Buddha's stand to nominate a candidate against Dalmiya with whose work Subhas was quite satisfied. Buddha's reaction after the victory of Dalmiya should be analyzed in this context of a serious rift in CPI-M. It is understandable that the CM was furious over the result of the election as it proved a loss of face for him, which happened probably because of Subhas's maneuvre. Hence, Buddha's instantaneous reaction branding Dalmiya as an 'evil force' was in reality directed towards Subhas Chakraborty rather than Dalmiya.[68]

I agree that money is one of the primary motivators for politicians to interfere in sports administration. Especially when we talk about hugely cash-rich BCCI, it seems certain that politicians could easily be tempted to utilize the financial muscle of that organization to serve their personal ends and fulfil their political ambitions. While the corrupt nature of our political leaders gives room for the argument that the latter could appropriate a handsome amount of money from BCCI treasury on different false pretexts to use during elections or remit directly to party funds, it is more important to note the kind of avenues and connections a place in the cricket administration could open up to these politicians thanks to the BCCI's immense control over various aspects of cricket's commercialization—sponsorship, television rights and so on. In brief, a BCCI chief has all the power to initiate worthy ventures and deals with world's lucrative business houses to satisfy his personal or wider interests.

A point that generally goes unnoticed with regard to the CAB elections is the way the media got divided in their representation of the countdown, course and aftermath of the event. While some of the newspapers *the Statesman* or *Bartaman* disapproved the chief minister's decision to nominate and support a candidate in the CAB elections, others such as *Aajkaal* or *Ganashakti* appreciated his action.[69]

Buddhadeb Bhattacharya's interference in the CAB elections 2006 is an integral part of the CPI-M's calculated drive to occupy all the societal spaces in Bengal. They have already done this in other spheres of society—in education, literary fields, journalism, performing arts, administration and so on. Now, it wants to control sports bodies as found recently in cricket's apex body in the state, the CAB.

As to why politicians are increasingly getting interested in cricket alia sports administration, it may be surmised that mass spectator sports like cricket have had a deep impact on Indian psyche. Hence, a high position in the BCCI or sports administration for that matter may help a person later on to build up his credibility at a social level thereby making a positive impact on the public psyche. This social popularity or credibility gained through a lucrative position in the sports administration could be safely invested as social capital while drawing popular favour during political election campaigns.

With regard to Jyoti Basu's stand in the debate over Buddhadeb Bhattacharya's interference in the CAB elections, one can notice subtle shifts in it. He was initially opposed to such intervention in sports and did not like Buddha's decision to field a candidate, particularly a serving police commissioner, against Dalmiya in the election. Then when the debate over the issue got momentum, he argued that since Buddhadeb had pointed to certain charges against Dalmiya, the latter himself should look into the matter as to why such charges were levelled against him. Finally, after Buddha gave his reaction after his candidate got defeated branding Dalmiya as part of an 'evil force', Basu said: 'I must make it clear that the Left Front had no candidate for the CAB president's post. Mukherjee was the Chief Minister's candidate and the fact is that he lost.' He also called for a discussion on the issue in the forthcoming meeting of the party's state committee.[70]

While it is well known that Buddhadeb Bhattacharya has had otherwise grievances against Dalmiya (viz., Dalmiya's appropriation of huge tracts of land at a cheaper price during Jyoti Basu's regime as the Chief Minister and his image as a defaulter in building a leather complex), his dislike of Dalmiya may not be simply confined to the person himself. In Buddha's regime, we have the emergence of a burgeoning business-cum-industrial community in Bengal, who no longer represent the old Marwari business community, who traditionally used to control the investment sector of Bengal economy. Hence, investigations need to be undertaken to explore this triangular nexus between business, politics and sport because Buddha's dislike of the traditional business interests in Bengal economy might have something to do with his crusade against Dalmiya. By fielding a heavyweight candidate such as Prasun Mukherjee against him in the CAB elections and defeating him in the process, Buddha wanted not only to put an end to his career as a cricket administrator, but to undermine the policy of Jyoti Basu and Subhas Chakraborty to stand by old business horses like Dalmiya.[71]

At the end of the discussion, Prof Jayanta Kumar Ray, president of the session and chairman of the institute, raised a very pertinent point:

The most worrisome aspect that comes out of this debate on recent CAB elections is that our ministers, neglecting their more important duties such as administering law and justice, begin to interfere in sports. The way the ministers and high officials are getting involved in different scams, the way they are getting used to misusing their power and position to satisfy their vested interests, the way they are undermining the security of public life as well as the state should become a matter of more serious concern to themselves and to the media. Appallingly, instead, they have become more interested in less important affairs like sports/cricket (CAB elections for instance). Mind it, what is happening in cricket centering on organizational elections may be tolerated, but what is taking place in the political administration of the country can't be tolerated.[72]

While we can clearly discern an ethical voice in the above comment, it must be recognized that motivated or ill-advised governmental or ministerial intervention in societal or cultural spheres will not help better the political image of the nation.

Conclusion

The BCCI elections of 2005–2006 as well as the CAB elections of 2006 confirmed the beginning of a new trend in Indian cricket—intrusion of mainstream politics into Indian cricket. The course of Indian cricket administration henceforth became intertwined with the art of 'political cricket' driven by political parties and factions and led by political personalities, such as Sharad Pawar or Buddhadeb Bhattacharya. Cricket administrators, such as Dalmiya—a mastermind in 'cricketing politics' globally—had to adapt to this changing order of Indian cricket administration. The question that naturally surfaces here is what makes politicians, such as Pawar, interested in cricket. People who had little interest in the sport earlier, suddenly became so much involved in a bitter game to control the destiny of the sport in our country. In my opinion, money is one of the motivating factors behind this changed attitude of the politicians towards the game. Given the corrupt nature of Indian ministers and officialdom, it is but expected that the lure of money the BCCI could now boast of could easily motivate politicians like Pawar to move into the helm of power. Of course, in a country like India where cricket is like a national religion, enjoying power and popularity by exercising control at the helm of BCCI is no less a motivating factor as well. At another level, it is an exercise in public relations; or in other words, an attempt to acquire a different kind of public profile. However, as the results of the two BCCI elections of 2004–2005 and the CAB election of 2006 as well as the mode of operation of the BCCI in the Pawar age clearly indicated, those who would be able to exercise and manoeuvre a mixture of the two trends, 'cricketing politics' and 'political cricket', would be successful to control the destiny of the game either at the central or at the regional level.

Notes and References

1. C.L.R. James, *Beyond a Boundary* (Durham: Duke University Press, 1993), quoted in Boria Majumdar, 'Willow Talk: Moolah and Mediation', *Sahara Time*, 13 March 2004, p. 22.
2. Ibid.
3. For details on the princely patronage of cricket, see Boria Majumdar, *Twenty-Two Yards to Freedom: A Social History of Indian Cricket* (New Delhi: Penguin/Viking, 2004), pp. 21–74.
4. For an elaborate discussion on these aspects of Indian cricket, see Boria Majumdar, *Once Upon a Furore: Lost Pages of Indian Cricket* (New Delhi: Yoda Press, 2004).
5. *The Statesman* (Kolkata), 23 September 2004, Sports page.
6. Ibid.
7. *The Telegraph* (Kolkata), 28 September 2004, p. 1.
8. Ibid.
9. *The Statesman*, 28 September 2004, Sports page
10. *The Telegraph*, 28 September 2004, p. 1.
11. Ibid.
12. *The Statesman*, 29 September 2004, p. 1.
13. Ibid.
14. Ibid.
15. Ibid.
16. Ibid.
17. *Ananda Bazar Patrika* (Kolkata), 28 September 2004.

18. *Ananda Bazar Patrika*, 29 September 2004.
19. *The Statesman*, 29 September 2004, Editorial.
20. *The Telegraph*, 30 September 2004, p. 1.
21. *The Statesman*, 30 September 2004, p. 1.
22. *Ananda Bazar Patrika*, 30 September 2004, p. 1, emphasis added.
23. Ibid., 1 October 2004, Editorial.
24. Ibid.
25. *The Telegraph*, 30 September 2004, p. 1.
26. *Ananda Bazar Patrika*, 1 October 2004, p. 1.
27. As one senior Congress leader was said to have dismissed the suggestion that 'such elections take place on party lines.' According to him, 'personal interests and networking are the key factors to determine the victor and vanquished in BCCI election.' *The Statesman*, 20 September 2005, p. 1.
28. *The Statesman*, 14 and 20 September 2005.
29. *The Telegraph*, 22 September 2005, p. 1.
30. *The Statesman*, 23 September 2005, p. 1.
31. Ibid.
32. Ibid.
33. *The Statesman*, 22 September 2005.
34. Ibid.
35. The order came in the wake of a petition filed by Kalighat Club, an affiliate unit of the Cricket Association of Bengal. For details, see *The Statesman* and *The Telegraph*, 22 September 2005.
36. Ibid.
37. *The Statesman*, 23 September 2005, p. 1.
38. *The Telegraph*, 24 September 2005, p. 1.
39. *The Statesman*, 24 September 2005, p. 1.
40. Ibid.
41. Ibid., Sports page.
42. Ibid.
43. *The Statesman*, 26 October 2005, Sports page.
44. Ibid.
45. *The Statesman*, 25 November 2005, sports page. According to this circular, the president of the BCCI, besides casting his vote as the authorized representative of his association, could vote only in the event of a tie and not otherwise. It also asked Delhi and District Cricket Association as well as the National Cricket Club in Kolkata to pass a resolution among them before attending the elections. The circular also declared that Bihar and Rajasthan had the right to vote and disqualified Jharkhand's claim to vote. The observer also ruled that should there be a contest for the president's post, the person contesting should be from West Zone as per the BCCI constitution (Rule 20), thereby leading to wide speculation that Ranbir Singh Mahendra would be debarred from contesting for the post for the second consecutive year.
46. Ibid., 26 November 2005, p. 1.
47. *The Statesman*, 29 November 2005, p. 1; *The Telegraph*, 29 November 2005, p. 1. While the observer's final rulings seemed to give a boost to Dalmiya and his associates to retrieve their numbers to win the election, the Pawar lobby remained convinced of a comfortable victory given the already-achieved alliance within their ranks.

48. *The Statesman*, 29 November 2005, p. 1.
49. *Ananda Bazar Patrika*, 30 November 2005, p. 1. As the Congress leadership swung into action and ensured that a state ruled by its chief minister went Pawar's way, the votes of Himachal Pradesh, Assam and Andhra Pradesh reportedly went in his favour following clear instructions from the former to its governments. This only reflected the developing closeness between the Congress and the Nationalist Congress Party at that time. See *The Statesman*, 30 November 2005, p. 1.
50. *The Statesman*, 30 November 2005, p. 1.
51. Ibid.
52. *The Telegraph*, 30 November 2005, p. 1.
53. *The Statesman*, 20 January 2007.
54. *The Statesman*, 31 July 2006, p. 1.
55. Ibid.
56. *Ananda Bazar Patrika*, 1 August 2006, p. 1.
57. *The Statesman*, 2 August 2006, Editorial.
58. *The Statesman* and *The Telegraph*, 1 August 2006, p. 1.
59. *The Telegraph*, 1 August 2006, p. 1.
60. Ibid.
61. *The Statesman*, 6 August 2006, p. 1.
62. *The Telegraph*, 6 August 2006, p. 1.
63. *The Telegraph*, 1 August 2006, p. 1.
64. Ibid.
65. *The Statesman*, 2 August 2006.
66. *The Telegraph*, 1 August 2006, p. 1.
67. Ibid.
68. Response of Dr Binoda K. Misra, a Fellow of the Maulana Abul Kalam Azad Institute of Asian Studies at the discussion on 23 August 2006 (hereafter *discussion*).
69. Response of Sanjana Joshi, Fellow of the Institute, *discussion*.
70. Comment of Amiya K. Chaudhuri, Fellow of the Institute, *discussion*.
71. Comment by a Fellow of the Institute who wanted to remain anonymous, *discussion*.
72. Comment of Jayanta Kumar Ray, the then Chairman of the Institute, *discussion*.

6

Asserting National Identity: The Decolonization of Bangladeshi Cricket

Introduction

Cricket in Bangladesh is rich in terms of tradition, culture and mass following. The game in colonial eastern Bengal, corresponding to modern Bangladesh, prospered as a popular sport under the joint patronage of the educated middle class and the native princes, who in their turn at times appropriated cricket to suit subversive purposes, or project a nationalist image. The political decolonization that took place with the emergence of Pakistan in 1947 did not provide the Bengalis of East Bengal/Pakistan their desired free play in cricket. Rather, the tradition of steady growth of cricket, a feature of the everyday life of colonial eastern Bengal, was stunted, and had to fight for its credibility and recognition, even without much avail, under the new Pakistani regime. Bengali cricket therefore continued to suffer under a new 'colonial hegemony' from 1947 to 1971. Post-independence, in the absence of their national team at international level, and given the success and impact of great performance by her two great neighbours—India and Pakistan—particularly during the 1980s and 1990s, common Bangladeshis began to support either of these two teams and worship cricketing icons of these nations. However, the country's rising status as a cricket-playing nation from the late 1990s went hand in hand with the common Bangladeshi's changing approach towards the game. With Bangladesh's smart performance in their World Cup debut in 1999 and her consequent accession to Test status in 2000, the masses of Bangladesh began to flex 'their' nationalist muscle by supporting 'their' national team and worship their 'own' players as icons in the new century. This trend of cricket culture, well established with the experience of the 2007 World Cup, declared the rise of Bangladesh as a cricketing nation and the decolonization of Bangladesh cricket. The hosting of the ICC World Cup in 2011 and its impact on the everyday life of Bangladesh may be said to have completed this process of decolonization, thereby transforming cricket into a nationalist obsession and as a marker of its national identity. This chapter intends to throw light at this complex and shifting process of decolonization of Bangladeshi cricket in a historical perspective. It also argues, in Bangladesh, which now shares a common South Asian cricket culture with the subcontinental Big Threes—India, Pakistan and Sri Lanka—cricket acts as a great leveller in a society ridden with political dissension and socio-communal tension. The passion and emotion, with which Bangladeshis play, watch and read about cricket, point to the game's increasing popularity and steady mediatization in the country.

Cricket in Colonial East Bengal: Origins, Introduction and Adoption

Although the earliest mention of cricket in Dhaka goes back to 1858,[1] Sylhet was probably the first to host a competitive cricket match of any worth in 1856.[2] This match drew the attention of the press as well: 'Perhaps the most interesting event ever recorded in the cricketing annals of Eastern Bengal, was the grand single wicket match between "service" and "non-service" that came off on the 24th instant on the parade ground of that humidly picturesque station Sylhet.'[3] Any cricket match of significance involving the natives was that of a match played at Old Lines (present-day Purana Paltan) in Dhaka between the Europeans and the natives in 1876.[4] The Englishmen took the match quite seriously and won it by a comfortable margin.[5] The *Bengali Times*, a contemporary newspaper, reported the match thus: 'England expected every man to do his duty, and nobly did those who had the least pretension to the name of Englishman respond to their country's call.'[6] It also described the technical aspects of the actual game in details, which bears testimony to the quality of contemporary sports journalism. For example, it commented on the way Mr Loyal, the highest scorer for the Europeans, got out as follows:

> A cautious fieldsman standing almost under his very nose, and who had escaped the batter's observation in the heat of excitement, bided his time, and the best player of the day was destined to fall an easy prey to miserable catch right into his opponent's hand.[7]

As regards the performance of the native players, the newspaper wrote: 'Poor fellows! They were always wrong, expecting the slow for the quick and vice versa.'[8]

It was these European officers and soldiers who introduced cricket to the natives in the cities. Muntassir Mamoon has argued that cricket was primarily a means of entertainment and leisure for the Europeans who used such matches as fruitful occasions of social interaction with lunch and drinks.[9] In support of his point, Mamoon refers to the description of a match between the Station and the Outsiders played in 1876: 'At about 2 P.M. numbers of ladies and gentlemen sat down and did ample justice to sumptuous tiffin provided by our former commissioner after which the cricket was resumed, and continued until sunset.'[10] This view, however, does not take into account the central importance of sport in the life and culture of the British colonial elite and military all over the world. As Richard Holt remarks:

> 'Joking' political incursions aside, British sports served overwhelmingly to express and enhance the solidarity of colonial society. Providing amusement for those far from home isolated amidst an alien and sometimes hostile population, sport was not so much a luxury as a necessity, a means of maintaining morale and a sense of shared roots, of Britishness, of lawns and tea and things familiar.[11]

J.E.C. Welldon, the Headmaster of Harrow from 1881 to 1885 and a fervent imperialist, provided the best possible conclusion that sports could deserve in the framework of British colonial empire-building:

> Englishmen are not superior to Frenchmen or Germans in brains or industry, or the science or apparatus of war ... The pluck, the energy, the perseverance, the good temper, the self-control, the discipline, the

co-operation, the *esprit de corps*, which merit success cricket or football, are the very qualities, which win the day in peace or war. … In the history of the British Empire, it is written that England had owed her sovereignty to her sports.[12]

The Dhaka Cricket Club was founded in early 1880s at the initiative of the enthusiastic teachers and students of Dhaka College. In fact, the British professors of the college played a leading role in promoting the game. The cricket team used to play practice matches at different places in Bengal. In 1883, it defeated the Krishnanagar College team. The lieutenant governor of Bengal, Rivers Thompson, who watched the match throughout, distributed rewards after the match.[13] In another match played at the Purana Paltan Cricket Ground in 1884, Dhaka College got the better of Jagannath College by 77 runs.[14] In the same year, a major controversy arose over the result of a match between the Presidency Cricket Club and the Dhaka Cricket Club at the Eden Gardens, in which both the college teams comprised some of the teaching staff as well.[15] As the latter won the match on the first day's score, some newspapers in Calcutta criticized the outcome and hinted at the defeat of the Dhaka Club in actuality. Newspapers in Dhaka strongly contested such a claim and argued that the result of the match was agreed on the suggestions from two Presidency professors—Rowe and Wheeler.[16] The Dhaka cricket team was led by Saradaranjan Ray, one of the best native cricketers of the time.[17] The fallout of the match was quite interesting. After being beaten by their arch-rivals, the Presidency students demanded the second match to be played by students only. Principal Booth agreed, but requested Saradaranjan to play as the captain. Saradaranjan, however, did not comply, and this dispute was said to have eventually led to his resignation from the college in 1887.[18] In 1891, Dhaka College also defeated Sibpur College by 47 runs.[19] The other legendary cricketer of Dhaka around this time was Basanta Kumar Guha.[20]

Thus, teams from eastern Bengal colleges and clubs started touring western Bengal quite regularly from the 1880s.[21] It was also noted that the rich Bengalis of Dhaka used to sponsor the Dhaka teams visiting Calcutta. Pratap Chandra Das, zamindar of Bangla Bazaar, donated ₹350 when the Dhaka cricket team went to Calcutta to play matches with the Presidency Cricket Club.[22] On its tour to play the Sibpur College, about ₹458 was raised as donation to bear the expenses of travel to and stay in Calcutta, of which Raja Rajendra Narayan Roy Bahadur and Babu Annada Prasad Roy Chaudhuri contributed ₹150 and ₹50, respectively.[23] It was also noted that people from different spheres of society—zamindar, barrister, teacher and doctor—all contributed according to their capacity.[24] Besides such financial assistance, the spectators and the newspapers never lost any opportunity to support the cause of a native team against the British sides. For example, one English newspaper once reported about such an encounter:

> The place was densely crowded by Native Spectators who caused great annoyance to the player while the game was going on, by shouting and clapping at any mishap of the opposite party in a most rude and unbecoming way, while they rather too vociferously applauded any piece of good luck that attended their own countrymen. But what was even worse, they managed to obstruct the ball from going as far it would have gone, had it not been stopped on its way by number of noisy Natives.[25]

Newspapers in Calcutta and Dhaka, on the other hand, used to be at cross with each other whenever a match between two college teams of the two cities took place. The newspapers also urged the middle classes, especially the students, to pursue cricket. As one vernacular periodical argued:

> Students are becoming idle by concentrating solely on their studies. They should therefore engage themselves in sports like cricket since students of Dhaka in recent times have excelled in both the organization and performance. They also quite often pay visit to Calcutta to play cricket matches, which add prop to both physique and entertainment.[26]

Thus, cricket became quite popular in Dhaka during the last quarter of the nineteenth century. This becomes more apparent when we find that 'leading members of the Presidency College Cricket Club were students from east Bengal, often belonging to families of modest means.'[27] Cricket gained more social currency when an inter-school tournament began in Khulna in 1890. The first year of the tournament comprised four school teams from Senhati, Bagerhat, Khulna and Daulatpur. In the first two knockout matches, Senhati and Khulna defeated Bagerhat and Daulatpur, respectively, and met each other in the final. The final aroused tremendous enthusiasm among the locals of Khulna. The commissioner of the Presidency Division and the magistrate of Khulna were present to witness the match. The match was not only keenly contested but wrought with a lot of tension among players exchanging hot words during the game.[28] In fact, this tournament took place three years before the start of Harris Shield of Bombay, erroneously regarded as the oldest inter-school cricket tournament in India.[29]

Cricket continued to flourish in Dhaka in the first two decades of the twentieth century. We get an interesting insight into this development in the following description:

> In east Bengal too, the period between 1900–20 saw an explosion in cricket enthusiasm. The partition of Bengal in 1905 had reestablished Dhaka's eminence as a capital of Bengal after a period of nearly 200 years. As the capital of eastern Bengal and Assam, Dhaka received a host of grants from the government. Though the annulment of the partition in 1911 once again reduced Dhaka to the status of a district town, it was accompanied by some compensatory promises from the government. Among these was the promise to establish the University of Dhaka, an institution that later emerged as a centre of sporting activity. The university contributed to enhanced economic, intellectual and political activity, with sport becoming an integral part of student life. However, with the institution developing into a hub of nationalist activity, governmental investment declined from the late 1920s, leading to a gradual decline in sporting activity.[30]

It has been argued that the development of sports in Dhaka since the last quarter of the nineteenth century had something to do with the considerable progress in civic matters and amenities under the tutelage of British civil servants, resulting in a noticeable rise in the standard of living.[31] Apart from a series of major civic development measures,[32] the municipality undertook the task of filling up tanks and establishing parks and playgrounds, thereby 'giving a fillip to sport in east Bengal'.[33]

First Attempt at Decolonization: Cricket Patronage and Nationalist Appropriation

The royal houses and the landed elites of Bengal had always taken a keen interest in the promotion of sports in the late nineteenth and early twentieth centuries. For example, the nawab of Dhaka and his

136 SPORT, CULTURE AND NATION

family, the royal houses of Cooch Behar, Natore and Mymensingh played a significant role in 'establishing cricket on a firm foundation in Bengal'.[34] According to Boria Majumdar, the growth of modern sports in Bengal from the late nineteenth century owed much to the joint patronage of the educated middle class and the native princes. He goes on to argue: 'Desire to attain recognition in British eyes together with the longing to defeat the British on their own turf were at the root of this initiative. To that extent, Bengali cricket was a nationalist enterprise.'[35]

The most prominent patron of sports from East Bengal in the early twentieth century was Jagadindranath Ray, the maharaja of Natore. In his venture to form a cricket team, the maharaja of Natore was in all probability driven by the urge to compete with the maharaja of Cooch Behar, who had already formed a very professional team comprising British players in its rank. Maharaja Nripendra Narayan Bhup Bahadur spent a lot of money to recruit professional coaches and players from England in order to train the aspiring Bengali players. He also gave the latter necessary exposure to play with the quality Indian and European cricketers from different parts of the country by arranging regular competitive matches.[36] Although the Cooch Behar team had earned renown in cricket at the turn of the nineteenth century, it was difficult to ascertain the quality of the native players because of the strong presence of Europeans in his team.[37] As Hemendra Kumar Ray argued, 'We, Bengalis, could not celebrate the victories of the Cooch Behar team much, because it could not boast of a purely Indian side.'[38] This probably spurred Jagadindranath on to form a quality cricket side comprising Indians alone. He had already created a cricket field along with garden house at a 45-acre land on the Bondel Road, which came to be known as the Natore Park.[39] He brought talented cricketers from around the country[40] to complement the Bengali talents at his disposal and formed a team that began to challenge the superiority of the European as well as other Indian teams of the country.[41] He was ably assisted in this venture by no other than Saradaranjan Ray, a leading intellectual as well as cricketer of the age. The maharaja encouraged a number of young Bengali players irrespective of their social affiliations such as class or caste to take up the field against the best of European sides.[42]

The latent motive of the maharaja in forming a quality Indian side seemed to be the desire to beat the British at their own game, thereby breaking the myth of the invincibility of the Raj at least on the cricket field. Sharing with his contemporaries, such as Surendranath Banerjee, the belief in the politics of association, petition and protest,[43] Jagadindranath probably wanted to utilize cricket as a cultural arena to challenge the British sense of superiority. Although he never overtly propagated such a 'nationalist enterprise' for his cricket venture, the impact of the success of his team against top European sides certainly aroused certain extent of nationalist sentiment in Bengal. As Hemendra Kumar Ray wrote in his obituary to the Maharaja:

> Whenever the Natore XI defeated the European teams of Calcutta, our chests swelled with pride. Before the formation of the Natore XI, we, Indians, were losers on most occasions. But with the formation of the Natore XI, Maharaj Jagadindranath turned the tables on the English. Whether it is a fault of ours or not, we do not regard games as something simple, rather we are affected by the results of these encounters. This is because this is the only arena where we are allowed to compete on even terms with the English. The English have always us as 'effete'. It is on the sporting field that we may counter such allegations. This is why we justifiably perceive a victory on the sporting field as a 'national victory' against the British.[44]

He went on to conclude:

> There is no doubt that the series of victories achieved by the Natore XI formed by the Maharaja incited the nationalist sentiment of the Bengali youth. It was a great contribution for which Bengal will always remember the Maharaja. By lavishly spending money and working hard to create a quality Indian side, he also showed his sense of patriotism.[45]

Thus, Jagadindranath's patronage of cricket may be said to have assumed the form of a cultural nationalist resistance against the British, which might also have an impact on the Bengali psyche in inspiring them to look at modern sports from such a perspective. In fact, he appropriated the very British virtues of games ethic—discipline, fair play and sporting spirit[46]—to inculcate among the young Bengali cricketers, and made them a determined fighting brigade to go all out for win on the sports field.[47] Some of his contemporaries attributed the Bengali excellence in cricket in the first quarter of the twentieth century to his initiative. According to them, 'one of the cherished ambitions of the Maharaja was to raise the Bengali youth to such a level of sporting excellence that they could equal and beat the British in all modern sports.'[48] For this very reason, he always took great pride in his appreciation of the Mohun Bagan Club that won the IFA Shield in 1911 by defeating a host of European sides as the first Indian team.[49] For him, Mohun Bagan became synonymous with patriotism.

Boria Majumdar has suggested that 'Bhadralok products of the public school system the English had imported, though overtly advocating the "games ethic", often employed sport as a tool of subversion.'[50] And he goes on to conclude with reference to Bengal cricket:

> the Bengalis did not play cricket simply to be like the British and to then defeat then on their own turf. Bengali cricket was not simply an act of mimicry. It sought to permeate ideas of self-respect, manliness and self-worth among the people. Educated men from middle-class backgrounds promoted cricket, trying to legitimise physical activity in Bengali society and win respect for the players. The sport emerged as the mirror wherein an Indian/Bengali identity started to reassess itself, and in that sense Bengal cricket was certainly part of a nationalist enterprise.[51]

The cricket-promotion initiatives of the maharaja of Natore certainly bear testimony to the above comment. In cricket, one could thus read into the princely patronage imperial emulation as well as nationalist enterprise, thereby signalling the first attempt at decolonization of cricket in eastern Bengal, alias modern Bangladesh.

Fighting against Hegemony: Cricket under Second Colonial Rule

During British colonial rule, the attempt to challenge and subvert British hegemony on the sports field was aimed at decolonizing sports in Bangladesh/India even before the actual political decolonization took place in 1947. The formation of Pakistan unfortunately did not provide the Bengalis their desired free play on the sports field either. Rather, the tradition of steady growth of modern sports, a feature of the everyday life of colonial eastern Bengal, however, had to fight for its credibility and recognition, even without much avail, under the new Pakistani regime. The tradition of steady growth of sports, a feature of the everyday life of colonial eastern Bengal, was stunted, and the organizers and players had to fight against heavy odds to earn what they deserved in the field of sport under the new Pakistani regime. In the context of political and social experience of suffering and struggle, the Bengalis of East Pakistan considered the Pakistan regime as a second colonial rule and tried to appropriate the sports field as a cultural arena to assert their national/ethnic identity both within and without East Pakistan against the policy of discrimination pursued by the hegemonic West Pakistani regime. Such occasions of assertion, however, were very rare before the emergence of independent Bangladesh in 1971, given the high-handedness and nepotism of the West Pakistani ruling elite, who controlled sports administration at that time. Bengali sports therefore continued to suffer under a new 'colonial hegemony' under the rule of Pakistan from 1947 to 1971.

After the Partition of India, eastern parts of Bengal that fell into the sovereign domain of the new Pakistan state came to be called East Pakistan. Any worthy discussion of the sporting life in East Bengal/Pakistan after the birth of Pakistan in 1947 brings us to the larger story of West Pakistan's political, economic and cultural hegemony in the eastern wing between 1947 and 1971. As Jayanta Kumar Ray noted in 1967:

> Since the emergence of Pakistan as an independent state, those who dominated the Central Government, remaining predominantly West Pakistani in composition ... have consistently tried to impose (and greatly succeeded too) a cultural, economic and political hegemony upon East Pakistan. The relative strength of cultural, economic and political motivations in this hegemonial design may be a matter of debate, but the design itself is not. Nor are its results, which are writ large on the face of East Pakistan.[52]

In such a context, argues Ray, 'The new East Pakistani elite, however, finds it almost impossible to achieve its legitimate cultural-economic-political goals because of the use of force and intrigues by the West Pakistani ruling authorities spearheading the military-bureaucratic complex.'[53] According to him, the frustrations of this elite were 'deep-rooted, widespread and represent genuine grievances of all East Pakistanis except those enjoying the patronage of the West Pakistani ruling clique in the then Pakistan.' 'A thorough acquaintance with these frustrations', he further points out, 'opens up the heart of an elite pining for democratic rights and the fulfilment of nationalist impulses.'[54] Many later writers more or less followed and refined the same line of argument offered by Ray much earlier.[55]

Thus, since the birth of Pakistan in 1947, there developed great imbalances in the growth of different sectors in the two wings, imbalances which inevitably intensified Bengali alienation. These imbalances ranged from discrimination in administration, bureaucracy and defence to educational, cultural and economic deprivation. The overwhelming dominance over East Bengal by West Pakistan, it is argued, was made possible by the powerful grip on the levers of power and decision-making held almost from the very beginning by 'the ruling military-administrative-industrial complex', based in West Pakistan.[56] The thoughtless policies pursued by the ruling elite only helped aggravate and deepen these imbalances to such an extent as to create a lasting bitterness between the two wings of Pakistan, resulting in the separation of East Pakistan and emergence of Bangladesh in 1971.[57] Thus, the people of East Pakistan smarted under what may be arguably described as 'internal colonialism' as 'the West Pakistani ruling circle persisted in practising cultural-economic-political domination upon East Pakistan in the entire period from 1947 to 1971.'[58]

Within this broader discourse of political, economic, social and cultural hegemony, Bengalis of East Pakistan suffered discrimination in different spheres of life, including sport. According to scholars like Boria Majumdar, 'any analysis of cricket in East Pakistan has to take into account the antipathy East Pakistanis feel/felt for their West Pakistani counterparts.'[59] According to him, 'sport in East Pakistan was not allowed to blossom and talented players were unjustly kept out of national sides.'[60] In fact, given the political instability of East Pakistan during 1947–1971 with democracy becoming a farce, as Majumdar further points out, it was quite natural that 'entertainment' lost its deserved place in the social context.[61] Naturally, therefore, the Bengalis had to bear the brunt of West Pakistani domination in the arena of sports as well.[62]

The discriminatory sports policy of the Pakistan regime was no more apparent in other sports than in cricket. Since the 1930s, because of the huge popularity of the Pentangular Tournament in Bombay, cricket had also gained social currency in Dhaka. Dhaka witnessed a lot of cricket being played in the 1940s, and the Dhaka Cricket League started in the 1950s. Dhaka's most renowned clubs in that period included Victoria, Dhaka Wanderers, Gymkhana, Ispahani and Eaglets. These clubs played a major role in popularizing the game in East Pakistan.[63] Domestic cricket between 1954 and 1968 was conducted in four leagues in Pakistan, which were officially part of the first class Quaid-e-Azam Trophy, in which the regional East Pakistani teams took part regularly.[64] More importantly, Dhaka became the first international cricket venue in East Pakistan. The Dhaka Stadium, which was the official venue for the East Pakistani sides' home matches, assumed historical significance when it came to host the second Test match of India's first ever official cricket tour of Pakistan in 1955.[65] It went on to host six more Test matches during the period of Pakistani rule.[66]

Despite the popularity of the game in East Bengal/Pakistan, it was very hard for the Bengali cricketers to get a berth in the national side of Pakistan. As a result, 'although Dacca was a regular stop for touring cricket teams, no local found a place in the Pakistan side.'[67] According to Shamya Dasgupta, 'The reason, quite simply, was prejudice against cricketers from East Pakistan.'[68] Hasan Babli tries to explain the absence of Bengali cricketers in the following words:

> It's not that players from East Pakistan were not competent enough. In fact, some of them were quite good. But they were deliberately ignored by the Pakistani selectors. Rather, it was alleged that Bengalis can't play cricket. They lack the strength of the wrist and can't stand up to adverse situation. Such stupid arguments were used only to keep Bengali cricketers away from the national squad. However, it was not only cricket that suffered as a result of the discriminatory policy of the Pakistani government, but Bengalis' education and economic development—all suffered the same fate.[69]

While West Pakistani cricketers, such as Ismail Gul, Tahir Hasan, Rouf Ansari, Mohammad Tahir and Sarwar Hossain, dominated and occupied the centre of attraction in Dhaka cricket, Bengali cricketers such as Chand Khan, Khwaja Amirullah Munni, Athar Ali, K.M. Omar Hicchu, Hassan, Abdul Latif, Sukumar Roy, Moinuddin Ahmed, Bakul, Masiuddin Ahmed Mantu, Abdul Mazid Koran, Lutfar Rahman Makhan, Raisuddin Ahmed, Altaf Hossain, Daulatuzzaman,

Shamim Kabir, Raqibul Hasan, Tanvir Mazhar Islam Tanna, Saiyad Ashraful Huq, S.M. Farooq and Safuqul Haque were no less competent and popular among the cricket-lovers.[70] Given due opportunity, many of them would have excelled as Test cricketers and earned renown in international cricket, thereby making the pages of history as Bengali cricketers.[71] On many occasions, however, worthy Bengali players faced discrimination or rejection on silly pretexts to make room for more influential West Pakistani counterparts. Even the only East Pakistani representative in Pakistan national cricket team was not a Bengali, namely, Niyaz Ahmed Siddiqi.[72]

Despite such a policy of discrimination pursued by the West Pakistani regime, the Bengalis of East Pakistan always fought for their 'national' cause, and, whenever they got an opportunity, they tried to prove their mettle on the cricket field, thereby asserting their 'national' identity. However, Bengalis in general became disgruntled over such neglect and injustices on the sports field.[73] Whenever a match between a West Pakistan team and an East Pakistan side took place, regional sentiments and wrath came to be aroused among the Bengalis of East Pakistan. Incidentally, when the Pakistan national team was playing a cricket match against the Commonwealth XI at the Dhaka Stadium on 1 March 1971, the news of President Yahya Khan's notorious decision to postpone the National Assembly was aired on radio around 1 P.M., leading to widespread dejection among Bengali spectators who protested against the decision vehemently by stopping the game immediately and chasing the Pakistani cricketers.[74]

Rise of Bangladesh as a Cricketing Nation

Bangladeshi passion for football as the most popular mass spectator sport gave way to the state's raising status as a cricketing nation from the end of the 1990s. While cricket progressed slowly as a popular game in independent Bangladesh since the 1970s, it was only at the turn of the century that the people and the government of Bangladesh came to appreciate the sport's potential as a socially viable politico-cultural tool to assert national identity in South Asia as also to prop up the process of nation-building. This fundamental transformation in the Bangladeshi approach to sport can be meaningfully understood in terms of the state's appropriation of cricket as a political instrument and economic means in an age when the country has also to cope with the challenges posed by globalization and its attendant ramifications such as economic liberalization, commercialism, mediatization and professionalism.

As already noted, cricket had always been popular in colonial Bangladesh—both in British eastern Bengal and in East Pakistan. However, despite the popularity it enjoyed, the game had to be reorganized after liberation. And it took more than two and a half decades for Bangladesh to arrive at a respectable stage of participation at the international level when it qualified for the 1999 World Cup finals by winning the ICC Trophy in 1997. While Bangladesh slowly made desired progress in cricket in terms of performance and organization in the first two and a half decades of Independence,[75] its cricket culture tended to remain 'colonized'. In the context of their nation's marginal presence and poor performance at the international level, Bangladeshi public used to support either Pakistan or India and admire Pakistani or Indian cricketers as idols at the international stage. Despite Bangladesh's absence from major international cricketing fixtures, people in large numbers followed passionately the cricketing prowess and rivalry of their two big neighbours, particularly when the latter played against each other on the soil of Bangladesh. 'Flags of the two countries were waved around, words were exchanged at will and the passion seemed no different from what one would expect to see around Mumbai or Lahore or, for that matter, at Sharjah.'[76] Pakistani cricketers, such ase Zaheer Abbas, Imran Khan, Javed Miandad, Wasim Akram and Ramiz Raja, and Indian nationals, such as Sunil Gavaskar, Kapil Dev, Ravi Shastri and Md Azharuddin, became the cynosure of all eyes. The support for Pakistan, however, was overwhelming till the late 1990s predominantly due to the religious factor, although, given India's crucial role in bringing about Bangladesh's freedom, support for India should have been natural. Pakistan team's charisma under Imran Khan's flamboyant personality, the team's high success rate against India, particularly in Sharjah, and their subsequent World Cup victory played a major role in making the majority of the Bangladeshis aggressive Pakistan fans. The situation began to change from the mid-1990s, as Dasgupta rightly points out, 'with the post-1971 generation taking centre stage.' The comeback of the Awami League to political power was also probably an important factor in transforming the mindset of the people:

> Basically, as the value of India to our country was propagated, and that filtered through to the masses, a slight shift could be seen. If today you see a fair number of Indian supporters, that's the reason. For the enlightened classes, the religious factor was overshadowed by the political factor.[77]

The rise of Sachin Tendulkar added more vigour, while the emergence of Sourav Ganguly as an international Bengali cricketing icon and a charismatic Team India under his leadership at the turn of the century made a fundamental impact on the psyche of cricket fandom in Bangladesh. Thus, the success and impact of great performance and stars of her two giant neighbours—India and Pakistan— in international cricket during the 1980s and 1990s made common Bangladeshis supportive of any of these two teams, and worshipper of cricketing icons of these nations. This in turn implied the growth of a 'colonized' cricket fandom in Bangladesh in the absence of the nation's powerful self-image as a cricketing force. Some major breakthrough was needed to change the image of Bangladesh cricket and its cricket culture. Bangladesh's win in the ICC Trophy of 1997 leading to her qualification for the World Cup, her smart performance in their World Cup debut in 1999 and her consequent accession to Test status in 2000 provided a series of such much-needed breakthroughs, bringing about in consequence a fundamental transformation in Bangladesh cricket for ever.

Bangladesh's performance in the sixth ICC Trophy held in Malaysia in 1997 gave her the permit to play in the World Cup for the first time. As Bangladesh reached the final of the tournament, it obtained the passport to the next World Cup. But people back home wanted to see their national team win the Trophy for the first time. As Bangladesh won the final match, thousands of fans thronged on to the ground to congratulate the team.[78] Back home in Bangladesh, the match seemed to have brought the everyday life to a standstill from office to court, while the roads became desolate as all assembled before the television or radio set. Ecstatic celebration followed the victory of Bangladesh, with the fans coming out of homes, offices, schools and colleges, markets and workplaces into roads to express their joyous excitement.[79] Later on the captain of the Bangladesh team, Akram Khan, recounted the true significance of the victory thus:

> Truly speaking, everything seemed to have changed after this victory. I think, not only in cricket, but in general Bangladesh came up to the world with a new identity. We emerged as a cricketing nation. Till date Bangladesh was known as a recurrently flood-hit country. But after the ICC Trophy win, global communities came to recognize Bangladesh as a cricketing nation.[80]

In fact, people all over the country became jubilant as the dream to play in the World Cup became true. At the same time, Bangladesh also became a regular ICC member with the right to play one-day internationals.

Bangladesh's maiden participation in the World Cup was crucial in changing the outlook of Bangladeshi masses towards the game. Till then they used to support either Pakistan or India in the competition for the Cup in the absence of 'their' team. It was time to shout for their 'own' team in 1999. The red-and-green brigade of Bangladesh would make the nation's presence felt and identity asserted in large parts of the world.[81] Bangladesh achieved its first victory in the World Cup against Scotland on 24 May. Then it went on to stage a big upset by defeating one of the tournament favourites, star-studded Pakistan, in their last group league match on 31 May. This win came to be regarded as a historic victory for Bangladesh on more counts than one. The comprehensive victory of Bangladesh over Pakistan in an otherwise unimportant match in Northampton became a watershed in the history of Bangladesh cricket primarily because this victory was considered by many, including the then ICC President Jagmohan Dalmiya, as a clear evidence of Bangladesh's growing stature as a cricket-playing nation and an ample justification for her elevation to Test status. The victory brought in its wake wild jubilation throughout the country. From Teknaf to Tentulia, people came out of their homes in joyous excitement once the last wicket of Pakistan fell. They never saw such a victory since that against the same Pakistan in the Liberation War of 1971.[82]

This victory instilled a lot of confidence into the hearts of an otherwise ailing nation, making the people aware of their potential in different fields of life.[83] The depiction of the event in different newspapers, albeit heterogeneous in nature, reflected the diverse contemporary meanings of the same: political, social, cultural and economic. The victory, it was noted, 'was one of the 120 million Bangladeshis people. Bangladesh has not seen such a victory since the Liberation, bringing tears of joy in the eyes of our people.'[84] For many, including politicians, litterateurs and intellectuals, the victory, comparable to the victory in the War of Liberation, was deemed to be a revenge against the atrocities committed by the Pakistan army against the Bangladeshi masses in 1971. Post 1999, it is said, there was a dramatic transformation in the status of cricket in the country. From office-goers to school students, the game became a fad with everybody in the cities. Cricket was fast challenging football's position as the number one sport in Bangladesh. The game, having shed its aristocratic restrictions, began to prosper at the grassroots of Bangladeshi society. From a beggar to a rich man, its popularity increased overnight.[85] As one writer aptly remarked, 'it has now become difficult to live life without cricket.'[86] In other words, cricket became an inescapable part of Bangladeshi life. The sale of cricket goods too increased by leaps and bounds. In the lanes and streets of Dhaka, young men could be found playing cricket with whatever they could gather.[87] Despite being a poor underdeveloped country, Bangladesh preferred to invest a lot to patronize and play international cricket to project a positive image at the global stage.

In the midst of jubilation and promise, shades of suspicion and controversy crept in. Many across the cricketing fraternity considered the match to be a 'fixed' one. The primary suspects were India and Pakistan, who—it was argued—wanted to appropriate the victory to make Bangladesh eligible as a Test-playing nation and thereby increase the weight of the Asian bloc in the ICC. For Dalmiya, to put it simply, entry of Bangladesh into the ICC meant an extra vote for himself and for the cause of South Asia when it came to any election. This is, however, not the place to investigate whether the match was fixed or not. What is more important is to appreciate that the impact of the victory on Bangladeshi society and culture was momentous and long-term while the implications of the victory for Bangladesh cricket were historic and far-reaching.

Whatever be the strength of allegations by the Western media about Bangladesh's victory against Pakistan, it did the trick for the dream to come true for the nation. Bangladesh acquired the long-cherished

Test status on 26 June 2000 amidst Western opposition and not too sober controversy. However, the accession of Bangladesh to Test status was the much-needed measure to open the floodgates of cricket enthusiasm for ever. Bangladesh again went wild with celebrations, probably a little out of proportion; yet the real cricket fan knew what it meant for the nation's cricket.[88] 'The passionate followers of cricket across the country and strong political support by the Government of Bangladesh' were considered to be the two key domestic factors precipitating Bangladesh's Test status.[89] As the former South African cricketer Ali Bacher noted during his visit to Dhaka, 'the game of cricket has great prospects in a country like Bangladesh where there is cricket on the streets, cricket in the schools, in the villages, a competitive league, and Friday cricket—drawing crowds of spectators who love the game in all its forms.'[90] Bangladesh's entry into Test cricket and its decent show in the first Test against India heralded the birth of a cricketing nation which was always in the making during the preceding three decades. Cricket by this time began to reach every sphere of social life while the new generation had already taken up cricket as their national sport.

As expected, Bangladesh did not have a smooth run in the thorny road of international cricket against the best of the Test-playing nations. In the next four years following her elevation to Test status, Bangladesh's performance in either Tests or one-day internationals did not do any justice to Dalmiya's decision. Barring occasional fighting moments and individual flurries, it suffered a series of miserable defeats in both formats of the game. In fact, from 2002 to 2003, noted Khondaker Mirazur Rahman, editor of banglacricket. com, 'Bangladesh made headlines in cricket media for wrong reasons when losing Test matches inside 3 days by a large margin was a norm.'[91] He recorded the transition of cricket of this distressing period thus:

> On many occasions, the newly promoted Tigers laid down without even putting up a fight. Unfortunately for Bangladesh, during this period Bangladesh did not manage to win a single match in any format against Test playing nations. After the infamous debacle in 2003 World Cup, Bangladesh cricket team went for a major overhaul. Dav Whatmore, the mentor of Sri Lanka's resurgence in world cricket, was handed the coaching job to lift the sinking Bangladesh cricket. He took the charge in June 2003 and Bangladesh started to make slow but steady progress in both

forms of the game. The improvement was more noticeable in the shorter version compared to the Test matches, but his main success was the ability to inject much needed confidence in the struggling team.[92]

Things, however, began to change from December 2004 when Bangladesh registered a memorable victory over India in its 100th one-day international match. It was followed by the nation's first Test match win at home against Zimbabwe in January 2005 after 34 Test matches. It was also Bangladesh's first Test series victory coupled with a one-day series victory against the same team in that series. The series win against Zimbabwe seemed to prove Dalmiya right, silencing his critics. It became apparent that Bangladesh was coming up on to the world stage with a new generation of cricketers: 'as is always the case with new cricketing nations just about finding their feet in the bigger world, Bangladesh cricket has spawned its share of standout performers; heroes, who have given the nation hope.'[93] Meanwhile, the government granted Mirpur Stadium and the surroundings to the BCB to establish a cricket-dedicated facility which would host international matches, and become the future home of a Bangladesh Cricket Academy. In June 2005, Bangladesh staged a major upset by beating World champions Australia in a NatWest Series one-day international match. The victory made a huge impact upon media representation of Bangladesh cricket in the West.

With the turn of the century, thus, cricket became an integral part of Bangladeshi national culture. Like literature, poetry and music, cricket came to be intertwined with the sense of Bengali/ Bangladeshi nationalism. Thus, the Bangladeshi nation in the new century was emerging through another secular cultural idiom, thereby breeding a new arena of cultural nationalism. The national cricketers were fast becoming the mass icons in Bangladesh at a time when the culture of intolerance among politicians was making the system of democracy virtually unsustainable in the confrontational environment of contemporary politics, 'where corruption, violence, mendacity, slander and incendiary rhetoric pollute the vocabulary of politics.'[94] While talented stars, such as Athar Ali Khan or Raqibul Hasan, gained huge popularity during their playing career, they did not have the opportunity to play Test cricket or too much of one-day cricket, and players such as Aminul Islam,

Habibul Bashar, Muhammad Rafique, Mohammad Ahsraful, Khaled Masud or Khaled Mahmud, who came to represent Bangladesh as a new Test-playing nation, became household names in the country. Interestingly, as Shamya Dasgupta rightly pointed out, 'along with the increasing popularity of the game in Bangladesh, as in India, the better cricketers have assumed the role of heroes, role models and icons.'[95] Mashrafe Mortaza, for example, became a national icon on the eve of the World Cup in 2007. More importantly, as Bangladesh was getting ready for the forthcoming World Cup, the cricket world could already take note of its potential to create major upsets: 'Over the years, Bangladesh's main mission has been to defy the odds and create an impression.... Nowadays, the skeptics and the hardcore critics of Bangladesh cricket think twice before making a comment about the Tigers.'[96]

Post independence, as I have already pointed out, in the absence of their national team at the international level, and given the success and impact of great performance by her two great neighbours—India and Pakistan—particularly during the 1980s and 1990s, common Bangladeshis began to support either of these two teams and worship cricketing icons of these nations. However, the country's rising status as a cricket-playing nation from the late 1990s went hand in hand with the common Bangladeshi's changing approach towards the game. With Bangladesh's smart performance in their World Cup debut in 1999 and her consequent accession to Test status in 2000, the masses of Bangladesh, commonly who used to support either India or Pakistan and admire Indian or Pakistani cricketers as idols at the international stage in the context of their nation's marginal presence and poor performance at that level, began to flex their 'nationalist' muscle by supporting 'their' national team and worshipping their *own* players as icons in the new century. The basis of this national support needed to be complemented by some standout and more consistent performances which Bangladesh targeted to achieve in the 2007 World Cup. The nationalist trend of cricket culture, which became well established after the experience of the 2007 World Cup in the everyday life of Bangladesh, may be said to have completed the process of 'decolonization' of Bangladesh cricket, thereby transforming the game into the marker of its national identity, to which we shall turn our attention now.

Cricket, Everyday Life and the Experience of World Cup 2007

The ICC World Cup 2007 was held at a time when a series of unstable events were rocking the social and political life of Bangladesh, and as a sense of despair, gloom and fear was breeding into the mass psyche as a result of continuing dissension and violence, the ICC Cricket World Cup of March–April 2007 came as a welcome distraction, as a safe refuge and as a social opiate for the masses. When the Bangladeshi populace seemed to become pathologically divided on political lines in their supposed loyalties towards the Bangladesh Nationalist Party, the Awami League or the Islamist groups, including the Jamaat-e-Islami, cricket came to act as new unifier transcending all divisive affiliations. Bangladesh defeated India and Bermuda at the Group stage to qualify for the Super Eight stage of the World Cup. Every moment of success of the Bangladesh cricket team in the 2007 World Cup was celebrated with a novel sense of nationhood and nationalism. All earlier debates about the nomenclature, character or future of nationalism in Bangladesh tended to be redefined in the context of Bangladesh's best ever performance in the World Cup. The new cricketing nationalism seemed to corroborate what Abul Kalam commented in a somewhat different context:

> The debate over Bengali and Bangladeshi nationalism often seems quite unnecessarily divisive, and affects the national image. The ultimate objective in nation-building is and ought to be qualitative improvement in cultural outlook, both behavioural and environmental. Bengalis are known to be proud of their culture, but there is a cohesive content in it beyond the politico-religious divide. The masses seem unaware of any existing divide in their nationhood. Hence there is a need for an enduring cultural consensus involving both the intellectuals and the elites.[97]

The experience of the 2007 World Cup made an all-pervasive impact on the everyday life of Bangladesh. The World Cup constituted a critical juncture in the transformation of cricket from a cultural passion to a nationalist obsession, signalling the decolonization of cricket in Bangladesh. Bangladesh's march into the Super Eight stage of the World Cup may be perceived as 'the moment of departure'[98] in the history of Bangladesh cricket, when a new brand of

Bangladeshi national identity began to assert itself through cricket. The enthusiasm that Bangladesh's qualification to the second round created was unique. One indication of this new trend was the unprecedentedly enthusiastic participation of the masses in the celebration of the achievement. Celebrations across the country knew no bounds.[99] Coincidentally, it was also the nation's Independence Day when Bangladesh created history to enter the next round of the World Cup. Bangladeshis from all walks of life, irrespective of their class, status or creed, joined hands to celebrate the memorable achievement on the day of Independence. Thus, cricket came to provide a unifying umbrella to assemble for all Bangladeshis.[100] The Independence Day of 2007 became special on account of this new unifier, asserting a new national identity of Bangladesh.

In the midst of cricketing nationalism that swelled the hearts of the masses in Bangladesh, voices of caution were also noted. As an unprecedented cricket fever engulfed the entire nation in the wake of Bangladesh's qualification into the Super Eight stage, Md Abdul Halim, a senior professor of Dhaka University, argued, 'we can't compete with the West in other spheres while we can beat them in cricket only. That is precisely the reason behind this mass cricket fever.'[101] Similarly, another professor of the University, Abdul Momin Chaudhury, considered the attempt to reckon cricket as a religion to be an expression of exaggerated emotional outburst of the masses. For him, a blend of media hype, commercialization and political appropriation was key to understanding such heightening status of cricket in everyday life.[102] At the same time, it was argued, the limitless jubilation in the wake of Bangladesh's success should not be complemented by any aggressive reaction in case of defeat. As one reader in a leading Bangladeshi daily commented:

> Aggression is not desirable in our cricket fandom. We don't want to be such a cricket-fad nation who burn the effigy of national cricketers or throw stones at the houses of the cricketers in the wake of a defeat. We don't have too many things for celebration in our country. It is only cricket which brings us moments of joy and glory under the red-and-green umbrella of nationalism at different points of time. Hence our love and goodwill should remain in tact for Bangladesh cricket team for ever. Similarly, these moments of glory be kept alive to make such moments long-lived in the near future.[103]

The experience of the World Cup 2007 showed that Bangladesh set up new standards in its cricket history in the West Indies, while more than 150 million Bangladeshis back home bathed in an unprecedented spate of cricketing nationalism. While Bangladesh's stunningly successful run ended at the Super Eight stage with the singular victory against South Africa, it had already come to be regarded as a strong cricketing nation by other illustrious Test-playing countries. For the first time, Bangladeshis remained indifferent to the unexpected early exit of India and Pakistan from the World Cup as they became concerned with the performance of 'their' country—Bangladesh. The decolonization of Bangladesh cricket was thus complete.

After the World Cup, Bangladesh also performed well in the first 20-20 (T20) World Cup. Meanwhile, Bangladesh cricket went through a spate of change as Australian Jamie Siddons took over as coach from Dav Whatmore. Initially, Jamie failed to keep the victorious momentum going and to lift the spirit of the team. As one writer points out, 'The World Cup success proved to be a false dawn of Bangladesh cricket as the Tigers failed to live up to the expectations and started to lose badly in both forms of the game. ... The bubble of expectations had been rudely burst, fans and media were clamouring for answers.'[104] While the Bangladesh's cricket boat was nearly sinking through 2008, some of its top players left the national team to play for more lucrative yet unsanctioned Indian Cricket League (ICL). This prompted a transformation in the national side, and a young group of players began to change the fate of Bangladesh from the end of 2008 so much so that when the former came back to join the national side in 2009, they found it hard to find their place in the team. In 2009, Bangladesh under the leadership of Mashrafe Mortaza and Shakib Al Hasan inflicted defeats on Zimbabwe and West Indies, followed up by its commendable performance against England in 2010. They also whitewashed New Zealand 4–0 at home in a five-match one-day series, with one match being washed out. More importantly, in Tests, although they could not win a single match, they raised the hope of winning against top quality opponents. A little more maturity and a proper balance in the team in terms of bowling and batting would surely have brought them home in most of these matches. As Khondaker Mirazur Rahman has rightly lamented:

One of the areas where we are still lagging far behind all other Test nations is our inability to take advantage of match situations. It's really baffling to see time and again we are losing matches after gaining some ground and reaching a position of strength. ODIs and Test matches alike, it's the same old story. We will dominate few sessions, few passages of play here and there and eventually throw it all out to succumb to a big defeat. Sometimes it seems that we are not probably good enough to challenge the opposition on a consistent basis, we probably don't believe in our abilities when we are on top, and lack the killer blow.[105]

The remedy he suggested is also worth mentioning: 'Our cricket administrators must look into this and take initiatives to arrange regular psychological sessions with leading sports psychologists and incorporate an experienced professional within our coaching staff settings for our tigers.'[106] And he concluded on an optimistic note on the eve of the 2011 World Cup:

Overall, I must stress that Bangladesh cricket is now in good shape and is ready to take the leap to the next level. Now, the cricket administrators of our country must take the initiative to keep the upward curve going and provide facilities to our boys, and create proper cricket infrastructure for sustainable development. Rest assured, Bangladesh is well on its course to be a top 5 cricket nation within the next decade.[107]

ICC World Cup 2011 and Bangladesh as a Host Nation

Since the World Cup in 2007, Bangladesh matured more as a cricketing nation, and cricket has become its de facto national obsession. While the country has not registered any noticeable progress in sports in general, its performance in international cricket improved much. The impact of this improvement upon the national culture of Bangladesh and consequent changes in her cricket culture are phenomenal. The hosting of the 2011 World Cup provided an opportunity to the nation to showcase both its maturity and potential as a cultural destination as well as a cricketing nation in terms of performance and culture. This section will try to show how Bangladesh rose up to the occasion to assert its identity at the international stage despite the critically uneven impact of the event on its polity, society and economy. The passion with which Bangladeshis now play, watch and read about cricket, to which I was an eyewitness during the 2011 Cricket World Cup, too, points to the game's universal popularity and mediatization in the country. Moreover, the game's rising importance as an emblem of nationalism within the state and as a marker of national identity at the international arena is a point that requires careful consideration. Bangladesh as a host nation of the World Cup has also showed that its citizens have preferred the Indian/Pakistani brand of aggressive fandom to its Sri Lankan counterpart of a mature sense of sportsmanship.

According to Sufia M. Uddin, 'Crucial to the success of nationalism is the construction of a single sustainable national culture that bonds people together in a convincingly imagined community. Traditions are created, intentionally sculpted to promote a particular nationalism.'[108] Invented traditions, argues Eric Hobsbawm, 'are highly relevant to that comparatively recent historical innovation, the "nation", with its associated phenomena: nationalism, the nation-state, national symbols, histories and the rest.'[109] In Bangladesh, as we have already noted, the masses commemorate a number of such traditions represented through certain secular occasions, including the Language Day, Independence Day, Pohela Boishakh and Victory Day, thereby reinforcing and securing the basis of a strong sustainable national culture. In this broader context, the ICC Cricket World Cup of 2011 could be seen as a grand cultural spectacle signifying the assertion of both nationalism and secularism at the international stage. While the standard binary of nationalism in Bangladesh in terms of juxtaposition between secular nationalism based on Bengali identity and religious nationalism based on religious identity is slowly being challenged by a third movement of fundamentalist Islam, the dichotomies and dissensions in Bangladeshi polity and society get submerged under the rubric of one national cultural idiom—cricket.

The country's new-found confidence as the host raised the expectations of the cricket-loving public as well. A nation obsessed with cricket was now expecting their team to perform well in the tournament. Thus Bangladesh as a host nation, which staged both the unveiling of the World Cup and the inauguration of the tournament, showed the potential of cricket as a complementary tool of nation-building and state-building. The very organization of the Cup therefore came to be seen as a political statement by the national government to assert Bangladesh's national identity at the global stage. In other words, the state left no stone unturned to showcase the vast potential of Bangladesh in front of the international public. The beginning of the World Cup coincided with the Language Day celebrations in the country centring around 21 February. This made the occasion a truly grand secular nationalist spectacle which became intertwined with the spirit of nationalism and secularism as expressed through the legacy of the language movement. As Sheikh Saifur Rahman nicely put it, 'Cricket has become a symbol of national integrity and patriotism to us because it is only this game that represents the image of a bright Bangladesh effacing the darker depiction of the country.'[110] As a co-host of the World Cup, Bangladesh had a wonderful opportunity to demonstrate that it could match any country when it came to hospitality and friendly warmth. One editorial on the day following the inauguration wrote, 'We hope the guests will like this lush green delta that has for centuries been known as an abode of peace-loving people. Let the World Cup further brighten our image. Let cricket promote friendship and understanding among the participating countries.'[111]

The cricket fever that gripped Bangladesh in the wake of the World Cup was incredible and amazing. Unlike on earlier occasions, the 2011 World Cup began with the Bangladeshi people being imbued with high hopes about the performance of their national team. In course of the last few years, the so-called minnow's sense of inferiority gave way to a sense of pride and confidence in 'our' players' ability to deliver for the country. People from all walks of life, irrespective of age, gender, class or creed, were expecting a smooth progress of their national team to the quarter final, a possible semi-final berth and not-too-impossible appearance in the final. As noted by a cricket correspondent,

The cricket craze can be attributed to the recent successes of the Tigers. They are no longer the minnows of international cricket, rather giant killers who are now becoming giants themselves. It is not surprising that the local fans are looking forward to a berth for the Tigers in the quarter finals at the least.[112]

The World Cup also became the greatest occasion for the Bangladeshis to show their prowess as cricket fanatics. In the course of only three decades, cricket, once regarded as a distant second to football in terms of popularity, became a national obsession. It has the ability to arouse passion, stir emotion and evoke debate; in other words, it thrives on spontaneity. As Golam Sarwar, editor of *Samakal*, argued:

> Tension and anomalies of politics are increasing our anxiety day by day. Can we not be able to sidetrack this daily conflict-generating and self-serving politics to concentrate on, and chime with, the spirit of cricket? Cricket would surely heal our everyday forms of desperation and frustration. Let us forget the toils of daily life and join the sea of joy of World Cup cricket.[113]

Hence, as the tournament would get under way, Bangladeshi people were expected to impress the cricketing world with their unmatched passion and fandom:

> Cricket, or to be precise our national team, now is a beautiful baby that everybody cares for, caresses, whose every step is followed with affection. This World Cup provides an ideal platform for Bangladesh to showcase their unbridled passion and love for the game. And as a hospitable nation that hardly needs an occasion to celebrate, we invite the cricket world to come and join the festivity. We can proudly claim we are cricket fanatics.[114]

All of Bangladesh's group league matches saw the same kind of excitement and emotions on the part of the Bangladeshi fans, although the nation could not reach the quarter-finals despite raising a lot of hope after beating England on 11 March. While Bangladesh's hard-earned victory against Ireland, England and the Netherlands brought unbounded joy, its meek surrender against the West Indies and South Africa generated widespread frustration and dejection.

Thus, with the 2011 World Cup, cricket craze has become an integral part of everyday life of the nation. According to Muntassir Mamoon, this craze would continue in the long run as cricket has become a long-term factor in public life in every nook and corner of the country. For him, in a poverty-stricken hopeless state of affairs, common Bangladeshis look forward to escape from their daily ailments in life and find solace in the success of cricket.[115] While there were many voices before and during the Cup to create the awareness among the cricket-crazy Bangladeshis about the importance of the spirit of sportsmanship, urging the acceptance of success and failure in the same spirit,[116] Bangladeshi fans tended to become prey to the 'Indian syndrome' of over-the-top behaviour. Thus, Bangladesh's progress as a cricketing nation, which has been phenomenal in the last one decade or so, implies its raising status not only in the realm of cricketing prowess or performance but more so in terms of cricket culture and fandom. The transition of cricket spectatorship and fan-fare which began in 2007 reached the culmination in 2011. Going beyond any cricketing assessment of Bangladesh's failure to deliver the expected, it may be argued, the sense of frustration lying beneath the apparent appreciation and recognition of the game as a national bond has begun to come out on the surface with the maturity of Bangladesh as a cricketing nation. The more it would become mature and stronger as a cricketing power, the greater would be the intensity of its fandom, which seems to have chosen the Indian and Pakistani brand of aggressive cricket culture rather than the Sri Lankan variety characterized by a mature sense of proportion.

Conclusion

Bangladeshi society is often shown to be divided between the secu-larists on the one hand and the religious Right and fundamentalists on the other, leading to what one scholar has called 'competing imag-inings of nationhood.'[117] Accordingly, she sees 'in an examination of invented traditions, commemorations, interpretations of particular events, and the intentionality behind the commemoration of a spe-cific combination of events' 'the struggle between religious national-ists and secularists.'[118] A further challenge to this apparent binary of nationhood comes from the marginalized voices of the 'non-Bengali' Bangladeshis, who represent another competing vision of cultural pluralism, urging the state to recognize their identities and expres-sions.[119] However, despite this so-called 'fragility of nationalism', strengthening the fact that 'a community can be imagined in a number of ways by the very nature of being imagined,'[120] such very ways can contradictorily reinforce the homogeneity of nationalism. In twenty-first-century Bangladesh, particularly in the aftermath of the hosting of the ICC World Cup in 2011, cricket has asserted its status as one such way of imagining a secular homogeneous nationalist identity. It also challenges the notion that the multiple imaginings of the nation in Bangladesh are 'constrained by the dominant cultures within which they are created and communicated; one is the universal (Islam), and the other is the local (Bengal).'[121] Cricket as a nationalist obsession transcends everything in Bangladesh, binding all in one knot from a rickshaw-puller to the prime minister, from a fundamentalist mullah to a westernized IT professional, from a poor farmer's wife to a high society lady or from a Hindu priest to a disgruntled Chakma. More importantly, cricket educates the Bangladeshi youth about national-ist ideology and instils in them a deep emotional attachment towards the nation thus imagined. Performing well or not, nationalism around cricket is not fragile as the other 'invented traditions' are argued to be, since it cuts across affiliations of race, religion, community or ethnicity. The religious fundamentalists and their lay followers, who do not agree with the idea of nationalist ideology, too, seem to have succumbed to the all-pervasive wave of cricketing nationalism in the wake of the World Cup. The impact of globalization and trans-national bonds makes this cricketing nationalism more stable and viable. Cricket, thus, redefines and rekindles Bangladeshi national-ism. Beyond the political rhetoric of struggle over the question of religious versus ethno-linguistic identity, cricket now provides a space where Bangladesh as a 'homogeneous' nation makes its pres-ence felt globally.

Notes and References

1. It is known from an English weekly that a match between Dhaka Station and Her Majesty's Fifty-fourth Regiment on 20 January 1958. While the Dhaka Station team comprised civil English officials, the regimental side consisted of English soldiers.
2. Muntassir Mamoon, 'Dhakay Cricketer Suru' (The Beginnings of Cricket in Dhaka), in Siddhartha Ghosh, ed. *Cricket Elo Banglay* (Cricket Comes to Bengal) (Kolkata: Subarnarekha, 2002), p. 72.
3. Quoted in ibid.
4. Ibid., pp. 72–73.
5. Winning the toss, the Europeans decided to bat first and put up a decent score of 130. The Native, in reply, surrendered meekly, scoring only 69 runs. Ibid.

6. Quoted in Mamoon, 'Dhakay Cricketer Suru', p. 73.
7. Ibid.
8. Ibid.
9. Ibid.
10. Ibid.
11. Richard Holt, *Sport and the British: A Modern History* (Oxford: Oxford University Press, 1989), p. 208.
12. Quoted in J.A. Mangan, *The Games Ethic and Imperialism: Aspects of the Diffusion of an Ideal* (London: Frank Cass, 1998), pp. 35–36.
13. *Dhaka Prakash*, 1883, quoted in Mamoon, 'Dhakay Cricketer Suru', p. 74.
14. Ibid.
15. The Dacca College team had Principal Booth, Prof. Tapper and Saradaranjan Ray in their ranks, while the Presidency had only Prof. Rowe with the team. For details, see Mamoon, 'Dhakay Cricketer Suru', p. 74.
16. Ibid.
17. Saradaranjan was the elder brother of famous Bengali writer Upendrakishore Ray.
18. Prasadranjan Ray, 'Bengalis and Sahibs: An Early History of Bengal Cricket', in *The Elite: Journal of the Calcutta Club* (Calcutta: Calcutta Club Ltd, 2002), pp. 2–3, quoted in Boria Majumdar, *Twenty-Two Yards to Freedom: A Social History of Indian Cricket* (New Delhi: Penguin/Viking, 2004), p. 166, fn.
19. *Dhaka Prakash*, 1891, referred to in Mamoon, 'Dhakay Cricketer Suru', p. 75.
20. Basanta Kumar was a son of the zamindari family of Bikrampur.
21. *Sakha*, February 1891, p. 24; *Sandesh*, November 1925, p. 292, referred to in Majumdar, *Twenty-Two Yards to Freedom*, p. 155, fn.
22. Mamoon, 'Dhakay Cricketer Suru', p. 75.
23. Ibid.
24. Ibid.
25. *Bengal Times*, quoted in ibid.
26. *Dhaka Prakash*, n.d., quoted in Mamoon, 'Dhakay Cricketer Suru', p. 77.
27. *Sakha*, 1890, p. 24, referred to in Majumdar, *Twenty-Two Yards to Freedom*, p. 155, fn.
28. *Sakha*, February 1890, quoted in Boria Majumdar, 'Satyai Oitihasik' (Truly Historic), *Ananda Bazar Patrika*, 8 November 2000.
29. The first inter-school cricket tournament in the country, the Harrison Shield, began in Calcutta in 1887.
30. Majumdar, *Twenty-Two Yards to Freedom*, pp. 165–166.
31. See Sarifuddin Ahmad, *Dhaka: Itihas O Nagar Jiban* (Dhaka: History and Civic Life) (Dhaka: Academic Press and Publishers Limited, 2001), pp. 196–256.
32. These measures included construction of new roads, improved conservancy, filtered water supply and health care services.
33. Majumdar, *Twenty-Two Yards to Freedom*, p. 157.
34. Ibid., p. 158.
35. Ibid., p. 135.
36. Charuchandra Mitra, 'Smarane' [Obituary], *Manasi o Marmabani*, Vol. 18.1, No. 6 (1926) (hereafter *Manasi o Marmabani*).
37. Ibid.
38. Hemendra Kumar Ray, 'Swargiya Maharaj' (Late Maharaj), *Manasi o Marmabani*, p. 552.
39. Ramakanta Bhattacharya, 'Jagadindra Jiban Panji' (The Life Record of Jagadindranath), *Manasi o Marmabani*, p. 526.

40. The list of native cricketers who played for the Natore side from 1901 to 1914 included Baloo, Vithal, Sibram Semper, Gazdar, Salamuddin Adi, Rezzak and Ganpat. Bhattacharya, 'Jagadindra Jiban Panji', p. 527.

41. Mitra, 'Smarane', pp. 579–580.

42. Mani Das and Kaladhan Mukhopadhyay were the two prime examples. For details, see Mitra, 'Smarane', p. 580. He also brought up a young boy, Srish Ray, son of a clerk at the Natore court, after being convinced of the latter's cricketing talent and potential. Unfortunately, the boy fell ill and, despite the Maharaja's best efforts, died shortly. For details on this incident, see Ramakanta Bhattacharya, 'Maharaja Jagadindranath', *Manasi o Marmabani*, p. 563.

43. At the instance of Surendranath, Jagadindranath became the president of the Natore Political Association in 1886 at the age of 18. He joined the Bangiya Byabasthapak Sabha as a representative of the Rajshahi Municipality in 1894. He was at the helm of the anti-Partition movement of 1905 from its very beginning, and presided over the famous Town Hall protest conference. Bhattacharya, 'Jagadindra Jiban Panji', pp. 526–527.

44. Ray, 'Swargiya Maharaj', pp. 552–553. Translation by Boria Majumdar, *Twenty-Two Yards to Freedom*, p. 34.

45. Ibid., p. 553.

46. For a detailed discussion of his sporting spirit with illuminating examples, see Purnachandra Ray, 'Krirakhetre Jagadindranath' [Jagadindranath in the Field of Sports], *Manasi o Marmabani*, pp. 585–588.

47. Dwijendranath Basu, 'Maharaj Jagadindranath', *Manasi o Marmabani*, p. 638.

48. Ibid., pp. 637–638.

49. Ibid., p. 637. For an elaborate discussion on the historical significance of this victory, see Kausik Bandyopadhyay, '1911 in Retrospect: A Revisionist Perspective on a Famous Indian Sporting Victory', *International Journal of the History of Sport*, Vol. 21, Nos. 3–4 (2004).

50. Majumdar, *Twenty-Two Yards to Freedom*, p. 135.

51. Ibid., p. 170.

52. Jayanta Kumar Ray, *Democracy and Nationalism on Trial: A Study of East Pakistan* (Simla: Indian Institute of Advanced Study, 1968), p. 1. A brief but useful discussion of the nature of West Pakistani hegemony over East Pakistan during 1947–1971 and the consequent emergence of Bangladesh is available in Md. Mahbubur Rahman, *Bangladesher Itihas: 1947–71* [History of Bangladesh: 1947–71] (Dhaka: Somoy, 1999).

53. Ibid., p. i.

54. Ibid.

55. See, for example, Kamal Hossain, *Muktijuddho Keno Onibarjo Chilo?* (Why the Liberation War Was Inevitable?) (Dhaka: Maola Brothers, 1998); Rounaq Jahan, *Pakistan: Failure in National Integration* (Dhaka: The University Press Limited, 1994); Muntassir Mamoon and Jayanta Kumar Ray, *Proshashoner Andarmahal: Bangladesh* (Inside the Administration: Bangladesh) (Dhaka: Pallab Publishers, 1988); Md. Mahbubur Rahman, *Bangladesher Itihas: 1947–71* (History of Bangladesh: 1947–71) (Dhaka: Somoy, 1999); Muhammad Jamir Uddin Sarkar, *Pakistane Gonotantrer Biparjay ebong Bangladesher Abhyudoy* (Crisis of Democracy in Pakistan and the Emergence of Bangladesh) (Dhaka: Catharsis, 2008); Hasan Zaheer, *The Separation of East Pakistan: The Rise and Realization of Bengali*

Muslim Nationalism (Dhaka: The University Press Limited, 2001); Shaikh Maqsood Ali, *From East Bengal to Bangladesh: Dynamics and Perspectives* (Dhaka: The University Press Ltd, 2009).

56. D.R. Mankekar, *Pak Colonialism in East Bengal* (Bombay: Somaiya Publications, 1971), p. 22.
57. Almost a spurt of vernacular writings deals with this theme of West Pakistani discrimination, East Pakistan's resistance and the road to the liberation of Bangladesh. See, for example, Muhammad Iftekharul Islam Khan, *Basanta Bhushito Bangladesh Rashtrer Abhyudoy* (Emergence of the State of Bangladesh adorned with spring) (Dhaka: Ayon Prokashon, 2008); and Rehman Sobhan, *Bangladesher Abhyudoy: Ekjon Pratyakkhadarshir Bhasya* (Emergence of Bangladesh: An Eyewitness Account) (Dhaka: Maola Brothers, 1998).
58. Muntassir Mamoon and Jayanta Kumar Ray, *Civil Society in Bangladesh: Resilience and Retreat* (Dhaka: Subarna, 1998), p. 11.
59. Majumdar, *Twenty-Two Yards to Freedom*, p. 134, fn.
60. Ibid. Majumdar refers to his interviews with Qamruzzaman (Dhaka Press Club, 7 September 2001) and Prof. Muntassir Mamoon (Dhaka, 5 September 2001) to substantiate his view. Both are said to have blamed West Pakistani ruling circles for their country's decline in cricket.
61. Boria Majumdar, 'Oitihya Chhilo, Tabu Parini: Amader Byabosabuddhi Nei' (We had tradition, yet we failed: We lack commercial sense), *Ananda Bazar Patrika*, 9 November 2000.
62. During my visit to Bangladesh in 2007 and 2008, I spoke to a number of scholars and journalists on the viability of this argument. Almost all of them agreed that the West Pakistani government pursued a policy of discrimination in the field of sports as well. Discussions with Muntassir Mamoon, Professor of History, Dhaka University (Dhaka: 16 and 28 March 2007); Ahmed Kabir, Professor of Bengali, Dhaka University (Dhaka: 17 March 2007); Abdul Momin Chaudhury, Professor of History, Dhaka University (Dhaka: 28 March 2007); Md. Abdul Halim, Professor of International Relations, Dhaka University (Dhaka: 28 March 2007); Ajoy Barua, veteran sports journalist, *Dainik Sambad* (Dhaka: 29 March 2007).
63. Hasan Babli, *Antarjatik Crickete Bangladesh* (Bangladesh in International Cricket) (Dhaka: Khelar Bhuvan, 1994), p. ix.
64. Shamya Dasgupta, 'Bangladesh Cricket: Scoring on Passion, but Little Else …', *Sport in Society*, Vol. 10, No. 1 (January 2007), p. 163.
65. Babli, *Antarjatik Crickete Bangladesh*, p. ix.
66. These matches included the drawn Test between Pakistan and New Zealand in November 1955, Pakistan's first win in the venue against West Indies in March 1959 and her only loss to Australia in November 1959, three drawn Tests against England in 1961–1962 and 1968–1969 and against New Zealand in 1969–1970.
67. Dasgupta, 'Bangladesh Cricket', p. 164.
68. Ibid.
69. Babli, *Antarjatik Crickete Bangladesh*, p. ix; translation by the author. For similar comments, see Ripan Biswas, *Moulik Cricket* (Fundamental Cricket) (Dhaka: Srijani, 2011), p. 19.
70. Ibid., p. xi.
71. Ibid.
72. Mahmood, 'Kridabid der Birochito Bhumika', p. 146.

73. Brojen Das, a talented young swimmer, facing such discrimination, decided to prove his mettle differently and crossed the English Channel in 1959, creating a huge stir all over the subcontinent.

74. Ibid. Also see Jahanara Imam, *Ekattorer Dinguli* [The Days of 1971], (Dhaka: Sandhani, 1986), p. 1.

75. For an interesting personalized account of Bangladesh's progress in cricket, see Yousuf Rezaur Rahman, *Sentimental Journey: It's More Than Just a Game* (New York: Yousuf & Parveen, 2002). Another useful work in the same genre is: Omar Khaled Rumi, *Orthat* (That is) (Dhaka: Omar Khaled Rumi, 1990). For an academic discussion on the subject, see Kausik Bandyopadhyay, *Bangladesh Playing: Sport, Culture, Nation* (Dhaka: ICBS/Subarna, 2012), Chapter 4.

76. Dasgupta, 'Bangladesh Cricket', p. 175.

77. Jahangir Chowdhury's comment, cited in ibid.

78. Dilu Khandakar, 'Flashback Kuala Lumpur', *Ananda Alo*, Vol. 1, No. 25 (1 April 2006), p. 10.

79. Rejanur Rahman, 'Cricketer Ananda, Cricketer Alo' (Joy of cricket, light of cricket), *Ananda Alo*, Vol. 1, No. 25 (1 April 2006), p. 5.

80. Akram Khan, 'Cricket Jati Hoye Uthlam' (We became a cricketing nation), *Samakal*, ICC World Cup special issue, 2011, p. 32; Author's translation.

81. Dulal Mahmud, 'Durer Biswacup, Kachher Biswacup' (World Cup afar, World Cup nearer), *Saptahik Bichitra*, 30 April 1999, in Dulal Mahmud, *Stadium Er Sei Addata Aaj Aar Nei* (Adda at the stadium no longer exists) (Dhaka: Akhhorbritta, 2005), pp. 26–27.

82. *The Daily Janakantha*, 1 June 1999, p. 1.

83. Dulal Mahmud, 'Cricket Safari', in Mahmud, *Krirajagat*, 16 February 2003, in *Stadium Er Sei Addata Aaj Aar Nei*, p. 49.

84. *The Daily Janakantha*, 1 June 1999, p. 1.

85. Ibid., p. 15.

86. Dulal Mahmud, 'Crickete Je Proshner Uttar Sahaje Mele Na' (The question which is difficult to answer in cricket), in Mahmud, *Stadium Er Sei Addata Aaj Aar Nei*, p. 33.

87. Ibid., p. 24.

88. Omar Kureishi, 'Bangladesh move to the centre-stage', *The Dawn*, 5 July 2000, available at www.banglacricket.com, accessed on 20 September 2011.

89. Khondaker Mirazur Rahman, '10 Years of Test Status: Where Do We Stand Now?', *A Journey ... Test Cricket: 10 Years of Bangladesh*. Dhaka: Bangladesh Cricket Board, 2011, p. 7.

90. Cited in 'The History of Bangladesh Cricket', available at www.banglacricket.com, accessed on 25 September 2011.

91. Rahman, '10 Years of Test Status', p. 7.

92. Ibid.

93. Ibid., p. 177.

94. Zarina Rahman Khan, 'Decentralized Governance: Trials and Triumphs', in Rounaq Jahan, ed. *Bangladesh: Promise and Performance* (Dhaka: UPL, 2000), p. 344.

95. Dasgupta, 'Bangladesh Cricket', p. 179.

96. Rabeed Imam, 'Tigers "Mission Respect"', *Australia Tour of Bangladesh 2006 Souvenir* (Dhaka, 2006), p. 34.

97. Abul Kalam, 'National Self-Image, Policy and Leadership', in Abul Kalam, ed. *Bangladesh in the New Millennium: A University of Dhaka Study* (Dhaka: UPL, 2004), p. 104.

98. I have taken this term from Partha Chatterjee's celebrated work *Nationalist Thought and the Colonial World: A Derivative Discourse?* (London: Zed Books, 1986), Chapter 3, pp. 54–84. Chatterjee, however, used the term in an entirely different context.

99. For a detailed description of the celebration in the wake of Bangladesh's march to the Super Eight, see *Samakal*, 27 March 2007, pp. 1–2.

100. *Naya Diganta*, 27 March 2007, p. 2.

101. Interaction with Md. Abdul Halim, professor of International Relations, Dhaka University, Dhaka, 28 March 2007.

102. Interaction with Abdul Momin Chaudhury, professor of History, Dhaka University, Dhaka, 28 March 2007. He referred to the Sri Lankan example, which shows the mature ways of handling the pressure of international cricket in terms of victory or defeat.

103. Letter of M.R. Munna (Rangpur) at Reader's column, *Prothom Alo*, 28 March 2007, p. 8; Author's translation.

104. Rahman, '10 Years of Test Status', pp. 7–8.

105. Ibid., p. 9.

106. Ibid.

107. Ibid.

108. Sufia M. Uddin, *Constructing Bangladesh* (Chapel Hill: University of North Carolina Press, 2006), p. 122.

109. Eric Hobsbawm and Terence Ranger, eds. *The Invention of Tradition* (Cambridge: Cambridge University Press, 1983), p. 13.

110. Rahman, 'Cricket: Japone, Udjapone', p. 73; author's translation.

111. *Daily Sun*, 18 February 2011, p. 4.

112. Ibid.

113. Golam Sarwar, 'Cricket er Janye Bhalobasa' (Love for cricket), *Samakal Chakka*, ICC World Cup special issue, 2011, p. 3; Author's translation.

114. Al-Amin, 'The passion is here to stay', *Star Roar: World Cup Special*, February 2011, p. 15.

115. Interview with Muntassir Mamoon, Dhaka: 19 February 2011.

116. Dibakar Acharya, 'Jitte Sikhi, Harte Sikhi' (Let's learn to win and to be beaten), *Shaptahik Kagoj*, Vol. 3, No. 6 (20 February 2011), p. 37. The author described the aggressive reaction after defeat in a match as typically 'Indian' and urged the Bangladeshis not to emulate this culture, which only affects the reputation of the nation.

117. Uddin, *Constructing Bangladesh*, p. 142.

118. Ibid., p. 145.

119. For details on this, see Willem van Schendel, 'Bengalis, Bangladeshis and Others: Chakma Visions of a Pluralist Bangladesh', in Rounaq Jahan, ed. *Bangladesh: Promise and Performance* (Dhaka: UPL, 2000).

120. For details on this, see Partha Chatterjee, *The Nation and Its Fragments: Colonial and Postcolonial Histories* (Princeton: Prince University Press, 1993).

121. Uddin, *Constructing Bangladesh*, p. 151.

7

Cricket under Siege: Terrorism, Security and the Future of Cricket in Pakistan

Introduction

Cricket has become one of the most abiding national passions in South Asia in the last few decades. It has truly become an emblem of national pride as well as a unifying force in an otherwise politically turbulent, strategically sensitive and socio-ethnically divided region. Pakistani cricket is an integral part of the subcontinental cricket culture and economy now being led by India at the international level. However, as this chapter will argue, there is one non-cricketing factor which is going to decide the fate of Pakistan as a cricketing nation in the twenty-first century: the question of terrorism and human security.[1] Pakistan's image as a stable political entity began to face unpleasant questions relating to its alleged links with acts of global terrorism since the destruction of the World Trade Center on 11 September 2001. Post 9/11 incident, most cricket-playing countries sans South Asian nations refused to play in Pakistan for security reasons. As a result, cricket began to suffer not only as a game but also as commerce. The PCB had to incur huge losses due to a series of cancellation of visiting teams' tours, which included Australia, New Zealand, South Africa and the West Indies. As cricket exchanges between Pakistan and other South Asian nations depend mainly on bilateral relations based on the reciprocity of political goodwill on both sides, the latter continued to play in Pakistan to allay security fears embedded in the Western mind. However, in the aftermath of the terrorist attacks in Mumbai (26 November 2008), the process of confidence building between India and Pakistan received a major blow, as evidences clearly pointed to Pakistan's strong hands in the plot of the terror. Finally, the terrorist attack on the Sri Lankan cricketers and officials at the Gaddafi Stadium, Lahore, on 3 March 2009, may be regarded as the last nail in the coffin of Pakistan as a host cricketing nation. This might, in the long run, as I suggest, prove to be a blow to the cricketing solidarity of South Asia as well. With the decision of the ICC in April 2009 to cancel the World Cup matches in Pakistan, tension became manifest in the organization of the 2011 ICC World Cup to be hosted jointly by India, Pakistan, Sri Lanka and Bangladesh. More importantly, as this chapter forcefully argues, from the point of view of Pakistan, given Pakistan's lack of credibility in the avowed objective of containing terrorism, and the strong presence and growing influence of the Taliban in the country, security threats emanating from continuous acts of terror in the country, coupled with ever-rising social instability, religious fundamentalism and political tension, not to speak economic and environmental security threats, pose serious concerns for the nation in any efforts to recreate its image as peaceful democratic society where cricket could be pursued without fear. It is, therefore, important to understand that unless Pakistan could show real urge to mitigate the evil of terrorism and share the concerns of the neighbours, the role of sport as a tool of confidence building and bridge of peace in South Asia will continue to remain illusory in nature.

Cricket in Contemporary South Asia: Situating Pakistan and Her Cricket

Shaharyar Khan argued a few years back:

> In India and Pakistan—as indeed all over South Asia—cricket has assumed an all-consuming hold on people from all walk of life. From Quetta camel-cart driver to the Chennai professor, from the Lahore shopkeeper to the Bombay housewife, from the Dhaka student to the Colombo hotel waiter, cricket has become an overwhelming passion, its huge energy like incandescent lava flowing down a live volcano, ready to be channelled towards peace and harmony.[2]

Such pre-eminence of cricket in South Asian life has also led to its construction and interpretation in terms of political transition, social tension, economic transformation, diplomatic relations or cultural development. Cricket has been central to the social and political life of Pakistan since its emergence as an independent state. To quote Shaharyar Khan again, 'In Pakistan it (cricket) is the strongest unifying force amongst its people, young and old, rich or poor, man or woman, Shia or Sunni, Pathan or Sindhi. It brings a unity in peacetime only achieved in times of war.'[3] Cricket has provided 'one of the few sources of collective joy in a society that has had its fair share of woes.'[4] It is the de facto national game in Pakistan, if not her only 'secular' obsession in the last few decades. As B.K. Bangash aptly makes the point:

> Scholars who have made it their life's work to study Pakistan often conclude that the only thing that unites this discordant nation of tribes, ethnicities, cultures and languages is religion. In 1947 the nation was born as an Islamic state, a refuge for a persecuted minority fleeing the Hindu dominance of India, newly liberated from colonial rule. Yet 60-odd years later, even as contraband Johnny Walker is liberally poured into the glasses of those who can afford it, Shari'a, or Islamic law, is declared in a district not far from the capital as a concession to the Taliban. Islam no longer unites; it divides. In its place rises a new unifier: cricket.[5]

The passion with which Pakistani cricketers play the game, the emotion with which Pakistani masses watch their national team play, the admiration with which they worship their cricketing icons and the cricketing culture that has grown around this nationalist obsession are fascinating enough to invite comparison with those of India or Sri Lanka. As Javed Miandad nicely sums up in his autobiography:

> If ever I was struggling out in the middle, pushing for victory or staving off defeat, the sight of the Pakistan flag fluttering defiantly would warm my heart and keep me going. Whenever we played in Sharjah, I used to run laps around the ground before the start of a match.... The atmosphere was full of passion for Pakistan, and it would uplift us. It is this passion, this purely Pakistani passion, which has fuelled my cricket and has motivated me to do whatever I have been able to do.[6]

The story of Pakistani cricket offers an interesting repertoire of stunning performances, including exemplary success and appalling defeat, mass worshipping of its cricketing icons, public wrath against the national cricketers and politicization of cricket for diplomatic purposes.[7] With cricket's intensive professionalization, commercialization and mediatization since the 1990s, Pakistani cricket began to face the challenge of adaptation towards a changing order of the global game. More importantly, in twenty-first-century Pakistan, where true democracy begs place under the sun and where dissent is more powerful than cohesion, cricket provides a cultural space where all the dissents can converge for a Pakistani feat. Players from provincial cities and different ethnic–religious backgrounds are now well represented in the national squad. More importantly, cricket is no longer the preserve of the elite or the educated in Pakistan, 'it is the all-consuming passion of the common man, the worker, the clerk, the bus-driver, the student, the rag merchant, even the housewife.'[8] It has swept all other sports aside to become the number one sport of the country. Ace Pakistani cricketers are definitely considered as national heroes and respected for their feats. Cricketers receive official recognition: every cricket stadium has stands named after renowned cricketers, their pictures prominently displayed in cricket offices, dressing rooms and conference halls. While cricket has already served as a metaphor for the assertion of Pakistani identity, expression of cultural nationalism or feeling of emotional commonality,[9] it must emerge as a marker of the nation's international status as well as an instrument for flexing its economic muscle in the new century.

In the development of modern-day cricket, Pakistan's contributions are worthy of note on many counts. As Hanif Mohammad, a legendary Pakistan cricketer, commented:

> All types of tensions have been evident in Pakistani cricket. There have been factional struggles, biases and prejudices. But these are part of the human drama of our society. What is important, and rises above this all, is our record of achievements. It is an exceptional record over the past fifty years, specially given the circumstances and the difficulties. I was there at the start of our cricketing journey, and as I look back I see it as a record to be proud of it. It is important to reflect on the explanations. All the conflicts and tensions are a secondary issue; they add spice to the story, but first we have to see what the main ingredients were.[10]

Pakistan contributed to substantial changes in the international management of the game since the 1970s. In the process of inventive

and entrepreneurial changes that led to cricket's true professionalization in the 1980s, Pakistan played a central role. It joined hands with
India to democratize the process of decision-making in the international management of the game. It was this joint effort that helped
bring the organization of the World Cup to South Asia for the first
time in 1987: the true beginning of cricket's globalization across the
world and the beginning of the shift of the centre of cricket's economic and administrative gravity from the West to the East.

As already noted, like in India, cricket unites Pakistan: it is the
common thread that binds Swat to Sindh, Lahore to Larkana and
Quetta. Kids and youth play the game everywhere, in the fields of
Punjab and the rugged mountains of Baluchistan and the North-West
Frontier Province (NWFP). Cricket, earlier centred mostly in Lahore
and Karachi, has now stretched to Burewala, Multan, Sialkot, Swat,
Gilgit, Torkham and other relatively inaccessible areas. Cricketers
are now mostly drawn from across the country on the basis of merit
despite occasional instances of favouritism and partiality. This representative character of Pakistan cricket cutting across religious,
ethnic or regional affiliations has broken the elitist preserve of the
game, thereby making it open as career option to common Pakistanis.
Similarly, cricket craze has come to engulf the entire nation including all sections of people in Pakistan.[11] However, despite cricket's
immense popularity in Pakistan, it does not yet have the gloss and
glitter cricket in India is associated with. As one cricket commentator has remarked: 'it does not have a developed celebrity culture, nor
the economic clout that industry provides to Indian cricket.'[12] While
Pakistani cricketers are definitely hailed as national icons and celebrated for their sporting feats, their stature is not magnified beyond
limits and they are not viewed as greatest stars. This is probably due
to 'the limited reach of the media, and the fact sport cannot feed on
the financial clout of an expanding economy.'[13] That is why commercial benefits, including personal endorsement opportunities, are still
very limited to cricketers in Pakistan. Yet, playing cricket remains a
serious vocation in Pakistan. In fact, the growing representative character of cricket has definitely heightened the potential of the game as
a career option in the last two decades.

The challenge for Pakistan cricket in the new century is mani-
fold. But the most crucial point is how Pakistan cricket would adapt
to the changing priorities of the global game in the age of cricket's

continuous evolution as a highly commercial force. It requires not only talent on the field but immense professional ability and maturity off the field to channelize the new potentials cricket will thrive upon. However, the way the institutional mess and administrative incoherence produce a series of unpredictable and inexplicable changes in the recent past, stability is the catchword cricketers, administrators and fans in Pakistan should earnestly strive for. Exceptional talent needs to be balanced by professional management of the game by a stable and mature administration. However, as outlined in the introduction, the real threat to Pakistan as a cricketing nation emanates from continuous acts of terrorism and the related question of human security.

The Challenge of Terror and Security in South Asian Cricket[14]: Antecedents[15]

It is the cultural significance of cricket in South Asia which makes the sport a prime target of terrorism. The history of cricket's tryst with terrorism in South Asia goes back to the 1980s, particularly with the rise of Liberation Tigers of Tamil Eelam (LTTE) as a major terrorist outfit in Sri Lanka. On 21 April 1987, a car bomb killed more than 100 people at a bus station. As a result, the ongoing three-Test series between the touring New Zealand and Sri Lanka was cut to one. Five years later, New Zealand cricket team again faced a dilemma as a suicide bomb attack by a Tamil rebel killed four people outside the team hotel on 16 November 1992. Five players and the team's coach returned home on compassionate grounds after the incident. Finally, in 1996, cricket teams from Australia and the West Indies refused to play preliminary World Cup matches in Colombo a week after a huge bomb blast there killed 80 people and injured more than 1200. In July 2001, a New Zealand cricket tour again coincided with a suicide attack by Tamil Tigers, which closed Colombo's international airport. The attack claimed 14 lives, while 12 more got wounded in the pre-dawn attack. However, India and Pakistan together played a solidarity cricket match against Sri Lanka in Colombo to allay fears from the minds of the touring teams about the safety of cricketers in Sri Lanka.[16]

It was, however, the Al-Qaeda air attack at the World Trade Center on 11 September 2001 that changed for ever the security scenario and paradigm in South Asia in general and Pakistan in particular.[17] Since 2001, most of the international cricket tours in Pakistan got cancelled owing to security concerns, and Pakistan had to play its home series at neutral venues, such as Sharjah or Dubai. On 8 May 2002, New Zealand called off its ongoing cricket tour after a car bomb explosion in Karachi in front of the hotel where the visitors were staying, killing 13 people, including the team's physiotherapist and 11 French navy experts. In October same year, Pakistan played a home series against Australia at Sharjah, UAE, after the latter's refusal to tour over security concerns. Since May 2002 incident, Australia and New Zealand never toured the country, while England (2005–2006), West Indies (2006–2007) and South Africa (2007) played only once each in Pakistan. While the prospects of an Australian tour and the organization of the Champions Trophy in 2008 became very bright by the end of 2007, a series of major terrorist incidents upset everything. This fresh spate of terrorism began with the assassination of two-time Prime Minister Benazir Bhutto in a shooting and suicide bombing in Rawalpindi's Liaquat Bagh, killing up to 20 others and injuring many. It was followed by hundreds of killings in resultant internal repercussions and election-related violence, thereby gradually making the future of international cricket fixtures grim. On 11 March 2008, at least 24 people were killed and more than 200 wounded in twin suicide bombings in the eastern Pakistani city of Lahore. One of the attacks ripped apart Federal Investigation Agency building, killing 21, including 16 policemen. The other one hit the posh locality of Model Town, exploding close to Bilawal House, associated with PPP leaders Benazir Bhutto and her husband, Asif Ali Zardari.[18] Immediately, Cricket Australia postponed its forthcoming tour after taking independent security advice. As James Sutherland, the Cricket Australia boss, said: 'We've left no stone unturned in trying to ensure that the tour could proceed as planned, but at the end of the day for us the safety and security of our employees must come first.'[19]

In fact, by the end of July 2008, Australia and New Zealand players were advised not to travel to Pakistan for the Champions Trophy, raising the prospect of a possible boycott of the elite eight-team one-day tournament. New Zealand also cancelled its one-day series in Pakistan. In August 2008, the ICC postponed the Champions Trophy for 13 months after five of the eight teams confirmed they would not send a team due to security concerns. However, Cricket Australia decided to go ahead with an India tour days after a series of bomb blasts in New Delhi on 13 September 2008. In the blast, 20 people were killed and more than 90 injured, which happened a week before the Australian cricketers were due to arrive. Pakistani cricket authorities immediately accused their Australian counterparts of double standards. However, Australia duly appreciated the difference in security situations of the two countries and rightly decided to go ahead with the tour.

Security, Diplomacy and Indo-Pak Cricket in the Twenty-first Century[20]

In Chapter 4 of this book, I have elaborated in detail how cricket acted as a confidence-building measure in India–Pakistan diplomatic relations. It has been argued with much conviction that playing each other on a regular basis would definitely minimize the confrontational tension that usually accompanies rare occasions of cricket matches between India and Pakistan. If the two nations play cricket regularly, as it seemed in the light of reciprocal cricket tours between the two countries during 2004–2007, then perhaps cricket can move from being a metaphor for war to a vehicle of peace. However, it is important to remember that while the relation between Indian and Pakistani cricket boards—BCCI and PCB—was characterized mostly by friendliness and complementarity since the 1980s, despite several serious occasions of rift between the two countries at the political level, this relation too has recently become strained over Pakistan's alleged role in engineering terrorist attacks in India. The Mumbai terrorist attacks on 26 November 2008 may be said to have put an end to the days of goodwill between the two cricket boards. Added to this is the central problem of playing cricket in Pakistan, which the Western countries always pointed their fingers to: concerns of security and safety of players. This concern came to be shared and used by the BCCI as well in the aftermath of Mumbai attack to cancel India's tour of Pakistan. The question that naturally therefore arises: is it possible to pursue international cricket in Pakistan without fear of life any more? The assault on the Sri Lankan cricketers at the Gaddafi Stadium, Lahore, on 3 March 2009 confirmed that the concerns were true.

Given the way Indo-Pakistan cricket relations evolved over the years and particularly in the twenty-first century, it may be argued that cricket can act as a prop to confidence building only if the neighbours share with each other their concerns of national interest and security. Once one side falters or seems to falter in this approach to confidence building, the entire process of peace building receives a blow. In such situations, cricket exchanges between India and Pakistan also come to a halt. This happened in 1999 after the Kargil War and in 2001 after the terrorist attack on Indian Parliament House. It happened again in the aftermath of Mumbai terrorist attacks on 26 November 2008 as substantial evidence of Pakistan's link to this attack was detected. Hence, the Indian government promptly cancelled Indian cricket team's scheduled tour of Pakistan in February 2009. As India's sports minister, M.S. Gill, remarked in calling off the government's permission for the tour, 'You can't have one team coming from Pakistan to kill people in our country and another team going from India to play cricket there.'[21] Therefore, unless policy makers, diplomats and politicians of both countries take sincere and reciprocal steps in resolving the outstanding issues in foreign relations, cricket's viability as confidence-building measure would not be sustained in the long run.

From Mumbai 26/11 to Lahore 3/3: The Question of Human Security and Cricket under Siege

It is well known that when the Mumbai incident took place on 26 November 2008, the English cricket team was touring India. As the militants stormed the Indian financial capital, killing about 170 people in a series of attacks and the gunmen hit high-profile targets, including the Taj Mahal Hotel, where foreign teams normally stay, the England cricket team flied home from India on 28 November on security grounds. Two major sequels followed the attack. First, quite expectedly, India called off their Pakistan cricket tour after the government refused permission due to tension between the nuclear-armed neighbours over the military attack in Mumbai. Interestingly enough, despite BCCI's warnings about security situation in Pakistan, Sri Lanka agreed to step in to tour Pakistan in February–March 2009. Second and more important, despite wider security fears emanating from Mumbai attack, the England and Wales Cricket Board decided in early December to send their cricket team to play the Test series in India.

In fact, the Mumbai attack excited a much-awaited transformation in the paranoiac mindset of the Western governments, cricket boards and media that used to suffer from a climate of prejudice and fear about terrorist actions or suicide attacks. This mindset, according to Michael Roberts, 'is marked by a poverty of analysis, and indulges, and indulges in sweeping generalizations that are inattentive to the limitations of militant organisations, the regional differentiation in their capacities and their selectivity of targets.'[22] As Gary Kristen, coach of the Indian cricket team, remarked in that context, 'There is no way that security can be guaranteed wherever you are in the world. But you can't keep saying no. There are terrorism threats everywhere; even the UK is not immune from them.'[23] Prime Minister Gordon Brown's gentle suggestion to the England and Wales Cricket Board that it should consider a return to India to play their scheduled Test matches on a revamped programme was an indication of the strengthening resolve to refuse to kowtow to the global threat of militant violence.[24] It is also important to note that the paranoiac mindset towards global terror did not apply the same logic to the moment of the 7 July 2005 atrocities in London, when the Australian cricket team drove in to play their Test match at Lord's from 21 July. A former chief of the British special services stated in the aftermath of the Mumbai terror attack, anonymously, that the UK itself would not be prepared to handle the type of attack that Bombay weathered. Yet, this understanding still does not have too many sympathizers in the Western world. As Michael Roberts argues:

> So, in effect, we have one measuring rod for England and another for India. And, of course, there is yet another for Pakistan and Sri Lanka. Both are placed in the lowest rung of the unfamiliar-dangerous and fanatical.

Indeed, Pakistan has become a virtual pariah. It does not generate 70 per-
cent of the cricket world's revenues as India does. It is a Muslim country
and has Taliban sympathizers.... Add to this the image of the 'fanatical
Muslim terrorist', and those brave men of the cricketing paddock quickly
become whining cowards.[25]

This scheme of evaluation of terrorism and security in relation to
cricket has undergone major transformation in the last few years.
As India began to offer unthinkable riches from its 'wealthy vault'
with the unveiling of the Indian Premier League (IPL) extrava-
ganza from April 2008, cricketers from Australia and the West,
earlier averse to visiting South Asian countries in the smallest
prospects of security concern, decided to change their mindset and
approach towards terrorist activities and security concerns in India.
To give one example, the Australian and South African players on
the Rajasthan Royal squad playing in the IPL ultimately decided
to adhere to their contracts and play on in Jaipur and elsewhere
in India after eight serial blasts rocked that city on 13 May 2008,
leaving 63 dead and over 216 injured. To many of us, the England
cricket team's return to play the Test series in December 2008 may
therefore seem to be a continuity of this changed mindset moulded
powerfully by Indian cricket's strong economic clout. But one
should not discount the influence of such considerations as those
embodied in Prime Minister Brown's intervention. In a statement
following the Mumbai attacks, Kevin Pietersen, England's captain,
said: 'We're going to demonstrate in India that we're showing our
support to play Test match cricket. I think it's very important we
go and rub shoulder to shoulder with the Indian people in their time
of need.'[26] The point I want to make is: would the England cricket
authority or Pietersen do the same thing if the attack took place
in Pakistan? The answer is anybody's guess: No. It is now most
important for the cricket-playing nations outside South Asia to
make a decision about who can certainly be relied upon to provide
protection in case of a terrorist attack. And the decision has already
been made in two extremes after the attack on Sri Lankan cricketers
in Lahore on 3 March 2009.

Six Sri Lankan cricketers and their British assistant coach were
wounded and five police officers were killed when a dozen gunmen
attacked their bus as it drove under police escort to a stadium in the

Pakistani city of Lahore. The Test series was immediately cancelled and the cricketers were flown back home. Already in February, the ICC decided to move the Champions Trophy out of Pakistan after many members expressed reservations about touring the country, which became amply justified after the Lahore tragedy. The incident also nullified the hypothesis propagated by influential figures like Imran Khan that cricketers would never be attacked because they were so uniformly popular in Pakistan. As Kumara Sangakkara put things in perspective sometime after the attack:

> We have all had to grow up a bit more and not be so naive to think that sportsmen are somehow immune from the troubles of the world. The Munich Olympics were probably the last time a sports team has been targeted like this. We lived in a bubble thinking we were untouchable. That has gone now. The sense of security has disappeared. These threats are real, and not just confined to one section of society.[27]

One pertinent question that was being asked everywhere after the incident was: why cricket/cricketers became a target of the terrorists? According to Henry Clarke, the attack 'is an attempt to instill widespread terror through an attack the terrorists know will be widely publicised. *In short, an attempt to effectively terrify local Pakistanis by attempting to kill foreign cricketers.*'[28] He further asserts: 'International cricket no longer possible in Pakistan; therefore we should stop accusing foreign teams of discriminating against Pakistan vis-à-vis India. *The question here is of the survival of Pakistan, not of cricket.*'[29] Motives of terrorist organizations are to get maximum exposure for their efforts, sending strong messages to the world. Cricket coverage may be the ideal platform. As David Siddall argues:

> Cricketers are major stars competing on the world stage via mass TV networks to captured audiences in their millions. It is easy to see why terrorists want to share this stage and make it their own.
>
> No cricketers were killed but the perpetrators will be pleased with the sensational global headline.
>
> This goes further than cricket. Modern media sporting coverage gives any terrorist group the exposure they seek.
>
> The Lahore attacks will inspire terrorist groups to commit similar acts in the future.[30]

Haroon Lorgat, the CEO of ICC, stated: 'It is very obvious that the landscape and the thinking has changed dramatically.'[31] Lalit Mansingh, the former Indian ambassador to Washington and London, and one of India's most respected diplomats, said on television immediately after the attack on that fateful morning that the attack on a cricket team is the best way to destroy the confidence not just between India and Pakistan, but all of South Asia. The Lahore attacks are 'an indication of how rapidly Pakistan is rolling down the precipice—these are the signals of the creeping Talibanization of Pakistan', said Mansingh.[32] The Pakistanis are also anxiety-stricken. After the Lahore attack, popular Pakistani websites and blogs (for example, www.pkpolitics.com) were abuzz with comments on the attacks. Some blamed the Central Intelligence Agency (CIA), Moussad and Indian intelligence agency Research and Analysis Wing (RAW), but a large part of the reactions carried shame, anxiety, anger at their own government and helplessness and a dismal realization that no international cricket will be played in Pakistan for a long, long time. Not being able to watch, live, the best international players on their own soil is surely disappointing to Pakistani fans of the game. But more disturbing is the fact that the terrorists have taken control of something that has rarely been dragged into the circle of terrorism or religion this way before—cricket. According to former ambassador Mansingh, 'it's a signal to the rest of the world saying, keep your hands off Pakistan, we [the terrorists] are in control, we can do anything at any time.'[33]

Postscript: The Future of Pakistan as a Host Nation

The Lahore attack might not be the end for Pakistani cricket, but it could be the end for the kind of high-profile international cricket in Pakistan that its fiercely loyal home crowds love to see. The country was justly stripped of hosting the rights for the 2011 World Cup because of 'uncertain security situation' there. In fact, Ehsan Mani, the former ICC president, sounded the warning quite early after India cancelled its tour in December 2008: 'What I fear is that Pakistan is being pushed to the brink of isolation and Pakistan will have to do something about it.'[34] Unfortunately, Pakistan could not do anything about it; rather, the Lahore attack pointed to major security lapses on the part of the government. As ICC President David Morgan said in a statement, 'It is a regrettable decision (but) our number one priority is to create certainty and … deliver a safe, secure and successful event and the uncertainty created by events within Pakistan created a huge question mark over our ability to do just that.'[35] The cumulative impact of so much security-related disruption has not only damaged the prestige of the game and the country but also hit with a huge loss of revenue. To put it very simply, as Sarfraz Nawaz, the former Pakistani captain said, 'cricket in Pakistan is over for some years'.[36]

With a drastic deterioration in human security situation in Pakistan over the last seven years or so, thanks to a spate of terrorist attacks,[37] not only cricket-playing nations but any sportspersons from any part of the globe would think twice before visiting the country. As Mahela Jayawardene, the Sri Lankan skipper at the Lahore Test, admitted a changed perspective on life after the 3/3 attack on Sri Lankan cricketers:

> You realise there are more things to life that cricket. I just want to concentrate and enjoy the simple little things and make the most of every moment. I know that in this world nothing is sure right now; anything can happen if you are in the *wrong place at the wrong time*. It's not a negative thing; lots of people go through this in day-to-day life, people in the armed forces and even normal people. You appreciate their job even more now and try to contribute in some way.[38]

The basic question of human security has even transformed the contours of cricketing relations within South Asia. South Asian cricket-playing nations after the Lahore attacks have now appreciated the difficulty of playing in Pakistan as the cricketers' lives are at stake. As a result, the cause of solidarity in South Asian cricket is facing the danger of being undone by the cause of security. Even India now could easily point to security fears rather than to strains in political or diplomatic relations as the most plausible reason for not playing in Pakistan. But India along with Sri Lanka and Bangladesh need not be complacent in this regard either as terrorism looms large in the entire subcontinent as a whole.[39] The respective governments have the great responsibility to ensure that what has happened in Pakistan in recent years does not happen in the countries they govern. Otherwise the future of cricket in South Asia will be in serious jeopardy.

I would wind up my discussion with a few comments by cricketers and cricket fans, which actually sum up the grim realities of cricket both as a game and as commerce in Pakistan. Zaheer Abbas, the legendary Pakistani cricketer, strongly disapproved of the ICC decision to take the world Cup out of Pakistan:

> It's time that Pakistan cricket breaks its silence over what's been happening against it in recent times. The ICC took away the Champions Trophy and now it has deprived us of the World Cup. What else should happen before we break our silence? I would ask the PCB to make it clear to the ICC that we will boycott the World Cup if it is held in Asia. If Pakistan is unsafe for the event then there is no justification to have the World Cup in other parts of the subcontinent which are also within the range of terrorists. It's a great loss for Pakistan cricket and for that I would blame the ICC and India which has pulled out its support when we needed it the most.[40]

One immediate reply to his accusation came out on a website as follows:

> It's the perfect decision in my opinion. Now playing cricket is not important. Playing safe is important and the world cup should go on. And I don't understand why people like Zaheer Abbas blame INDIA for the cause. INDIA cancelled the trip for players' safety/security and not for any other personal/political reasons. But Sri Lanka went to play there and paid for it. Luckily no fatal incident for the players. Such an incident has not happened ever in Cricket history. Is that not a reason enough to cancel the tournament in Pakistan? I would request respectable person/cricketer like Zaheer Abbas not to add fuel to the flame and cause a new set of problems to the existing political tensions.[41]

The contestation between these two views can be resolved by a third comment posted by a non-resident Pakistani living in the USA:

> As a Pakistani living in the US and a cricket fan, I am in a state of total shock and disbelief—not at the decision made by the ICC, but at the reactions of former Pakistani cricketers and the PCB. Exactly what kind of massacre needs to occur before they realize that Pakistan is just not a safe place to host events at this point in time? If the PCB cannot provide

competent security to one visiting team, they certainly will not be able to successfully negotiate the security of a dozen teams. And let's not forget about the hundreds of thousands of cricket fans as well. Pakistan could have cleared all these fears and doubts with the recent tour of Sri Lanka. They failed. I understand that no country is 100% safe, but any country where a dozen terrorists sporting machine guns and rocket launchers can breach through 'President Style Security', manage to kill innocent civilians, injure foreign sportsmen, and to make matters worse, successfully escape without even a scar, is *Just Not Safe*.[42]

Unless Pakistan comes out of the imbroglio of domestic problems in politics, economy and society and becomes a secure place for foreigners to play without any fear of life, which only looks to be a distant possibility, international cricket will never return to Pakistan, depriving its millions of passionate fans the excitement of live cricket action.[43]

Notes and References

1. It is of relevance here to recount a few personal memories, related to my frantic attempt to manage a tour of Pakistan to do fieldwork during 2007–2008 while I was a Fellow at the Maulana Abul Kalam Azad Institute of Asian Studies (MAKAIAS), Kolkata. In late October 2007, I was to visit Kabul as part of an academic group from the MAKAIAS. I, along with Arpita Basu Roy, one of my colleagues, wanted to utilize the occasion to visit Pakistan as well as Kabul. While Arpita could manage to obtain the clearance from the Interior Ministry of Pakistan, thanks to the organizers of the conference she was to attend, and got her visa done in time, my clearance, despite the recommendation from the Pakistan Cricket Board, came only after I had come back from Kabul on 28 October. Arpita was fortunate enough to go en route to Islamabad on the same day only to find her in one of her lifetime experiences as Emergency was declared in Pakistan on 4 November, the day she was supposed to return on the expiry of her visa. She got stranded in Lahore as all international flights got cancelled indefinitely. All of us here could do nothing but pray for her safety in 'a country where anything can happen to anyone at any time'. Fortunately, she came out of the imbroglio in a few days, thanks to the support of some local Pakistanis.
   Next, I was invited to a Conference on Indo-Pak peace process to be held in Islamabad in early April 2008. The conference organizers, namely, the Islamabad Peace Research Institute, sent me air tickets and necessary documents to procure my visa. The clearance from the Interior Ministry was about to come. On 11 March, at least 24 people were killed and more than 200 wounded in twin suicide bombings in Lahore. One of the attacks ripped apart Federal Investigation Agency building killing 21, including 16 policemen. The other one hit the posh locality of Model Town exploding close to Bilawal House, associated with Pakistan Peoples Party (PPP)

180 Sport, Culture and Nation

leaders Benazir Bhutto and her husband, Asif Ali Zardari. Two immediate sequels followed on the very next day: Australia cancelled its forthcoming cricket tour of Pakistan, while I received a one-line letter from the conference coordinator saying that the conference was indefinitely postponed.

2. Shaharyar Khan, *Cricket: A Bridge of Peace* (Oxford: Oxford University Press, 2005), p. vii.

3. Ibid., p. viii.

4. Omar Noman, *Pride and Passion: An Exhilarating Half Century of Cricket in Pakistan* (Pakistan: Oxford University Press), 1997, p. 35.

5. B.K. Bangash, 'Pakistan's Cricket Attack: A Blow to National Psyche', 4 March 2009, available at http://www.time.com/time/world/article/0,8599,1882994,00. html?iid=sphere-inline-sidebar, accessed 7 October 2009.

6. Javed Miandad, *Cutting Edge: My Autobiography* (Karachi: Oxford University Press, 2003), p. 306.

7. For more layers on this, see Kausik Bandyopadhyay, 'Pakistani Cricket at Crossroads: An Outsiders Perspective', *Sport in Society*, Vol. 10, No. 1 (January 2007), pp. 101–119.

8. Khan, *Cricket: A Bridge of Peace*, p. 179.

9. A useful discussion on cricket, politics and identity in Pakistan can be found in Chris Valiotis, 'Cricket in "a Nation Imperfectly Imagined": Identity and Tradition in Postcolonial Pakistan', in Stephen Wagg, ed. *Cricket and National Identity in the Postcolonial Age—Following On* (London: Routledge, 2005), pp. 110–131.

10. Quoted in Noman, *Pride and Passion*, p. 16.

11. Khan, *Cricket: A Bridge of Peace*, p. 179.

12. Mathur, 'An Inside View of Pakistan', *The Sportstar*, 13 March 2004, p. 22.

13. Ibid.

14. For a general discussion on aspects of security and terrorism in contemporary South Asia, see: Major General Vinod Saighal, *Global Security Paradoxes: 2000–2020* (New Delhi: Manas, 2004); S.K. Khatri and Gert W. Kueck, eds. *Terrorism in South Asia: Impact on Development and Democratic Process* (Delhi: Shipra, 2003); Akmal Hussain, 'Terrorism, Development and Democracy: The Case of Pakistan', in Khatri and Kueck, eds. *Terrorism in South Asia*; P.R. Chari and S. Gupta, eds. *Human Security in South Asia* (New Delhi: Social Science Press, 2003); Rajesh M. Basrur, ed. *Security in the New Millennium: Views from South Asia* (New Delhi: India Research Press, 2001); N.C. Behara, ed. *State, People and Security: The South Asian Context* (New Delhi: Har-Anand, 2002); Major General Dipankar Banerjee, *Security in South Asia: Comprehensive and Cooperative.* (New Delhi: Manas, 1999); P.R. Chari, 'South Asian Security: A Conceptual Approach', in Banerjee, ed. *Security in South Asia.*

15. For a list of terrorist assaults on subcontinental cricket, see 'Timeline: Cricket and terrorism', 3 March 2009, available at http://www.guardian.co.uk/sport/2009/mar/03/timeline-cricket-attacks (accessed 6 October 2009); 'Timeline: Cricket and terrorism', available at http://www.channel4.com/news/articles/world/asia_pacific/timeline+cricket+and_terrorism (accessed 6 October 2009); Asif Ali, 'Timeline: Cricket and Pakistan, a troubled history', 3 March 2009, available at http://www.timesonline.co.uk/tol/sport/cricket/article583681.ece (accessed 6 October 2009).

16. Some interesting insights on this World Cup and this particular event are offered in Paul Dimeo and Joyce Kay, 'Major Sports Events, Image Projection and the

Problems of "Semi-periphery": A case Study of the 1996 South Asia Cricket World Cup', *Thrid World Quarterly*, Vol. 25, No. 7 (2004), pp. 1263–1276.

17. For discussion on the changing security scenario in Pakistan, see Amitabh Mattoo, 'Pakistan', in Banerjee, ed. *Security in South Asia*, pp. 75–112; Saba Gul Khattak, 'Questioning the Security Discourses: The Case of Pakistan', in Behara, ed. *State, People and Security*, pp. 149–175.

18. Declan Walsh, '24 killed in twin Lahore suicide blasts', *The Guardian*, 11 March 2008.

19. 'Australia postpone Pakistan tour', 11 March 2008, available at http://news.bbc. co.uk/sport2/hi/cricket/7288996.stm (accessed 14 October 2009).

20. For a more detailed discussion on cricket's importance in India–Pakistan diplomatic relations, see Kausik Bandyopadhyay, '*Feel Good, Goodwill* and India's *Friendship* Tour of Pakistan, 2004: Cricket, Politics, Diplomacy in Twenty-First-Century India', *The International Journal of the History of Sport*, Vol. 25, No. 12 (October 2008), pp. 1654–1670. Also see Emily Crick, 'Contact Sport: Cricket in India-Pakistan Relations Since 1999', *South Asian Survey*, Vol. 16, No. 1 (2009), pp. 59–79; and Kausik Bandyopadhyay, 'Cricket as Confidence Building Measure: Sports, Culture and Regional Cooperation in South Asia', *Man & Development*, Vol. XXX, No. 1 (March 2008), pp. 121–132.

21. Quoted in Sashi Tharoor, 'Fantasies and Realities', in Shashi Tharoor and Shaharyar Khan, *Shadow Across the Playing Field: 60 Years of India-Pakistan Cricket*, New Delhi: Roli Books, 2009, p. 18.

22. Michael Roberts, 'Whine or play cricket', *Himal Southasian*, Vol. 22, No. 1, January 2009.

23. Cited in ibid.

24. Roberts, 'Whine or play cricket.'

25. Ibid.

26. Ibid.

27. Alex Brown, 'We have all had to grow up', available at http://www.cricinfo.com/magazine/content/story/399535.html, 15 April 2009 (accessed 12 November 2009).

28. Henry Clarke, 'Cricket and terrorism', 4 March 2009, available at http://kalimna. blogspot.com/2009/03/cricket-terrorism.html, accessed 6 October 2009; bold in original.

29. Ibid; bold in original.

30. David Siddall, 'Cricket and Terrorism: A Huge problem', 3 March 2009, available at http://ezinearticles.com/?Cricket-and-Terrorism-A-Huge-Problem&id=2165194 (accessed 7 October 2009).

31. 'Attack leaves Pakistan facing uncertain future at home', 3 March 2009, available at http://www.guardian.co.uk/sport/2009/mar/03/pakistan-attack-sutralia-new-zealand (accessed 7 October 2009). Lorgat, in a personal interaction with the author, also revealed that the cancellation of World Cup matches in Pakistan was solely due to the uncertain and inadequate security situation prevailing in the country. Discussion with Haroon Lorgat, Oxford, 22 July 2009.

32. Manjeet Kripalani, 'Cricket and terrorism: Barbarians at Lahore's gates', 3 March 2009, available at http://www.businessweek.com/globalbiz/blog/eyeonasia/archives/2009/03/cricket_and_ter.html (accessed 7 October 2009).

33. Ibid.

34. 'Pakistan risks isolation, warns ICC chief', *The Mercury*, 24 December 2008, p. 17.

35. 'World Cup matches moved out of Pakistan', 17 April 2009, available at http://www. cricinfo.com/ci-icc/content/story/400154.html?wrappertype (accessed 7 October 2009).

36.   M. Ilyas Khan and Gordon Farquhar, 'Pakistan faces loss of cricket tours', *BBC News*, 3 March 2009, available at http://newsvote.bbc.co.uk/mpapps/pagetools/print/ news.bbc.co.uk/2/hi/south_asia (accessed 7 October 2009).

37.   To give one small piece of statistics, the number of terrorist attacks that hit different parts of Pakistan in October 2009 alone was more than 300. For details, see Hasan Zaidi, 'Pakistan on the Brink', *India Today*, 16 November 2009, pp. 42–51, in which the author, examining the current state of affairs in Pakistan, raises a serious question: 'With a wave of terror attacks, its army battling jihadis, the political system deeply divided and its economy in tatters, Pakistan is close to collapse. Can it be saved?' (p. 43).

38.   Sriram Veera, 'Jayawardene on recovering from Lahore attack: "I told myself it's just another day"', available at http://www.cricinfo.com/ipl2009/content/story/401270. html, 24 April 2009 (accessed 12 November 2009); emphasis added.

39.   Remember how the second Indian Premier League had to be shifted from India to South Africa in April–May 2009 as the IPL schedule clashed with the Parliamentary elections held during the same time and the central government expressed its inability to provide adequate security arrangements to hold the event during that period. Similarly, the Bangladesh government had to halt all visits by foreign teams in March 2009 as it could not guarantee them adequate security after more than 70 people died in a coup by rank-and-file border guards against their superiors in Dhaka on 25–26 February 2009.

40.   'World Cup matches moved out of Pakistan.'

41.   Posted by SATTY77 on 18 April 2009 at 07:27 AM GMT on http://www.cricinfo. com/ci-icc/content/story/400154.html (accessed 7 October 2009).

42.   Posted by Desiguy007 on 18 April 2009 at 7.40 PM GMT on http://www.cricinfo. com/ci-icc/content/story/400154.html (accessed 7 October 2009); emphasis added.

43.   Bangladesh has become the first country to have agreed to play in Pakistan since the terrorist attacks on Sri Lankan cricketers in March 2009. However, the final decision of the Bangladesh Cricket Board rested on the security clearance from the International Cricket Council, and ultimately it decided against the tour.

8

Sport, Culture and Nation: Field Notes from Colombo and Kabul

As has already been noted in the Introduction, academic studies on sports culture in South Asia to date have mostly concentrated on Indian examples, ignoring the unique dimensions of the same in other countries of the region. Chapters 6 and 7 of this book have tried to partially redress this imbalance by analyzing the case of cricket in Bangladesh and Pakistan. This chapter will attempt to assess the nature of sports culture—particularly its cricketing variety—in Sri Lanka and Afghanistan, albeit in a different way. In order to understand and appreciate the impact of sports/cricket on the public life in these two countries, I would narrate some personal reminiscences and observations I gathered during my visits to Sri Lanka in November 2008 and to Afghanistan in October 2007. The visits enabled me to have a first-hand experience of the attachment, passion and emotion of the people towards one of their most popular sports, cricket, especially at a time when both the countries were undergoing turbulent political and social situation. Thus, the chapter offers an ethnographic commentary on the nature of sports culture in contemporary Sri Lanka and Afghanistan.

Understanding the Lankan Way: Cricket Culture in Sri Lanka

Cricket, one of the most abiding national passions in Sri Lanka in the last few decades, has truly become an emblem of national pride as well as a unifying force in an ethnic-strife-ridden state, particularly since Sri Lanka's historic World Cup victory in 1996.[1] The story of Sri Lankan cricket shares similarity with other South Asian counterparts like India and Pakistan on more counts than one. Yet, that cricket in Sri Lanka has always been interestingly different compared to how the game is conceived and appreciated in India or Pakistan was a major finding of my field trip to Colombo on 2 November 2008. To start with a layman's perspective, while visiting different places in and around Colombo, I used to speak to my driver Jayantha who was an intelligent guy having a reflective mindset to comment on the importance and impact of cricket in public life of contemporary Sri Lanka. He agreed that even though cricket is the greatest mass spectator sport in Sri Lanka, people have always retained a unique sense of control in so far as the response to win or defeat is concerned. He also argued that it is the cricketers, and not the film stars, who are regarded national heroes and icons in public perception.

Mahinda Wijesinghe, one of the most knowledgeable old cricket buffs of the country, with a lot of contributions to the nation's cricket,[2] raised a number of interesting points about Lankan cricket in an engaging discussion: White racism against the subcontinental teams, the loopholes in ICC laws, contrast between the behavioural pattern of the cricketing mass in India and Pakistan on the one hand and Sri Lanka on the other (importance of big money in Indian case), and cricket as a great leveller in Sri Lankan society.[3] He also gave a number of suggestions for the improvement of the game. In course of time, I also met a number of fascinating cricketing personalities of Sri Lanka: Premasara Epasinghe, one of the legendary sports administrators, persons and writers of Sri Lanka and private secretary to the Minister for Education in 2008; Ranjit Fernando, the greatest Sri Lankan cricket commentator of contemporary times; Mr Chandra Schafter, the chairman of Janashakthi Insurance, which published the most exhaustive work on Sri Lankan cricket till date[4]; and Chandrika Haturasinghe, the coach of Sri Lanka A national team.

It may be of relevance here to reproduce the views and opinions of less renowned people closely related to cricket in Sri Lanka for a long time. For example, at the Nondescripts Cricket Club, I spoke to one of the oldest cricket officials of the country, Leo Wijesinghe. Leo seemed to be a little indifferent to my queries about the culture of Sri Lankan cricket. He tended to suggest that being a small country and having lesser attendance of spectators at cricket grounds, the game never went beyond limits in Sri Lanka. As he argued, neither the cricketers nor the fans have ever tried to win by any means; rather, they played or watched it in the spirit of the game.[5]

During my visit to the Social Scientists' Association, I met Ananda Wakkumbura, a staff of the association, who spoke about the evolution and history of cricket in Sri Lanka. He cautioned me about any generalization on the nature of cricket culture in Sri Lanka. For him, although the Sri Lankans have mostly shown a sense of maturity in their response towards the game, the ground-level realities were slowly, but surely, changing. The high dose of nationalism injected into the game by the media has made a major impact upon the youth who have begun to express their fanatic sentiments on and off the field in recent times. If one visits any of the one-day matches played between Sri Lanka and any visiting sides, one would easily see these things happening quite frequently.[6]

Another interesting person I met was Ralph Gunawardena, a former bankman and cricket promoter. As to the resilient nature of cricket culture in Sri Lanka, he argued that it is because of the Sri Lankans' ingrained sense of tolerance and compassion which Buddhism has imparted to them over the years. He also stated how the evolution of school cricket for more than a century helped Sri Lanka to become a disciplined cricketing nation. The role of public schools in this regard went beyond their educational structure as the schools founded on local initiative such as Nalanda and Ananda also followed in the footsteps of the Royals and the Thomas so far as the importance of cricket in the curriculum was concerned. But while the recruitment of cricketers for the national team was mostly confined to the prestigious schools of Colombo till the mid-1990s, the 1996 World Cup victory provided a new momentum to the provinces to come up with cricket as well. He urged that it is important to spread the game beyond Colombo and provide the basic infrastructure to the local youth to motivate and mobilize them in cricket. While most cricketers of earlier times used to be very educated and fluent in English due to their affiliation to the public schools of Colombo, many now come through an experience of only cricketing skill without the glamour of city-bred English education. Ralph wished that he would be able to do something viable to promote cricket in the regions by the middle of 2009. However, he seemed to be hesitant with regard to the LTTE's position on a Sri Lankan cricket victory, especially the 1996 World Cup victory, although he tended to agree with me that cricket must be a great leveller in Sri Lankan society.[7]

In the Colombo University, the discussion with some of the teachers of the Department of Sociology, including Dr Sasanka Perera and Dr Subhangi Herath, proved fruitful. Subhangi, although by no means much interested in cricket, gave her views on the mature character of cricket culture in Sri Lanka. She referred back to Robert Knox's work on Sri Lanka,[8] a seventeenth-century text based on his experiences as a traveller in Ceylon, to point out the nature of tolerance and compassion which the people of Sri Lanka were possessed with from ancient times. For her, this temperamental balance of Sri Lankan culture emanated from Buddhism, although she strongly opposed to accept that, given the warfare of the last two and a half decades, Sri Lankans any longer really conform to the fundamentals of that religion. She admitted that cricket, or for that matter, sport in Sri Lanka, is looked upon only as a 'sport' and not, as it happens to be India or Pakistan, as part of a life-and-death equation. That is why the Sri Lankans never put too much emphasis on the non-sporting dimensions of cricket. Subhangi made an important observation on how there has developed a fiercely competitive attitude among urban middle-class families to send their children to prestigious schools and thereby to cricket, while in the rural areas, such competitive attitudes could not develop due to lack of opportunities.[9]

As to the generalized view that Sri Lankans display remarkable maturity in accepting both win and loss in cricket in the same spirit, Sasanka pointed out that it is also important to keep in mind the few occasions of fan violence that have occurred in Sri Lanka. However, he argued that the ingrained tendency towards syncretism in Sri Lankan culture and life must have kept it in check and made sure such occasions remain rare and do not escalate. Since there have been two major ways to look at sport as profession, particularly in India, one being sport as an avenue to a job and the other being sport itself as a job, the experience of Sri Lanka has been quite similar to India. After Sri Lanka's attainment of the Test status in 1982, people all over the country gradually became attracted to the game as a road to a secure job. However, it was only after the nation's World Cup victory of 1996 that cricket itself emerged as a career option. The impact of the victory was such, as Sasanka recollected, that the LTTE declared a national holiday to celebrate the same. Although they mostly emphasized the feat of Muralitharan in the victory, nobody could deny that the high tide of 'Sri Lankan' nationalism also swept over them. This shows the power of cricket as a great leveller.[10]

Subhangi also drew our attention to the case of Susanthika, the Olympic medallist for Sri Lanka, who came from a very poor lower-class background. Susanthika, once elevated to the status of cultural icon in Sri Lanka, had a tough time in adjusting to the new status structure of society, given her poor educational and economic background. Many criticisms poured upon her as she tried to make those adjustments, particularly with respect to her behavioural patterns. Another faculty member pointed out how the Muslims in Sri Lanka mostly support Pakistan when Sri Lanka and Pakistan play against each other.

The most fascinating revelation during my field trip in Colombo came from a half-an-hour telephone discussion with Ajith Perera. It was a voice from a man whose career as a Test umpire was cut short by an accident on 12 November 1992 when a tree fell upon his car on his way back home soon after collecting the letter of appointment from the Sri Lanka Cricket Board to the National (Test match) Panel, which confirmed him as the Field-of-Play umpire for the first Test between New Zealand and Sri Lanka to be held the following week and standby umpire for the third Test. This accident made him permanently disabled. A chemist by profession, Ajith had the unique distinction of becoming the first Sri Lankan to have proven expertise on the laws of cricket: a test umpire, a scorer, an examiner on laws of cricket and a training instructor. After he became disabled, he continued to show his passion for the game by writing on it. A journalist as well as a cricket writer, Ajith's most enduring contribution seems to be his pioneering role in initiating a voluntary campaign in Sri Lanka for the recognition of accessibility of the disabled in the cricket stadia. As he pointed out, nearly 15 per cent of the population in Sri Lanka are affected with mobility. Yet, public buildings and sports stadia in the country are not amenable to the movement of such people. This is something which Ajith described as the 'denying of opportunities' or even a kind of 'violation of human rights' to a large number of people all over the globe. Ajith's campaign can therefore be regarded as an initiative to prevent marginalization of disabled people from different spheres of life. A man of 'ability in disability', Ajith urged the media to take up this issue globally as a moral duty so that awareness is created to that effect, and some concrete actions are taken to ameliorate the problems of disabled peoples' accessibility to sports grounds.[11]

My meeting with Neil Wijeratne, a lawyer and sportswriter, was an interesting one. Neil proved to be an amazing person as well as a great collector of sports and other literary writings, particularly on and from India. Although a lawyer by profession, he can be described as a sports historian, a statistician, a recorder journalist and an author. He has written a lot on Sri Lankan sport—particularly rugby—in both English and Sinhala, while he has authored a number of literary and journalistic works as well. Neil spoke to me uninterruptedly about his career, his interest in sports, his experiences, his works, his journalistic skill, his present research and, most importantly, his strong views on sports in Sri Lanka. He frankly stated his disapproval of the way Sri Lankan cricket evolved after the World Cup victory. That is why he did not really focus on cricket any longer and mostly concentrated on other sports, including rugby and soccer. He was then amassing information to write a history of school cricket in Sri Lanka and the history of Sri Lanka's accession to Test cricket. While Neil's explanation of Sri Lankan cricket culture, being more mature in understanding, followed the same logic of colonial public school system, he pointed to one interesting reality in Sri Lankan sports map. As he argued, while international cricket is most popular in Sri Lanka, when it comes to the domestic front, it is rugby, than cricket, which attracts greater public attention.[12]

My discussion with Trevor Chesterfield, the prolific cricket columnist of *The Indian Express* and a cricket writer of great merit, gave me a lot of thoughts to verify the inferences I drew on Sri Lankan cricket till then.[13] Trevor, a New Zealander by birth, seemed to be an interesting man of insight, albeit a little ethnocentric as well. As we got plunged into an absorbing discussion on subcontinental cricket, including the typicality of Sri Lankan cricket culture, his Sri Lankan wife Paula also offered her observations on the subject from time to time. Trevor's strong views about cricket cultures in various countries (although he later sent me an SMS saying that he is 'essentially strongly apolitical and an egalitarian by nature') opened up newer vistas of understanding for me. However, Trevor's points incited me to brief certain points of difference between the two cricket cultures: Indian and Sri Lankan. First and foremost, I found senior and national cricketers of Sri Lanka assisting their juniors—be they school/club cricketers or national A side—whenever they get an opportunity to do this. I learnt from Trevor that it is a part of their contract with the Sri Lanka Cricket. But I had a feeling that it was also an urge from their heart that they have made it a practice, or you can say tradition, to do that consistently during and after their cricketing careers. This 'urge' has something to do with their ingrained sense of nationalism, commitment and discipline which characterize Sri Lankan cricket since the beginning. However, one must not confuse this Sri Lankan 'nationalism' with its Indian counterpart. In Sri Lankan cricket, nationalism means a sense of commitment to the national team (or for that matter to the nation) as well as to the game itself. The commitment to the game implies the vindication of the public school spirit of discipline and fair play in cricket. This somewhat uniquely colonial tradition of Sri Lankan cricket culture is marked by a lack of excesses in behavioural pattern of the cricketers in striking contrast to its Indian counterpart. The same experience can be had from the nature of Sri Lankan cricket spectatorship which rarely shows any over-the-top reactions in response to wins or losses. This has been typical of an island society, which still perhaps suffers from an inferiority complex, emanating from a sense of isolation from the mainland geographically, culturally and economically. Yet, it was cricket that gave the people of Sri Lanka the first taste of national superiority globally, and that with a certain amount of consistency. The World Cup victory of 1996 changed things a lot so far as the spread and popularity of the game and the development of infrastructure and finance of cricket were concerned. But it did not really change the disciplined culture of cricket in Sri Lanka. Although there might be stray incidents of violence during cricket matches over the last two decades, these occurrences still remain in the nature of an aberration. It is more a mature appreciation of the game and, more importantly, a mature response to the outcome of it which still constitute the core of Sri Lanka's cricket culture.

When one compares the Sri Lankan experience with the Indian one, one is also struck by the cricketers' exclusivity in the latter case. Since in Sri Lanka, cricketers are quite accessible outside the purview of the game, they could afford to move around at their will and go to any ground to help out the kids or juniors to improve the standard. In India, even if the national team cricketers do have the urge to help their juniors, they cannot really afford to do so at will, not to speak of the absurd situation of them going out to shop with their families without proper security. The fans would just simply crowd them out so much that they could always be in trouble in getting out of the lovable congestion of such fandom. However, Indian media plays a major role in exciting too much passion about cricket and the cricketers, while the Sri Lankan media keeps it in proportion. That is why cricketers in both countries, despite being greatest cultural icons in the eyes of the public, are treated differently. While Sri Lankan cricketers can afford to lead a normal carefree life outside the game, their Indian counterparts are not so fortunate to do so. The latter's exclusivity, in creating which the media plays a critical role, has become a source of glamour as well as irritation for them.

It may be of contextual interest here to reproduce the perceptive comments of an old lady named Suthami on certain aspects of cricket culture in Sri Lanka. Aged about 70, Suthami was my hostess at Horton Gardens, where I stayed during my trip to Colombo. Although she had not much interest in cricket or sports, Suthami reflected that one of the other reasons for the relative absence of violence in cricket spectatorship in Sri Lanka was the fact that in a small island like her or, for that matter, in small cities, such as Colombo, Galle, Kandy or Dambulla, it was always easy for the police or security forces to control the people in case of any such occurrence. She further pointed out that in local football, incidents of violence do occur mostly because the crowd draws on heavily from the lower rungs of society while cricket spectators constitute a mixed lot in which elites and middle classes still set the ball of discipline and control rolling.[14]

It would be fitting to wind up this discussion with the observations of Saadi Thoufeeq, one of the best cricket journalists of contemporary Sri Lanka. His views seemed crucial in my order of things since they represented the journalistic point of view on Sri Lankan cricket writing. Thoufeeq drew attention to the plight of sports magazines and books published in Sri Lanka. This would never succeed, as he pointed out, given the high price of newspaper/print in Sri Lanka as well as the availability of cheaper Indian sports magazines like the

Sportstar. He ascribed the lack of production of books on cricket to the same reason. Moreover, as he felt, compared to India, given a very small market of readers and an underdeveloped publishing industry, publishers in Sri Lanka are reluctant to take the risk of publishing too many books on cricket or sports, either in English or in national languages—Sinhala and Tamil.[15]

The culture of cricket that has evolved in Sri Lanka over the last two decades has proved to be an aberration in South Asia. Compared to its more illustrious subcontinental counterparts, which are known for their over-the-top behaviour and excesses of passion over cricket and its attendant nationalism, cricket worship and fan culture in Sri Lanka have always shown a sense of proportion and mature appreciation of the game. Average Sri Lankans' mature reaction to both exemplary success and appalling defeat of their national team does not really conform to the Indian or Pakistani variant of two extremes from mass worshipping of its cricketing icons to public wrath against national cricketers. Future researches should attempt to explain this typical Sri Lankan sense of maturity in appreciating the greatest mass national obsession in a country plagued by continuous ethnic war and political trouble for a long time. With cricket's intensive professionalization, commercialization and mediatization since the 1990s, Sri Lankan cricket began to face the challenge of adaptation towards a changing order of the game in South Asia, led by India. More importantly, in twenty-first-century Sri Lanka, it may be suggested, cricket provides a cultural space where the traditional Sinhalese-Tamil dissent can be submerged under a Sri Lankan feat.

Visit to Kabul: Perspectives on Sport, Society and Culture in Afghanistan

Afghanistan has been a hotbed of political turmoil over the past three decades. This turmoil, from time to time, was accompanied by tribal clashes, religious dissensions, social cleavages and cultural purges. The takeover of Kabul by the Talibans in 1996 marked the beginning of a distinct phase in Afghan history as it, apart from its self-defined political massacres and religious prosecutions, imposed a series of restrictions and bans on the socio-cultural life of the Afghan people. The Taliban rule either prohibited or controlled most of the popular cultural activities, such as television, internet, movies, music or sports. The worst victims, however, were the Afghan women whose behaviour, activity and movement came to be completely regulated by the Taliban. The end of Taliban rule in late 2001 after the 9/11 incident raised hope for a restoration of peace and security, as it was followed by a constitutional process to establish democracy in the country. Post-Taliban, Afghanistan's major aim, thus, has been to restore political and social stability, and economic and cultural development.

Being a part of the scholarly exchange trip to Kabul undertaken by the MAKAIAS, Kolkata, from 21 to 28 October 2007, I had the rare opportunity to visit the offices of the AREU, ANDS, Pajhwok Afghan News, Afghanistan Football Federation and Afghanistan Olympic Committee. The visits were useful in collecting information about some interestingly changing trends of society and culture in post-Taliban Afghanistan with special reference to sporting activities. I took some useful interviews, and had some relevant discussions at these places, which included persons such as Dan Rath, director, Communications and Advocacy, AREU; Attaullah Asim, Strategy Process Coordinator, ANDS; Javed Ahmed Hamim, regional editor, Pajhwok Afghan News; and Sayed Mahmood Zia Dashti, vice president, Afghanistan National Olympic Committee. Overall, certain inferences could be drawn on the basis of our discussions and interviews in Kabul.[16]

Afghanistan under Taliban rule had to face sanctions from global sports bodies like the International Olympic Council. There was also a strict prohibition on women's participation in, or watching of, sport. Post-Taliban, the socio-cultural scenario began to change radically as most of the orthodox restrictions, especially those on women, were gradually removed while the international ban on Afghanistan's participation was also lifted. This provided a booster for a renewal of interests in modern sports like football, cricket, judo or athletics among both men and women. While, for Afghan men, sport has become an arena for the assertion of national identity, women have taken it as a means of emancipation and empowerment. Yet one must not exaggerate the extent to which forms of popular culture like television, films, music or sports play a role in the process of women's empowerment. As Dan Rath, director, Communications and Advocacy, AREU, argued:

> The recent development of women sports owing to increasing participation of women in sports helps break the shackles of societal and cultural restrictions imposed on women in earlier regimes. But as one moves out of Kabul to regions the situation changes according to the priorities of the local sentiments.

In fact, women's access to sports since 2001 has increased steadily, and the international media has given a wide publicity to this development as a mark of progress. However, it must be noted that women's access to sporting activities is limited to certain urban pockets of the country such as Kabul. In other regions, where the control of the central government does not seem to be too strong, and regional leaderships or powers seem to have a large sway over the situation, women do not really enjoy such freer access to sports or other forms of popular culture. As for general development of sports across the war-torn nation, Rath argued:

> Facilities for promoting sports in the country were all destroyed during the Taliban period. Still the Afghans remain a soccer-crazy people. Whenever an occasion of a soccer match comes to the fore, people come together. This provides an excellent opportunity for healthy interaction among people of differing identities and affiliations. At the same time, support bases sometime lead to realignments of social relationships and identities. In recent times, cricket as a popular sport is taking off in Afghanistan. Other indoor sports like badminton, volleyball and basketball urgently need infrastructural booster as the facilities have all been destroyed. Right now, the Olympic Committee is in the process of building an indoor stadium for these sports.
>
> While sport in Afghanistan has been officially declared as a part of a planned effort of the Afghanistan Olympic Committee (AOC), direct cooperation from the govt. has been sporadic. What is most required is the growth of awareness among the sports bodies, the government as well as the players. Other countries, especially the neighbouring states and the global sports bodies should be made aware of the sporting space and international presence of Afghanistan. Sponsorship could be one very important prop for the development of modern sports facilities in conflict-ridden Afghanistan. The AOC has at present 31 sanctioned sports for the Afghans.[17]

Security is one of the major predicaments for popular cultural activities like sport to develop in Afghanistan. To reproduce Dan Rath's words again:

> It still looks a remote idea to organize international sporting events like cricket or soccer tournaments involving its South Asian neighbours in Afghanistan simply because of security reasons. Although people would take immense interest in such a venture, it will be a challenging task for Afghanistan to achieve such a goal. Rather, given the security situation, smaller indoor sports like badminton, volleyball or taikandu have greater potential to flourish.

More importantly, as Kabul is being rebuilt now, some measures are taken to ensure the basic infrastructure of the city. But in the process of normalization of life through long-term development, argued Rath, sport can play an important role. Hence, he felt, both public and state support is necessary to create more and more sports pitches, which will also sustain the environment-friendly atmosphere of the country.[18]

Apart from common threats to human security, especially in the regions, landmines constituted another source of insecurity for infrastructure building for sports in post-2001 Afghanistan. In fact, the creation of sports grounds or pitches and building of stadiums have long been a prime requisite there. But the process to this end has been very slow because the acquisition and utilization of land has proved to be a very critical process given the continuing fear of landmines across the country. For example, as Javed Ahmed Hamim, regional editor, Pajhwok Afghan News and advisor to the Afghanistan Cricket Federation (ACF) points out:

> [T]he municipality in Kabul had twice provided plots of land for building the cricket stadium, but the land could not be used for fear of mines. The ACF has a working agreement with the Kabul University, enabling the cricketers to use a part of the university ground for practice. Recently the ACF has been able to find and acquire another plot of land, and has initiated the work for building its coveted stadium. It is expected to accommodate a modest 10–15,000 people.[19]

Going by the assurance of the United Nations Mine Action Centre for Afghanistan (UNMACA), landmines should no longer remain a security threat any more in the cities.

Javed Hamim, who joined the Pajhwok Afghan News in 2001 after the fall of the Taliban, became an advisor to the ACF after 2004. He argued that the Afghan refugees who had gone to Pakistan during post-Soviet occupation period and imbibed the game there came back to their home country after 2001 and played a leading role in popularizing the game in Afghanistan. The ACF was founded in 2002. It became an ICC-elect member in 2003 and got the membership of the Asian Cricket Council (ACC) subsequently. Presently, Afghanistan has U-15, U-17, U-19 and Senior national teams. Hamim identified the basic problems for sports like cricket in the country: lack of governmental support, lack of infrastructure, particularly absence of sports grounds (cricket pitches) and stadiums, insufficient funding and sponsorship and corruption. The government is not in a position to support sports like cricket materially since it is preoccupied with more crucial aspects of reconstruction and development. In Kabul, there was only one stadium for all sports, namely, the Ghazi Stadium, which was also used for other purposes such as conferences or ceremonies. While there were a few open patches for playing football or volleyball, cricket pitches were nearly invisible. In AFC's bid to develop a sustainable infrastructure in cricket, the ACC, the BCCI and the PCB have come forward to provide some support in terms of finance, infrastructure, capacity building and exchange trips. The Afghan national teams visited Pakistan to play friendly matches to judge and improve upon their standard of play, while some players visited the Madras Rubber Factory (MRF) Foundation Pace Academy, Chennai, in India for better training. These exposures have certainly helped the national team perform better in recent times.[20]

In Hamim's opinion, security is not a big problem in present Afghanistan for the development of cricket. Once the new stadium is built up, given the growing craze for cricket among average Afghans, cricket will definitely take off as the country's most popular sport. The print and visual media has been truly instrumental in generating this kind of interest in cricket in the last few years. Yet gloom comes back when we take a look at the poor payment of players. There is no system of payment by the clubs as well. Limited funding comes mainly from banks, mobile companies or other sponsoring agencies. But most of the sponsorship deals are ailed by corruption.[21]

To provide one example of the government's perspective on the importance of sport, Attaullah Asim, Strategy Process Coordinator,

ANDS, Kabul, clearly stated that, 'sport falls in the less priority area in their programme.' 'The National Olympic Committee is expected to look after the development of sports in tandem with the Ministry of Cultural Affairs.' However, given the socio-economic problems, such as poverty, unemployment and insurgency, he recognized sport to be a tool of mobilization as part of the grand strategy for reconstruction and development. Emphasizing on the importance of youth associations, he argued that youth energies need to be channelled into peaceful cultural pursuits like sports.[22]

Sayed Mahmood Zia Dashti, vice president, Afghanistan National Olympic Committee, gave a realistic appraisal of the sporting scenario in contemporary Afghanistan:

> Afghanistan got IOC recognition in 1935 and made its first ever appearance in the Berlin Olympics of 1936. The Olympic Committee of Afghanistan was founded in 1950. It was also a founder member of the Commonwealth, and participated in all the Games till the onset of Taliban regime. In 1999 Afghanistan National Olympic Committee faced a ban from the IOC, only to be waived in April 2002 after the fall of the Taliban. During Taliban regime, women were also debarred from participating in any sports whatsoever. Afghanistan participated in the 2002 Busan Asian games as well as the 2004 Athens Olympic, albeit without any worthy performances on the track. The major problems of development of sports in present Afghanistan are: lack of infrastructure—gymnasium, pools or sports pitches and other basic amenities for sports. With the exception of the Ghazi Stadium, no other sports stadiums or specialized pitches are available. Players are very poorly paid—$20 per month at the maximum. The sports controlling bodies hardly receive any major support from either the government or the United Nations. The assistance from the neighbouring countries has not also been quite substantial in this regard. Hence, a strong budgetary support is required to really boost up the potential of sports in the country.[23]

It is very important that Afghanistan asserts its presence in the international sporting map. This would also help soothe the differences of various sorts in contemporary Afghanistan and add prop to the nation-building process.

Thus, in the process of transition from a fundamentalist authoritarian rule to a progressive democratic state in Afghanistan, sport plays a critical role. As has already been pointed out, Afghanistan during the Taliban rule faced not only political and economic sanctions from different countries but also suspension from international sports bodies like the International Olympic Committee. Such international proscription coupled with internal political strife left little enthusiasm for sports among the Afghan people, with a substantial part of them fleeing to either Pakistan or Iran as refugees. Although the Taliban government tried to appropriate sport as a tool to legitimize its authority at the international stage, as this chapter points out, that did not seem to spur the Afghan youths to support the venture enthusiastically, and a sort of stultification of modern sporting activities took place in Afghanistan. The Afghan refugees, who fled from Afghanistan with the onset of Taliban rule, on the other hand, used sport to assert their ethnic/national identity in exile, particularly as a mark of protest against the Talibanization of popular culture, including sport. Moreover, the prohibition on women to engage in or watch any sporting activities was a bane for the development of women's sports in the country.

With the restoration of a democratic government after the end of Taliban rule, the socio-cultural scenario began to undergo radical transformation with the waiver of most of the orthodox restrictions, especially those on women. The international ban on Afghanistan's participation in various sports tournaments was also withdrawn. As a result, men and women began to take active part in modern sports like football, cricket, judo or athletics. These sporting spaces became a new arena for the assertion of national identity, particularly for men. Women, on the other hand, have taken on sports as a means of emancipation and empowerment. Hence, it may be argued, sport becomes a useful ploy in contesting and negotiating the gendered discourse that pervaded Afghan society for long. The instrumentality of sport in contemporary Afghan society is also linked with the nation's urge for peace, development and progress as Afghan youths have increasingly preferred to replace guns with bats, and bullets with footballs. Media representations since the fall of Taliban rule too depict sports like football, cricket or other Olympic sports as viable means of cultural regeneration, a medium of social unity and a vehicle of peace. The national euphoria over the win of the only Olympic medal by an Afghan in both the 2008 Beijing Olympics and the 2012 London Olympics validates this argument.[24]

The Afghan government's desire to utilize sport as a useful prop in the process of building a peaceful progressive democratic nation state becomes apparent when we find the government as well as the apex sports associations of the country seeking support from neighbouring countries like India and Pakistan to rebuild their sporting infrastructure. The question, therefore, arises: can we really envisage some prospects of regional cooperation through collaboration in the sphere of sport? People from different social affiliations, and especially from the sports bodies I came across, are all of the view that popular cultural activities like sport can act as viable means of cultural regeneration, medium of social unity and vehicle of peace and regional cooperation. The role India or Pakistan have played so far in the regeneration of sporting interest and reconstruction of sporting infrastructure in Afghanistan certainly bears testimony to this point. Thus, sport emerges as a legitimate field of enquiry insofar as the politico-socio-cultural transition of Afghanistan from Taliban to post-Taliban regime is concerned.[25] The aim of future research should be to focus on this transition using sport as a lens and, in turn, to examine its relevance and importance in the present Afghan polity, society and culture.

Notes and References

1. For details on the various aspects of Sri Lankan cricket and its impact on the masses, see: Jayadeva Uyangoda, ed. *Cricket, Lovely Cricket! Sports in Culture, Class and Nation in Sri Lanka*. (Colombo: Social Scientists Association, 2007); Michael Roberts, 'Ethnicity in Riposte at a Cricket Match: The Past for the Present', in Michael Roberts, ed. *Exploring Confrontation: Sri Lanka—Politics, Culture and History* (Switzerland: Harwood Academic Publishers, 1994); J.A. Mangan, 'Imperial Origins: Christian Manliness, Moral Imperatives and Pre-Sri Lankan Playing Fields—Beginnings and Consolidation', in J.A. Mangan and Fan Hong, eds. *Sport in Asian Society: Past and Present* (London: Frank Cass, 2003); Suvendrini Perera, '"Cricket with a Plot": Nationalism, Cricket and Diasporic Identities', *Journal of Australian Studies*, June 2000; Trevor Chesterfield, 'Cricket in Sri Lanka: In Need of a Messiah', in Boria Majumdar and J.A. Mangan, eds. *Cricketing Cultures in Conflict: World Cup 2003* (London: Routledge, 2004); Michael Roberts, 'Sri Lanka: The Power of Cricket and the Power in Cricket', in Wagg, ed. *Cricket and National Identity in the Postcolonial Age*; Michael Roberts, 'Landmarks and Threads in the Cricketing World of Sri Lanka', in John Gemmell and Boria Majumdar, eds. *Cricket, Race and the 2007 World Cup* (London: Routledge, 2007); Michael Roberts, 'Wunderkidz in a Blunderland: Tensions and Tales from Sri Lankan Cricket', *Sport in Society*, Vol. 12, Nos. 4–5 (2009): 566–578. For an interesting discussion on Sri Lanka's road to 1996 World Cup victory, see Tyronne Fernando, *Kings of Cricket: Sri Lanka's Path to Victory at World Cup '96* (Colombo: Deepanee Publishers, 1998).
2. See Mahinda Wijesinghe, *Sri Lanka Cricket at the High Table* (Colombo: The Author, 2008).

3. Interview with Mahinda Wijesinghe, cricket specialist and senior cricket writer (Colombo: 3 November 2008).
4. S.S. Perera, *The Janashakthi Book of Sri Lanka Cricket: 1832–1996*, ed. S. Muthiah (Colombo: Janashakthi Insurance Ltd., 1999).
5. Discussion with Leo Wijesinghe, official of the Nondescripts Cricket Club (Colombo: 4 November 2008).
6. Discussion with Ananda Wakkumbura, Social Scientists Association (Colombo: 4 November 2008).
7. Interview with Ralph Gunawardena, retired bank manager and cricket promoter (Colombo: 5 November 2008).
8. Robert Knox, *An Historical Relation of the Island Ceylon* (1681), ed. J.H.O. Paulusz (Dehiwala: Thisara Prakashakayo, 1989).
9. Discussion with Subhangi Herath, Senior Lecturer, Department of Sociology, Colombo University (Colombo: 6 November 2008).
10. Discussion with Sasanka Perera, anthropologist and Senior Lecturer in History, Department of Sociology, Colombo University (Colombo: 6 November 2008).
11. Telephone discussion with Ajith Perera, former Test umpire and leader of disabled movement (Colombo: 6 November 2008).
12. Discussion with Neil Wijeratne, sports historian, journalist and author (Colombo: 8 November 2008).
13. Discussion with Trevor Chesterfield, sports writer (Colombo: 10 November 2008).
14. Discussion with Suthami, an old lady and owner of a guesthouse apartment called Horton Gardens in Colombo (Colombo: 9 November).
15. Interview with Saadi Thoufeeq, leading cricket journalist of Sri Lanka (Colombo: 10 November 2008).
16. However, one must be careful that the inferences drawn from these interactions, which mostly reflect the situation in Kabul, should not be always generalized for the regions of the country.
17. Discussion with Dan Rath, Director, Communications & Advocacy, Afghanistan Research and Evaluation Unit (Kabul: 24 October 2007).
18. Ibid.
19. Interview with Javed Ahmed Hamim, Regional Editor, Pajhwok Afghan News (Kabul: 24 October 2007).
20. Afghanistan's performances in the Asia Cup and T-20 World Cup in 2014 bear testimony to this point.
21. Interview with Javed Ahmed Hamim.
22. Interview with Attaullah Asim, Strategy Process Coordinator, Afghanistan National Development Strategy (Kabul: 25 October 2007).
23. Interview with Sayed Mahmood Zia Dashti, vice president, Afghanistan National Olympic Committee (Kabul: 27 October 2007).
24. Rohullah Nikpai won both the medals in 68-kg category in tae kwon do.
25. Unfortunately, there is virtually nothing so far as academic discussion on Afghan sports is concerned. The only work that deals with the traditional Afghan game Buzkashi is: Sreedhar and Mahendra Ved, *Afghan Buzkashi: Power Games and Gamesmen* (Delhi: Wordsmith, 2000). Very recently, one popular work on cricket has come from Tim Albone: *Out of the Ashes: The Extraordinary Rise and Rise of the Afghanistan Cricket Team* (UK: Virgin Books, 2011). One popular fictional work on Afghanistan cricket is also worthy of mention in this regard: Timeri N. Murari, *The Taliban Cricket Club: A Novel* (New Delhi: Aleph Book Company, 2013).

Epilogue

Sports history, it can be justly claimed, is peoples' history. Starting from this premise, the present work has studied the role of sport in shaping peoples' lives, cultures and identities in colonial and postcolonial times with particular reference to football in India and cricket in South Asia. What has followed, therefore, is not a broad social history of sport in South Asia. Rather, the work concentrates on exploring the relationships among the national, regional and local through the lens of two major mass spectator sports of South Asia. In considering sport as a mirror of society, the book does not give much weight to results and scores, lists and tables, data and statistics (although they prove invaluable when used as tools of analysis). Rather than describing particular matches or engaging second-hand discussions of tactics and the like, it has tried to study what sport meant and why it mattered in relevant contexts. In other words, as already outlined in the Introduction, the work is pursued with the premise that social history of sport can be meaningfully understood only by looking beyond the sports field.

The chapters on Indian football have tried to bring into focus some key issues in the game's contextualization in colonial and postcolonial times. While football, as a marker of community representation and diverse identities, has undergone important transformations over the last century, India's downward performance as a football nation has run in contrast to Indians' staggering passion for the global game. Interestingly, the game's prospect as a career option has definitely progressed in the age of globalization, giving opportunities to both the youth and to communities under duress as in the Northeast of India. As India wakes up to stage the under-17 World Cup in 2017, it is high time to address the issues and problems that still ail Indian football, and the chapters on Indian football in one way or other contextualize these issues and problems in a historical perspective.

In the realm of cricket in South Asia, as the book has tried to indicate, if the game can be considered a potential confidence-building measure in the normalization and progress of contemporary Indo-Pakistan relations, sport's overall importance as a key weapon in regional cooperation in South Asia needs to be considered with greater introspection.[1] There are certain recent examples that can augment insights into this process. In 1996 when Australia and the West Indies refused to play their World Cup matches in Sri Lanka for security concerns, India and Pakistan went there to play friendly matches to alleviate any such preconceived fears of security. This step also revealed a lot about the cricketing solidarity of the South Asian nations. The huge efforts India or Pakistan put to accord Bangladesh the 'Test status' in international cricket or the recent attempts to regularize South Asian Association for Regional Corporation (SAARC) tournaments and South Asian Games could be judged in this light. Thus, if meaningfully employed, sports such as cricket could act as a useful medium of cultural exchange/people-to-people contacts among the South Asian nations. Afghanistan, for example, received support—both infrastructural and financial— from its neighbours like India and Pakistan to promote sports in the country in order to engage the youth energy into peaceful social channels and cultural pursuits. More importantly, since the late 1980s, South Asian nations led by India began to control the fortune of global cricket economy. In fact, it won't be too much to say that the centre of gravity of world cricket has shifted from England to South Asia. The way India, Pakistan, Sri Lanka and Bangladesh— four major SAARC countries—snatched away the bid to host the ICC World Cup of 2011 from Australia–New Zealand and staged it bears testimony to this point. Finally, the organization of a successful sports event, like the Football World Cup or the Cricket World Cup, as the cases of Korea–Japan (2002), India–Pakistan–Sri Lanka (1996) or India–Sri Lanka–Bangladesh (2011) have illustrated respectively, can help rebuild the urban infrastructure and economic strength of a group of nations. The SAARC countries should therefore strive for organizing such mega events in collaboration with each other. However, the straining in Indo-Pak relations since November 2008 and the attack on Sri Lankan cricketers in Lahore in March 2009 created chinks in South Asian cricketing solidarity. It is therefore important to understand that unless the South Asian nations—individually as well as together—cannot show real urge to mitigate the evil of terrorism and share the concerns of the neighbours, sport's role as an instrument of cooperation will continue to remain limited in nature.

South Asian cricket has now become a fascinating phenomenon globally, thanks to its successful commercialization and attendant cultural transformations in the last two and half decades or so. Cricket has become closely intertwined with various manifestations of power and culture in the region: politics, national identity, security, and diplomacy. One of the key markers of cricket's importance in twenty-first-century India, for example, has been its political character, manifested in electoral politics of the BCCI and regional cricket associations. The increasing politicization of cricket and legal battles associated with it invite comparisons with other South Asian cricket powers, namely, Pakistan, Sri Lanka and Bangladesh. In fact, the Indian case in this regard offers an interesting comparison and contrast to experiences in those countries. In Pakistan and Bangladesh, for example, political authority—be it democracy or dictatorship—has always remained movers and shakers of the destiny of respective cricket authorities, namely, Pakistan Cricket Board and Bangladesh Cricket Board. In Sri Lanka, while democratic governance is enshrined in the constitution of the Sri Lanka Cricket, the relationship between politics and cricket has become one of the key features of cricket administration. A study of cricket board elections at central and regional levels in India, as offered in this volume, makes way for potential research to understand on how power play, personality conflicts and political imperatives influence cricket in other cricket powerhouses of South Asia.

The phenomenon of South Asian cricket has transformed the cricket culture across the world since the 1990s. In this process, cricket has become the representative of national identity and security. The forces unleashed by globalization played a critical role in redefining the unique cricketing culture in South Asia. Studies have been far too less on this new cricketing culture of South Asia and its patterns of unity and diversity in various states of the region. More importantly, researches into the evolution of cricketing politics and culture in South Asia sans India have also been scanty. The last three chapters in the volume are therefore expected to generate future forays into that domain.

The present work, using sport as a lens, has tried to consider some relevant themes of social history, and brought forth some important issues of political and cultural history of contemporary India as well as South Asia. It concentrates on exploring the relationships between culture, politics, national identity and regional cooperation in the history of modern sports in this region. The macrocosm of sports in South Asia (football and cricket in particular), into which I have tried to weave the microcosms of national and regional scores, is expected to generate future forays into more specialized regional and local studies. As James Walvin has suggested, 'more emphasis needs to be placed on local studies without losing sight of the broader context.'[2] *Sport, Nation and Culture* also shares Walvin's notion that 'general structures do indeed have a place, but they will inevitably be subjected to the qualifications of specific and local peculiarities.'[3] Walvin has further remarked:

> Like many other forms of social behaviour, sporting activity is largely socially and historically determined. Thus the sports historian and sociologist need to reach beneath the surface, behind the obvious facts of sporting history, if their studies are to be any more than yet another quasi-antiquarianism masquerading as serious social history.[4]

The present work, in the same vein, adopts a more didactic approach, which considers sport as a mirror of society. However, there is one area which has not really come under the purview of this work—the role of capital in the world of sports in India or South Asia. Global capital now plays a crucial role in the development of sports as well as in the organization of mega sports events across the world. Future research should concentrate on this theme while exploring various aspects of sport in the region.

Sport, Nation and Culture has thus intended to bring to light the importance of sport in colonial and postcolonial times in terms of football in India and cricket in South Asia as an essential cultural experience, a political tool, a social instrument and a commercial force. In this sense, it intends to contribute to the growing body of literature on the history of sport in South Asia. More importantly, viewing sport as an integral part of popular culture, the work also attempts to make a contribution to the wider historical literature on popular culture in modern South Asia. Second, as the work is based on an eclectic interdisciplinary approach, it really follows neither the 'Sports Studies' paradigm nor the 'Cultural Studies' paradigm, fashionable of late. Rather, the study is conceived within the broader contours of 'Social History', of course drawing necessary methodological support at times from other paradigms and disciplines. In this context, the work addresses the question of viability of placing the history of sport in what Ramachandra Guha calls 'a ghetto of its own'.[5] While a history of sport can become a viable area of study in its own right, I would argue that it is best pursued within the wider perspective and methodology of historical discipline. In other words, as Guha rightly asserts: 'the attempt should rather be to use ignored or previously marginal spheres, such as sport ... to illuminate the historical centre itself.'[6] Finally, the work pursues the study of contemporary history in terms of methodological exercise. That is why it has also tried to identify questions that still need to be asked, raise issues that urge serious debates and offer insights that can stimulate future research.

Notes and References

1. Most of the works on regional cooperation in South Asia have failed to appreciate the due importance of sport in that context. See, for example, Dipankar Banerjee, ed. *SAARC in the Twenty-First Century: Towards a Cooperative Future* (New Delhi: India Research Press, 2002); K.K. Bhargava et al., eds. *Shaping South Asia's Future: Role of Regional Cooperation* (New Delhi: Vikas Publishing House, 1995); K.K. Bhargava, I.N. Mukherjee, Bimal Prasad and C.D. Wadhwa, *South Asia: Towards Dynamism and Cooperation* (Bombay: Popular Prakashan, 1994); Jamil Choudhury, ed. *Cultural Cooperation in South Asia: The Search for Community* (New Delhi: Manohar, 2002); Devendra Kumar Das, ed. *SAARC: Regional Cooperation and Development* (New Delhi: Deep & Deep, 1992); Bimal Prasad, ed. *Regional Cooperation in South Asia: Problems and Prospects* (New Delhi: Vikas Publishing House, 1989).
2. James Walvin, 'Sport, Social History and the Historian', *The British Journal of Sports History*, Vol. 1, No. 1 (1984): 10.
3. Ibid.
4. Ibid., p. 8.
5. Ramachandra Guha, *A Corner of a Foreign Field: The Indian History of a British Sport* (London: Picador, 2002), p. xiv. This has actually happened with the histories of women and environment.
6. Ibid.

Index

About the Author

Kausik Bandyopadhyay teaches History at West Bengal State University, Barasat, Kolkata. Prior to this, he taught at Kidderpore College, Kolkata, and at the Department of History, North Bengal University. He was a Fellow of the International Olympic Museum, Lausanne (2010). A former Fellow of the Maulana Abul Kalam Azad Institute of Asian Studies, Kolkata (2006–2009), he is the Academic Editor of *Soccer and Society* (London: Routledge). His areas of research interest include Social and Cultural History of Modern India, Popular Culture in South Asia, History of Sport and Contemporary South Asia.

Dr Bandyopadhyay is the author of *Bangladesh Playing: Sport, Culture, Nation* (2012); *Scoring Off the Field: Football Culture in Bengal, 1911–80* (2011); *Playing for Freedom: A Historic Sports Victory* (2008); and *Playing Off the Field: Explorations in the History of Sport* (2007); co-author of *Goalless: The Story of a Unique Footballing Nation* (2006); editor of *Why Minorities Play or Don't Play Soccer: A Global Exploration* (2010) and *Modernities in Asian Perspective* (2010); issue editor of *Asia Annual 2008: Understanding Popular Culture* (2010); and co-editor of *Fringe Nations in World Soccer* (2008) and *Sikkim's Tryst with Nathu La: What Awaits India's East and Northeast?* (2009). He has also published a large number of articles in national and international journals.